KENT HULL is currently Director of Legal Services for the National Center for Law and the Handicapped in South Bend, Indiana. He graduated from the University of Illinois College of Law and has worked in legal services and public interest law. As an attorney, he has been involved in the rights of physically handicapped people particularly in the areas of higher education and accessibility in architecture and transportation. He has lectured across the U.S. on the rights of physically handicapped people.

PAUL HEARNE is a graduate of Hofstra University School of Law and former executive director of The Handicapped Persons Legal Support Unit in New York City.

Also in this Series

THE RIGHTS OF ALIENS	31534	$1.50
THE RIGHTS OF CANDIDATES AND VOTERS	28159	$1.50
THE RIGHTS OF EX-OFFENDERS	44701	$1.95
THE RIGHTS OF GAY PEOPLE	24976	$1.75
THE RIGHTS OF GOVERNMENT EMPLOYEES	38505	$1.75
THE RIGHTS OF HOSPITAL PATIENTS	39198	$1.75
THE RIGHTS OF MENTAL PATIENTS	36574	$1.75
THE RIGHTS OF MENTALLY RETARDED PERSONS	31351	$1.50
THE RIGHTS OF MILITARY PERSONNEL	33365	$1.50
THE RIGHTS OF OLDER PERSONS	44362	$2.50
THE RIGHTS OF THE POOR	28002	$1.25
THE RIGHTS OF PRISONERS	35436	$1.50
THE RIGHTS OF REPORTERS	38836	$1.75
THE RIGHTS OF STUDENTS	32045	$1.50
THE RIGHTS OF SUSPECTS	28043	$1.25
THE RIGHTS OF TEACHERS	25049	$1.50
THE RIGHTS OF VETERANS	36285	$1.75
THE RIGHTS OF UNION MEMBERS	46193	$2.25
THE RIGHTS OF WOMEN	27953	$1.75
THE RIGHTS OF YOUNG PEOPLE	42077	$1.75

Where better paperbacks are sold, or directly from the publisher. Include 25¢ per copy for mailing; allow three weeks for delivery.

Avon Books, Mail Order Dept., 250 West 55th Street, New York, N.Y. 10019

AN AMERICAN
CIVIL LIBERTIES
UNION HANDBOOK

THE
RIGHTS OF
PHYSICALLY
HANDICAPPED
PEOPLE

Kent Hull

with a chapter on
Employment Rights by
Paul Hearne

General Editor of this series
Norman Dorsen, *Chairperson ACLU*

A DISCUS BOOK/PUBLISHED BY AVON BOOKS

THE RIGHTS OF PHYSICALLY HANDICAPPED PEOPLE is an original publication of Avon Books. This work has never before appeared in book form.

Portions of this book contain material published in the *Federal Register,* as well as other United States governmental publications, and are appropriately identified in the footnotes following each chapter.

AVON BOOKS
A division of
The Hearst Corporation
959 Eighth Avenue
New York, New York 10019

First Discus Printing, December, 1979

DISCUS TRADEMARK REG. U.S. PAT. OFF. AND IN
OTHER COUNTRIES, MARCA REGISTRADA, HECHO EN
U.S.A.

Printed in the U.S.A.

This book is for my parents,
Virgil and Idella Hull
and
my parents-in-law,
Paul and Helen Ickes

A Note about Jack Achtenberg

This book began as a project by the late Jack Achtenberg. After Jack's tragic death in 1976, I undertook the work. While I have had the benefit of an outline he prepared, I wrote from my own sources and gave the book my own emphases, which varied from what he had planned to write.

I hope he would have liked this book. He was a dedicated and tenacious fighter for the rights of his fellow disabled (he probably would insist on that word) citizens. Jack's death occurred, as many know, because of the inaccessibility to wheelchair users of a public thoroughfare, where Jack was forced to travel in the street. He died after having been struck by a hit-and-run driver. That event serves as well as any to remind that the living of a life by handicapped people, despite legal rights and social concern, remains, not just in psychological or philosophical contexts, a risk.

Contents

	Preface	11
	Introduction	13
I	The Quest for Equality	17
II	A Primer on Rights	43
III	The Right to Access: Architectural Barriers	65
IV	The Right to Access: Transportation	95
V	The Right to Education: Preschool, Elementary, and Secondary	121
VI	The Right to Education: Postsecondary	157
VII	The Right to Employment	175
VIII	The Right to Live in the World	223
	Conclusion	231
	Appendix A: Model White Cane Law	233
	Appendix B: Michigan Handicappers' Civil Rights Act	237
	Appendix C: Architectural Barriers Ordinance of Prince George's County, Maryland—Declaration of Purpose	249
	Appendix D: North Carolina Statute	251

Preface

This guide sets forth your rights under present law and offers suggestions on how you can protect your rights. It is one of a continuing series of handbooks published in cooperation with the American Civil Liberties Union.

The hope surrounding these publications is that Americans informed of their rights will be encouraged to exercise them. Through their exercise, rights are given life. If they are rarely used, they may be forgotten and violations may become routine.

This guide offers no assurances that your rights will be respected. The laws may change and, in some of the subjects covered in these pages, they change quite rapidly. An effort has been made to note those parts of the law where movement is taking place but it is not always possible to predict accurately when the law *will* change.

Even if the laws remain the same, interpretations of them by courts and administrative officials often vary. In a federal system such as ours, there is a built-in problem of the differences between state and federal law, not to speak of the confusion of the differences from state to state. In addition, there are wide variations in the ways in which particular courts and administrative officials will interpret the same law at any given moment.

If you encounter what you consider to be a specific abuse of your rights you should seek legal assistance. There are a number of agencies that may help you, among them ACLU affiliate offices, but bear in mind that the ACLU is a limited-purpose organization. In many communities, there are federally funded legal service offices which provide assistance to poor persons who cannot afford the costs of legal representation. In general, the rights that the ACLU defends are freedom of inquiry and expression; due process of law; equal protection of the laws; and privacy. The authors in this series have discussed other rights in these books (even though they sometimes fall outside the ACLU's usual concern) in order to provide as much guidance as possible.

These books have been planned as guides for the people directly affected: therefore the question and answer format. In some of these areas there are more detailed works available for "experts." These guides seek to raise the largest issues and inform the nonspecialist of the basic law on the subject. The authors of the books are themselves specialists who understand the need for information at "street level."

No attorney can be an expert in every part of the law. If you encounter a specific legal problem in an area discussed in one of these handbooks, show the book to your attorney. Of course, he will not be able to rely *exclusively* on the handbook to provide you with adequate representation. But if he hasn't had a great deal of experience in the specific area, the handbook can provide helpful suggestions on how to proceed.

Norman Dorsen, Chairperson
American Civil Liberties Union

The principle purpose of this handbook, and others in this series, is to inform individuals of their legal rights. The authors from time to time suggest what the law should be, but the author's personal views are not necessarily those of the ACLU. For the ACLU's position on the issues discussed in this handbook, the reader should write to Librarian, ACLU, 22 East 40th Street, New York, N.Y. 10016

Introduction

The publication of this book as a part of the American Civil Liberties Union's Handbook Series has a significance beyond the merits of the book itself. As I argue, the belated acknowledgment by our system of public law that the civil rights of handicapped persons merit many of the protections afforded other minorities was an event of great importance in our national life. The battles now being waged against discrimination may obscure that initial victory, but the publication of a book on the rights of physically handicapped persons by one of our preeminent civil-liberties organizations marks the seriousness of the issue, not only for handicapped people but for everyone concerned about freedom and equality in our nation. Accordingly, I have written this book not only for handicapped people, but for all who care about the civil rights of their fellow human beings. It is entirely appropriate for others to be concerned, because, apart from idealistic reasons, they have a stake in the contributions which millions of handicapped persons will be able to make to our national life.

When I began work on this book, in the early months of 1977, it was clear that important legal developments were imminent. The United States Court of Appeals for the Seventh Circuit had held that §504 of the Rehabilitation Act of 1973 provided affirmative rights which could be enforced by means of a private right of action. Soon, courts throughout the nation followed that decision and began granting remedies to handicapped litigants. The White House Conference on Handicapped Individuals, the Transbus Mandate for accessible public transportation, and the promulgation of regulations by the Department of Health, Education and Welfare to implement §504 for recipients and federal financial assistance continued the progress in legal rights. But as this book went to press, the optimism and hope of 1977 were endangered by fears of inadequate enforcement of existing laws and threats of retrenchment in the gains achieved.

The opposition emerging to the achievement of equal rights for handicapped persons reflects an anxiety about the capacity of our society to meet sometimes uncertain obligations—in many ways, it is a fear of the unknown. The guarantee of civil rights for handicapped persons will require a daring and willingness to risk defeat in some circumstances, just as the great initial effort to eliminate racial discrimination required a similar courage. That our society may not be as willing to take that risk today as it was two decades ago perhaps says as much about where we have gone as a people as any other fact.

This book is limited not only in the sense, as the General Editor points out, that it *alone* does not constitute all of the law relevant to the topics discussed, but also in that the choice of topics reflects my view of the most pressing in the movement to achieve equal rights at present. I have not, for example, dealt with the details of public assistance programs and Social Security or with matters which are solely the concern of certain groups of handicapped persons. I have attempted to deal with the general topic of civil rights of all physically handicapped people, with illustrative examples of the application of rights to specific types of handicapping conditions. Essentially, this is a survey of basic rights that have been established in recent years, intended to give readers a sense of what these new developments mean. I have excluded the public assistance and special statute matters to concentrate on the broader issues.

My debts for this book are many and all cannot be acknowledged individually. But several do require special thanks.

First, to the American Civil Liberties Union, for sponsorship of the book, and to Norman Dorsen especially for encouragement, suggestions, and patience. I also owe thanks to Judith Riven, John Holliday, Lois Levin, and others at Avon Books.

Second, to my colleagues at the National Center for Law and the Handicapped, Inc., some of whom have read portions of the manuscript and all of whom—in one way or another—have influenced my thinking about the issues in this book. I must mention several persons specifically—my secretary, Delores Dant Fain, who typed the manuscript, and seven law students from Notre Dame Law School—Brian Higgins, Brenda Joiner, Ted Maloney, Beth Meier, Gaye Lynn Moorhead, Witold Sztykiel, and Paula Wiseman who assisted in research, proofreading, and citation-checking.

A third debt is to a group of lawyers and other advocates, some of whom were directly involved in cases discussed, for their time and effort in offering criticism of various chapters.

A final debt, but the foremost in importance, is to my wife, Jean, who has put up with this book as she puts up with me generally.

I should add a word about words. Throughout this book, I have used the term "handicapped" and not "disabled" or some other term. I am well aware that many of the people whose rights are discussed in these pages reject the word "handicapped." My choice of "handicapped"—apart from any personal opinion on the merits of various terms—is because this is a book about law and I am a lawyer. In most of the legislation and cases I discuss, "handicapped" is the term used; additionally, for legal purposes, the term "disabled" may have a fairly limited meaning, particularly with respect to public assistance law, which does not encompass all the persons I wish to address.

I

The Quest for Equality

One day in August 1870, a man named David T. Sleeper was making his way along a road near the small New Hampshire town of Sandown. At that time in his life, David Sleeper was blind, although he had once been able to see. Despite his handicap, he worked as a farmhand and, we are told, he was capable of many kinds of farm work: chopping wood, felling trees, mowing, reaping, threshing grain, digging potatoes, planting, and hoeing—"although with difficulty the first time hoeing corn." He was considered "a good man to hire."

He customarily traveled the roads of his community on foot and alone. His manner of crossing the bridge at Sandown was to feel his way across with his cane and sometimes to rely on the bridge railing for guidance. On this day, the railing was broken. When he attempted to cross, midway across the bridge he stepped off the edge and, with no railing to protect him, fell into the water.

He brought suit against the town for the injuries he suffered, alleging that the town had been negligent in failing to keep the bridge railing maintained. A jury awarded a verdict in his favor.

When the town appealed the case to the Supreme Court of New Hampshire, it argued that Sleeper himself had been negligent in traveling, as a blind person, unaided on the highways in his customary way of traveling. The immediate significance of this contention was that if Sleeper had been negligent (or, as lawyers say, contributorily negligent), he would have been barred from recovering damages for his injury.

17

Sleeper's lawyers argued that the highways are intended for use by all persons—including the handicapped —and that the roads must be made reasonably safe for handicapped persons. They contended that it would be unreasonable to require Sleeper to take someone with him every time he traveled or to require him to make special inquiries about the changed conditions of the road since he had last traveled them. He was entitled to presume that the town was keeping bridges and roads in a reasonably safe condition for him and for all others.

The Supreme Court of New Hampshire upheld the lower court's judgment in favor of David Sleeper. In its opinion, the court rejected the notion that Sleeper had been negligent in traveling alone:

> Blindness of itself is not negligence. Nor can passing upon the highway, with the sight of external things cut off by physical incapacity of vision in the traveller, be negligence, in and of itself, any more than passing upon the highway when the same things are wholly obscured by the darkness of night.

The court cautioned that a blind individual must make allowance for threats to his safety resulting from blindness and that many acts, safe for sighted persons, would constitute gross carelessness by a blind person. But David Sleeper had not been careless. He had the same right to assume the existence of a bridge railing as any other traveler. The court refused to accept the often-stated view that handicapped persons risk injury as they attempt to lead active lives:

> Blindness is no more negligence than near-sightedness, and probably no more likely, on the whole, to contribute to an accident; and whether any one of the senses be wholly obliterated, or only obscured and partially destroyed, cannot, as we see, make any difference with the application of the rule.

David Sleeper's case deserves consideration from several viewpoints. In one sense, it represents, succinctly, the dimensions of today's handicapped civil rights movement. At least three issues presented in this case are fundamental to the current demand by physically handicapped persons for equal rights under law.

The first issue is mobility. Sleeper asserted his right to move throughout his community in order to make his living. This is the same right of physical mobility asserted today by handicapped persons seeking access to public buildings and public transportation. But underlying the demand for physical mobility and access is the asserted right to participate in the social life of our communities (neighborhood, city, nation); the larger issue is whether one can move throughout a culture, concretely and symbolically, to enjoy the benefits of society and to contribute to the needs of society. The late Jacobus ten Broek, a blind lawyer and political scientist, expressed this larger concern eloquently:

> Movement, we are told, is a law of animal life. As to man, in any event, nothing could be more essential to personality, social existence, economic opportunity —in short, to individual well-being and integration into the life of the community—than the physical capacity, the public approval, and the legal right to be abroad in the land.

The second issue presented in *Sleeper v. Sandown* is the demand that society make accommodations for the limitations of physically handicapped persons. In *Sleeper,* the New Hampshire court held that the town must keep the bridge in repair, not only in a way that would take into account the protection of sighted persons, but also in a way that would protect blind persons. The town had a duty to blind persons in this respect.

In this early idea of a duty to handicapped persons is the genesis of a modern legal concept: that accommodations must be made to limitations of handicapped persons. We live in a world arranged, designed, and constructed to exclude handicapped persons. To overcome such barriers, the people and organizations which control the buildings, jobs, and services of our society must make changes to enable handicapped persons to have access. Accommodation in the *Sleeper* case meant a well-maintained bridge railing; today it means access to buildings, appropriate public education programs, and work arrangements structured to meet the needs of handicapped persons.

There are limitations to the accommodations principle —one set of regulations dealing with employment, for example, requires reasonable accommodations to "the known physical or mental limitations of an otherwise qualified handicapped applicant or employee" but provides an exception to federally assisted programs which "can demonstrate that the accommodation would impose an undue hardship on the operation of its program." The law and regulations create only a framework for the implementation of the concept of reasonable accommodation; the application of the concept is a continuing process.

The third issue presented is the demand that the ability of handicapped people be determined on an individual basis, and not on the basis of preconceived stereotypes about classes of handicapped persons. The New Hampshire court explicitly detailed the capabilities of David Sleeper as a hired man. The court's awareness of the facts, and of his reputation as a good worker, probably had some effect on the outcome of the case. The court seemed to suggest that Sleeper was not to be considered a blind person with limitations, but a blind person capable of working and living a worthwhile life. In order to help him realize the potential he had demonstrated, the court seemed to say, he must be allowed the freedom to travel. A century after this case, a blind public school teacher won the right to teach sighted children in the Philadelphia public schools because she also was able to demonstrate a record of achievement and show the similar successes of blind teachers in general. This principle of determination on the basis of actual ability, not preconceived stereotypes, is critical to the achievement of equal rights for handicapped persons.

The *Sleeper* case is noteworthy for one final reason. The handicapped rights movement is a relatively new force in our society. Yet this nineteenth-century case has within it the potential for widespread change. *Sleeper v. Sandown* was not the first, and certainly not the last, case establishing a right of handicapped persons to move freely through society with accommodations made for their needs. The potential of these cases was never realized. As late as the 1970's, blind persons and other handicapped persons were still fighting to overcome the prejudicial attitudes held by the defendants in the New Hampshire case. Yet the possibility of change existed long before recent statutes and laws. The modern quest to achieve legal equality for physically handicapped persons is, therefore, well-grounded in our legal past.[1]

Does the present concern over legal equality for handicapped people reflect a new direction in our national policy?

Yes. Public policy toward handicapped people has, throughout most of our history, been directed toward "taking care" of handicapped persons. As Sar A. Levitan and Robert Taggart have written, the problems of the disabled have been "conceptualized and measured from a medical perspective." The fundamental policy, stated by another writer, was one of benevolent paternalism, which protected handicapped people and allowed them "to live in seclusion and with as little pain or discomfort as possible."

Our public policy stood on two contradictory premises. One premise was that the problems of handicapped persons were serious enough to merit the intervention of national and state government. Federal legislation provided for federal grants to states for rehabilitating handicapped individuals and preparing them for employment. Yet, despite the recognized national interest in enabling handicapped persons to be gainfully employed, a second assumption undercut the rehabilitation program. This second premise was that the government would develop and recommend appropriate policies to facilitate the placement of rehabilitated individuals, but action generally would be limited to imploring and beseeching. In short, there was no provision for enforcement of rights of handicapped persons. It is this contradiction within our public policy—at one time an acknowledgment of the serious problems faced by handicapped people, at the same time an unwillingness to use the powers of government to achieve effective change—which has been the basic impediment to legal equality for handicapped persons.

The irony which handicapped persons faced was the conflict between repeated public declarations recognizing their problems and continued official unwillingness to do anything substantial to meet those problems. The change which occurred, mostly in the 1970s, was the enactment of legislation which enlisted the civil rights enforcement powers on behalf of the handicapped rights movement. Yet the old passivity remained deeply embedded in the attitudes of governmental officials. As late as 1976, a federal district judge held that one of the major federal statutes prohibiting discrimination against handicapped persons was merely "precatory," a legal term to describe language which entreats, requests, and recommends, as distinct from language which directs and commands. The essence of this judicial holding was that the long-awaited civil rights provision had no teeth in it. While an appellate court reversed that decision, the case demonstrates the reluctance with which courts and other agencies of government recognized the civil rights imperative in present federal legislation.[2]

What brought about the change in national policy from passive benevolence to active enforcement of civil rights?

One factor was the militancy of handicapped people themselves. They sought to adapt, to their own needs, the success of the American civil rights movement of the 1960s. That movement had achieved both the practical benefits of better lives for minorities and the less tangible, but equally important, benefits of a greater awareness of the rights of minorities by the American public. While recognition of handicapped people as a minority deserving civil rights protection was not immediate, the similarities between their situation and the status of other minorities compelled acceptance of the argument that handicapped persons deserved civil rights protection.

A second factor was the recognition by legislators and the public of the enormous price this nation paid because of discrimination against handicapped persons. The cost was not only economic, but psychological in terms of wasted, frustrated lives. The statistics alone, as Senator

Birch Bayh has stated, are appalling. While the figures vary with different sources, there is no doubt that, in terms of employment only, handicapped people are clearly disadvantaged. One source has estimated that only 47.8% of handicapped people aged 16 to 64 were employed (compared to 65.1% of the same group in the general population); another source, that only 5.6 million of 36 million handicapped persons are employed; and yet another source that only 800,000 of 22 million handicapped adults are employed.

Whatever the numbers involved, it was clear that handicapped people were a wasted resource. In its first annual report, the Architectural and Transportation Barriers Compliance Board (the federal agency established to enforce the Architectural Barriers Act) concluded, "For the most part, they are a hidden population, isolated in a household environment and restricted from contributing their talents as active members of the community." Even more direct was the summation of David Williamson, then executive director of the National Paraplegia Foundation: "They have less income, less education, less employment, and more poverty."

The cost was also increasing. The continuing birth of children with handicaps, the mounting toll of persons injured in traffic, the returning wounded war veterans from Vietnam, the number of older persons with mobility handicaps—all influenced the passage of laws which would guarantee legal equality to handicapped persons. By 1974, there was no doubt that Congress recognized the need for urgent reform, when it enacted amendments to the Rehabilitation Act of 1973:

The Congress finds that . . .

(3) there are seven million children and at least twenty-eight million adults with mental or physical handicaps;

(4) it is of critical importance to this Nation that equality of opportunity, equal access to all aspects of society and equal rights guaranteed by the Constitution of the United States be provided to all individuals with handicaps. . . .

(7) all levels of Government must necessarily share

responsibility for developing opportunities for individuals with handicaps. . . .

The reform was long overdue, but the change in direction and the rationale were unmistakable.[3]

**Are the civil rights laws enacted on behalf of handi-
capped persons similar to civil rights provisions protecting
other minorities and women?**

Yes. The major federal statutes protecting the civil
rights of handicapped persons clearly reflect the influence
of earlier laws prohibiting other kinds of discrimination.
§504 of the Rehabilitation Act of 1973, as originally
enacted, provided:

No otherwise qualified handicapped individual in the
United States [as defined by the Act] shall, solely by
reason of his handicap, be excluded from the participation in, be denied the benefits of, or be subjected to
discrimination under any program or activity receiving Federal financial assistance.

In 1978, §504 was amended to apply to the federal
executive branch also.

§504 was modeled on Title VI of the Civil Rights Act
of 1964, which provides:

No person in the United States shall, on the ground
of race, color, or national origin, be excluded from
participation in, be denied the benefits of, or be
subjected to discrimination under any program or
activity receiving Federal financial assistance.

A second statute, enacted before §504, is Title IX of the
Education Amendments of 1972, which incorporates the
Title VI language in a provision pertaining to sex discrimination in education programs or activities receiving
federal financial assistance.

The close relationship between §504 and Title VI and
Title IX is apparent, not only from the language of the
statutes, but also from the legislative history of §504.
Reports of the Congressional committees which considered the proposals to prohibit discrimination against
handicapped persons stated:

Section 504 was enacted to prevent discrimination against all handicapped individuals . . . in relation to Federal assistance in employment, housing, transportation, education, health services, or any other Federally-aided programs. . . .

[The section] was patterned after, and is almost identical to, the antidiscrimination language of Section 601 of the Civil Rights Act of 1964 . . . and Section 901 of the Education Amendments of 1972. . . . The section therefore constitutes the establishment of a broad government policy that programs receiving Federal financial assistance shall be operated without discrimination on the basis of handicap. . . .

Moreover, Congress specified that the administrative enforcement procedures for implementing §504 should follow procedures already established to carry out Title VI.

Additionally, in §503 of the Rehabilitation Act, Congress required "affirmative action" in the employment and advancement of qualified handicapped individuals by many federal contractors. The legislative history of §504 also includes a requirement of affirmative action.

The antidiscrimination provisions pertaining to handicapped persons are similar, not only because of the general legislative scheme, but also because of the use of terms well established in other areas of civil rights law.[4]

Is there any significance in the relationship between such handicapped rights provisions as §503 and §504 and other statutes pertaining to discrimination on the basis of race or sex?

Yes. From a political standpoint, the similarity between the handicapped rights laws and other civil rights laws underscores the determination by Congress that discrimination against handicapped persons is of the same sort (and just as serious as) the discrimination faced by persons because of race or sex. The significance of this determination by Congress is that it serves to rebut the notion that discrimination against handicapped persons is somehow "different" and not amenable to legal remedies provided for other kinds of discrimination. Congress is declaring that discrimination against handicapped people can be remedied in ways similar to those established for other problems.

From a legal standpoint, the relationship between the handicapped rights provisions and other civil rights laws is significant because it guides courts and administrative agencies in implementation of the law.

In *Lloyd v. Regional Transportation Authority*, one question was whether §504 created mandatory rights enforceable by handicapped persons. The Court of Appeals, finding that §504 did create such rights, relied not only on the legislative history of §504, but also upon other cases interpreting Title VI of the Civil Rights Act of 1964. In one of those Title VI cases, the Supreme Court had construed the rights of Chinese-speaking children in the San Francisco public school system to have classes conducted in Chinese. The Supreme Court had held, "There is no equality of treatment merely by providing students with the same facilities, textbooks, teachers, and curriculum; for students who do not understand English are effectively foreclosed from any meaningful education."

The Court of Appeals, in the *Lloyd* case, cited this language, and paraphrased it to apply to the rights §504 provides to handicapped persons in the context of public transportation:

> Under these [federal] standards there is no equality of treatment merely by providing [the handicapped] with the same facilities [as ambulatory persons] . . . ; for [handicapped persons] who [can] not [gain access to such facilities] are effectively foreclosed from any meaningful [public transportation].

Like courts, administrative agencies can develop policies to implement handicapped rights provisions by applying guidelines established in other areas of civil rights. In regulations promulgated to implement Title VI programs administered by the Department of Health, Education and Welfare, HEW established guidelines defining the discrimination prohibited. Among specific acts prohibited are:

—Provision of any service, financial aid or other benefit to an individual which is different, or is provided
in a different manner, from that provided to others
under the program;

—Subjection of an individual to segregation or separate treatment in any matter related to his receipt of
any service, financial aid, or other benefit under the
program;

—Restriction of an individual in the enjoyment of any
advantage or privilege enjoyed by others receiving
any service, financial aid, or other benefit under the
program.

When HEW later promulgated regulations to implement §504, the regulations carried over some of the same
concepts and even, in some provisions, the same language
of the Title VI regulations. Among the specific acts prohibited under the regulations are:

—Provision of different or separate aid, benefits, or
services to handicapped persons or to any class of
handicapped persons unless such action is necessary
to provide qualified handicapped persons with aid,
benefits, or services that are as effective as those
provided to others;

—Employment policies which limit, segregate, or classify applicants or employees in any way that adversely affects their opportunities or status because
of handicaps (but note the discussion of the *Trageser*
case in the employment chapter for possible limitations on this concept);

—Program accessibility policies in existing facilities
which do not give priority to methods that offer programs and activities in the most integrated setting
possible.

Also significant to the establishment of civil rights for
handicapped people is the practice in a number of states
of enlarging the coverage of existing civil rights laws to
include handicapped persons. In states such as Illinois,
Indiana, New York, and Washington, various laws already protecting civil rights of minorities were amended
to include handicapped persons. Indeed, §504 itself orig-

inated as an attempt to amend Title VI of the Civil
Rights Act to include handicapped persons within the
coverage of the Civil Rights Act. Whether by incorpora-
tion directly into existing civil rights laws or by inclusion
of existing language and concepts into new provisions,
the rights of handicapped persons are part of established
civil rights policy.[5]

Have there been past laws and cases which blatantly denied equal rights to handicapped persons?

Yes. In 1919, the Supreme Court of Wisconsin permitted a school board to exclude a physically handicapped student from a regular public school partly on the
grounds that he was alleged to have created a distraction
in the school because he drooled. The court's opinion
described what the school authorities found objectionable:

> He . . . has an uncontrollable flow of saliva, which
> drools from his mouth onto his clothing and books,
> causing him to present an unclean appearance. . . .
> It is claimed, on the part of the school board, that
> his physical condition and ailment produces a de-
> pressing and nauseating effect upon the teachers
> and school children; that by reason of his physical
> condition he takes up an undue portion of the teach-
> er's time and attention, distracts the attention of
> other pupils, and interferes generally with the disci-
> pline and progress of the school.

The court acknowledged that he appeared "normal mentally" and that he had kept pace with his peers, but de-
ferred to the school board's assertion that "the teachers
had difficulty in understanding him, and he was not called
upon to recite as frequently as the others for the reason
that he was slow in speech, requiring more time to recite
than the other pupils." The school board had wanted the
boy placed in a special public school for handicapped
students. The court concluded that whatever right the
boy had to an education in the public school would be
contingent on his presence in the school not being "det-
rimental to the best interests of the school." The court upheld the school board's action in excluding him. One

Justice on the court dissented, arguing that there was no evidence that the boy was disruptive and that, in light of a state constitutional provision guaranteeing a free public education to all children, the school board should not be granted such broad discretion in excluding students.

The issues raised in this case illustrate the prejudice against physically handicapped persons that the legal system has permitted. The discrimination against the student was purposeful and intentional, and similar to racial, ethnic, or sexual discrimination. The school board's determination was provoked by subjective, personal prejudice against him, not by a determination that he was unfit to participate in school. Moreover, the thrust of the board's efforts was to banish him to a segregated institution, where he would be out of sight from those offended by his personal appearance. It is very unlikely that such a decision would be upheld today; this case, nevertheless, demonstrates attitudes toward handicapped people that are still present in our society. Other states and cities have passed statutes and even state constitutional provisions excluding handicapped persons from public school systems. The characterization of handicapped persons as "social outcasts" is well supported by history.[6]

Has the problem of stereotypes about handicapped persons impeded their achievement of equal rights?

Yes. There is evidence that opinions about handicapped persons by nonhandicapped persons are formulated more on the basis of categorical judgments about the class to which handicapped persons belong than on the basis of the characteristics of individual handicapped persons. A report by an international group of experts convened by the United Nations to study the problem of architectural barriers to handicapped persons concluded that the "social barriers we have evolved and accepted against those who vary more than a certain degree from what we have been conditioned to regard as normal" were as serious as the physical barriers. The panel concluded: "More people have been forced into limited lives and made to suffer by these manmade obstacles than by any specific physical or mental disability."

Robert Bogdan and Douglas Biklen have described

the way that stereotypes operate to hinder handicapped persons:

> Although inaccurate, a stereotype is often stead-fastly maintained. . . . First, peers and culture sup-port the transmission of stereotypes and therefore constantly reinforce them. Second, groups like the handicapped are isolated, have few opportunities for intimate relations to develop between themselves and so-called normal people, and consequently have little chance of disproving the stereotypes. Last, and per-haps most important, handicapped people are treated in ways that correspond to their stereotypes and are rewarded for living up to others' images of them. . . . Thus they learn the role of the handicapped and fall victim to the self-fulfilling prophecies. . . .

Handicapped persons encounter many stereotypes. One of the most important developments in the civil rights of physically handicapped persons is the legally guar-anteed opportunity to combat these stereotypes.

Two cases demonstrate how the legal system can be used to combat stereotypes. In *Hairston v. Drosick,* school officials had excluded from regular classes a child with spina bifida, which had left her with incontinence of the bowels and a noticeable limp. The court found that she was of "normal mental competence and capable of performing easily in a regular classroom situation." The school district had attempted to require the child's mother to come to the school on a daily, intermittent basis to assist the child, a task impossible for the mother in light of other family responsibilities.

The court noted the opinion of a medical specialist rec-ommending that the student be permitted to attend public school, and the lack of contrary evidence on the part of the school and concluded:

> There are a great number of other spina bifida chil-dren throughout the State of West Virginia who are attending public schools in the regular classroom situ-ation, the great majority of which have more severe disabilities than the plaintiff child. . . . The needless exclusion of these children and other children who

are able to function adequately from the regular classroom situation would be a great disservice to these children.

Stereotypes, and the misinformed attitudes underlying them, are serious problems to most handicapped groups. Jack McCallister, executive director of the Epilepsy Foundation of America, has written of the stereotyping problems faced by persons with epilepsy:

> The vast majority of these individuals have seizure disorders which can now be completely controlled or alleviated by the use of anticonvulsant medication. Yet many of our country's current state laws and policies are still based on medical and psychological concepts which have long been discredited by enlightened discoveries.
>
> These obsolete laws and practices frequently prevent persons with epilepsy from getting an education, driving automobiles, finding jobs, or obtaining insurance protection for themselves and their families. . . .

In a case involving a schoolteacher applicant denied employment because she was blind, the problem of stereotyping was also evident. The woman, a college graduate certified to teach English, applied for a high school teaching position. School officials first told her that, at most, a blind teacher would be permitted to teach only blind students (who apparently were segregated in a separate school). They would not permit her to teach sighted students, or even to take the Teachers Examination, a prerequisite to teaching sighted students. Among the fears expressed was that she would not be able to maintain discipline, correct papers, and keep records.

Five years after her initial inquiry, school officials permitted her to take the Teachers Examination (which she passed), but would not offer her employment with seniority dating from her initial application. In the lawsuit which followed, the United States Court of Appeals for the Third Circuit, affirming the decision of a lower federal district court, held that the denial to the applicant of the opportunity to demonstrate her qualifications violated her rights to due process guaranteed by the Fourteenth Amendment to the United States Constitution. By requiring due process in such situations, the court has provided an opportunity to combat the stereotypes and groundless fears about handicapped persons which prevent their integration into society. The lower court specifically noted expert testimony at the trial which demonstrated that, with minor support services, blind teachers have an exceptional record of successful teaching. Finding that an oral examination given the blind applicant did not evaluate the applicant fairly, the court concluded:

> The grading of the oral examination was based, at least in part, on misconceptions and stereotypes about the blind and on assumptions that the blind simply cannot perform, while the facts indicate that blind persons can be successful teachers. . . . [In this case], however, the interviewers frequently did not give her an opportunity to explain how she might overcome her handicap, nor did the interviewers have sufficient background information to properly evaluate the prospects of a blind applicant for a teaching position.

The due process principle illustrated in these cases—that, in determining the abilities of handicapped persons to participate in certain activities and to accomplish certain tasks, the determination must be made on the basis of specific abilities of the individuals involved and not on the basis of stereotyped, categorical judgments about the handicapped class to which the individuals belong—is fundamental to the success of the handicapped rights movement. Handicapped people must not be denied the opportunity to show what they can do. This principle is also established in laws and regulations pertaining to the educational placement and the employment of handicapped persons, matters which will be discussed later.[7]

In addition to stereotyping, what other attitudes toward handicapped people interfere with their achievement of equal rights?

It is not unusual for nonhandicapped persons to feel uncomfortable, or even fearful, about handicapped persons. Studies by psychologists indicate that such reactions are not uncommon, although the discomfort of nonhandicapped persons may be camouflaged under "saccharine words" that deny such feelings. But studies also indicate that with increased interaction between handicapped and nonhandicapped persons, particularly when handicapped persons are in situations where their abilities are evident, the fears and discomfort decrease, and handicapped persons are better accepted.[8]

Is integration into the common social, political, and cultural life of our nation important to handicapped persons in their quest for equality?

Yes. Integration is extremely important. Many public statements by handicapped persons and their advocates reveal an urgent concern that handicapped people be able to participate throughout our society. Inherent in this concern is a concurrent desire to be independent and to be able to make choices in the direction of individual lives.

The Architectural and Transportation Barriers Compliance Board heard testimony to this effect at hearings on transportation accessibility in 1974:

> A recurring theme throughout much of the testimony was the need for individual mobility by the handicapped. A key word was "choice," and expressed was the desire of the disabled to move freely and independently in society unimpaired by the physical and attitudinal barriers that restrict their choice of transportation, housing, education, recreation, and employment.

The integration issue emerges clearly in policy-making hearings concerning public housing for handicapped persons. During the 1968 Congressional hearings on the proposed Architectural Barriers Act, an official of the Department of Housing and Urban Development acknowledged that "Although there is some sentiment for projects for the handicapped only, we have found more general agreement that colonies of the handicapped are not desirable, and that their development would be contrary to current rehabilitation objectives." The statement of Max Starkloff at hearings conducted by the Architectural and Transportation Barriers Compliance Board in

1975 well expresses the importance of integration: ". . . the real problem is not the door too narrow for the wheelchair or the building accessible only by stairs. It is the isolation, both physical and psychological, that surrounds disabled people. . . . Total integration is the number one priority." [9]

What effect has the segregation of handicapped persons, together with the stereotyped and fearful attitudes toward them, had on handicapped people as they tried to live full lives?

In many cases, the effect has been a crippling sense of inferiority. Erving Goffman, the sociologist, in his famous study *Stigma: Notes on the Management of Spoiled Identity,* has written that the consequence of stigma is "the reduction in our minds from a whole and usual person to a tainted discounted one." He found that stigmatized persons faced ostracism, feelings of inferiority, and tendencies by so-called "normals" to "impute a wide range of imperfections on the basis of the original one." The testimony of handicapped persons supports Goffman's conclusion. Justice William O. Douglas has described his boyhood experience with polio:

> In retrospect, I see that this period is when I became a loner. Throughout my life I have enjoyed company but seldom sought it out. I preferred to eat lunch alone. I preferred to walk or exercise alone. I became a very lonely introspective person. . . . I had read what happened to cripples in the wilds; the crippled deer or fawn or bird did not have much chance to survive its natural enemies. . . . Nature protected only the strongest and the best, and man, including myself, was much the same, I thought. Only strong men could do the work of the world. . . . By these standards I was a failure.

Another handicapped individual has expressed the same attitude eloquently:

> One simply does not have to be Freud to understand that a physical handicap carries with it certain deci-

sive psychological ramifications, chief among them
the anxiety-provoking question of whether or not one
can make it—economically, socially and sexually—
on one's own.

The present movement to achieve equal rights for
handicapped persons reflects not only a change in national public policy toward handicapped persons, but
also a change in the attitudes of handicapped persons
themselves from defensiveness and inferiority to self-
acceptance and assertiveness.[10]

How many handicapped persons are there in the United States?

The exact number is difficult to ascertain. The Architectural and Transportation Barriers Compliance Board
has estimated the number at approximately 22 million
people, or 10 percent of the United States population,
with "physical impairments which restrict them from normal daily activities." A report by the General Accounting
Office estimated a range in the handicapped population
from 18 to 68 million, "depending mainly on how handicapped is defined." A report by Educational Facilities
Laboratories and the National Endowment for the Arts
provides this summary:

There are no certain figures about the number of
handicapped people in the United States. Estimates
range from one out of eleven working adults ages
16–64 according to a 1970 U.S. Census Bureau sam-
pling which excluded children and the elderly, to one
out of every four, or 51.1 million Americans according to a 1971 National Center for Health Statistics
survey which excluded institutionalized and military
populations. Additionally, the Council for Exceptional Children estimates that one out of every ten
school-age children is handicapped and it is reasonable to assume that many people over age 64 and the
major portion of those living in institutions are also
handicapped. Therefore, while there are no definitive
figures for the total number of handicapped people,
it is certain that inaccessible facilities restrict and im-

pair a remarkably large number of United States citizens.[11]

Has lack of enforcement by the agencies charged with implementation of the handicapped civil rights provision been a problem?

Yes. At the federal level alone, at least three agencies have been criticized for slowness and lack of direction in carrying out their responsibilities under various laws.

The Department of Health, Education and Welfare, and its Office for Civil Rights, have been under continual criticism since 1973 because of tardiness in the promulgation of regulations to implement §504. HEW had responsibilities to develop regulations not only for its own programs, but also guidelines for other executive departments in their implementation of §504. HEW did not announce regulations for its own programs until the spring of 1977, and promulgated guidelines *for the process of developing regulations* for other departments and agencies in January, 1978. There is continuing concern among handicapped persons that enforcement of §504 by the federal government will not be adequate to combat the discrimination in federally assisted activities.

The Urban Mass Transportation Administration (UMTA) has also faced severe criticism, as well as lawsuits, for failure to implement its responsibility to mandate accessible transportation services for handicapped persons. A 1977 report by the General Accounting Office concluded:

Before 1975 the Urban Mass Transportation Administration was passive in carrying out [a 1970 law declaring that elderly and handicapped persons have the same right as other persons to use mass transit and mandating that "special efforts" be made to plan and design mass transit so that the handicapped would have access]. As a result, mass transit grants awarded to local transit officials seldom addressed the needs of elderly and handicapped persons. Some recent regulations should prove helpful, but more can be done.

The requirement announced in 1977 that, after September 30, 1979, local transportation authorities were required to purchase the "Transbus" (a vehicle accessible to many handicapped persons) has generated greater hope about UMTA's future policies. But skepticism about UMTA persists in the face of "interim regulations" which provide for limited, segregated, and insufficient levels of service to meet the transportation needs of handicapped persons. The "Transbus mandate" itself was only a partial victory until carried out, and the concern that the effective date of the mandate might be delayed by political factors was recently realized when the September 30 date was dropped.

A third agency which has met criticism is the Architectural and Transportation Barriers Compliance Board. Criticism of the Compliance Board has been mixed with criticism of the Architectural Barriers Act, which was once described as "an ineffectual policy statement rather than . . . a master-plan for a mandatory program." With amendments to the Act to make it more clearly mandatory and with amendments to the Rehabilitation Act, some criticism may abate. Several recent citations against agencies charged with violations marked the beginning of formal enforcement actions by the Compliance Board. The 1978 Amendments to the Rehabilitation Act were aimed at making the Board a more effective enforcement agency, as well as enlarging the Board's membership.

Criticism has been directed toward the Department of Labor, for tardy and ineffective enforcement of §503. Continued monitoring of the agencies charged with enforcing the handicapped civil rights laws is essential to the achievement of the goals of those laws.[12]

Has there been a "backlash" against the change in national policy toward equal rights for handicapped persons?

It may not be appropriate to characterize the reaction as "backlash," but at least two issues have been raised which indicate resistance. Employers have expressed concern that the reasonable accommodations requirement of some legal provisions may result in high costs. Partly to meet such criticism, the Department of Health, Education and Welfare commissioned an "inflationary impact statement" on the projected costs of implementation of §504. The report stated, "for most combinations of types of handicapping conditions and job category 'reasonable accommodations' will require either no or only minor outlays. . . . "

A second source of resistance has come from colleges and universities concerned about the requirements of §504, particularly the program and activity accessibility requirement. School officials have expressed the concern that the costs of altering existing buildings could be high. Partially in response to the complaints, HEW has interpreted §504 to mean that, "A recipient is not required to make structural changes in existing facilities where other methods are effective in achieving compliance" with the program accessibility requirement. "Other methods" may include reassignment of classes or services to accessible buildings and assignment of aides to handicapped persons (although carrying of handicapped persons is strictly limited.) There is a question of whether this HEW regulatory provision meets the intent of Congress in enacting §504. One gesture by Congress to meet the general problem of accessibility in higher education is the consideration of funds for colleges for purposes of meeting federal accessibility standards, itself a matter of controversy.[13]

Has the movement to achieve legal equality for handicapped persons been undertaken entirely at the federal level?

No. Many states have laws protecting the civil rights of handicapped persons. Some state laws reach beyond the scope of the federal provisions. Additionally, some counties and cities have adopted provisions protecting the civil rights of handicapped persons, particularly on the subject of architectural barriers. Therefore, any claim for discrimination on the basis of handicap should look to federal, state, and local laws as basis for relief. State and local laws may often be found as amendments to existing legislation or, in some cases, as statutes and ordinances dealing exclusively with the rights of handicapped persons.

NOTES

1. The New Hampshire case is *Sleeper v. Sandown*, 52 N.H. 244 (1872); ten Broek, *The Right to Live in the World: The Disabled in the Law of Torts*, 54 CALIF. L. REV. 841 (1966). (Professor ten Broek's famous article suggested the *Sleeper* case to me, *ibid.* at 868); *e.g.*, the HEW §504 regulations reasonable accommodations in employment section §84.12 (these regulations are those which apply to HEW recipients and are codified at 45 C.F.R.; throughout this book citation will be to the regulations as they appeared in the May 4, 1977 *Fed. Reg.*, 42 *Fed. Reg.* 22676); the Philadelphia case involving the blind teacher is *Gurmankin v. Costanzo*, 411 F. Supp. 982 (E.D. Pa. 1976), *aff'd.*, 556 F.2d 184 (3rd Cir. 1977); for a second case involving a blind teacher see *Bevan v. New York State Teachers Retirement System*, 74 Misc. 2d 443, 345 N.Y.S. 2d 921 (1973).

2. Sar A. Levitan and Robert Taggart, *Jobs for the Disabled* (Baltimore, 1977) xi; Comment, *The Forgotten Minority: The Physically Disabled and Improving Their Physical Environment*, 48 Chicago—Kent L. Rev. 215, 219 (1971); for the early federal legislation see the discussion in *id.*; the 1976 federal case was *Lloyd v. Illinois Regional Transportation Authority*, 75 C 1834 (N.D. Ill. 1976), *reversed sub nom., Lloyd v. Regional Transportation Authority*, 548 F.2d 1277 (7th Cir. 1977).

3. Senator Bayh's statement is at 123 Cong. Rec. No. 66, S6127 (April 21, 1977); employment statistics are in the Senator's statement as well as in the United States Department of Transportation, *The Handicapped and Elderly Market for Urban Mass Transit* at 8 (1973) and in Comment, *Equal Employment and the Disabled: A Proposal*, 10 Columbia Journal of Law and Social Problems 457, citing S. Rep. No. 319, 93rd Cong., 1st Sess. at 8 (1973); the ATBCB statement is in the Board's *First Report to the Congress of the United States* at 1 (1974) and David Williamson's statement is in the Board's report, *Freedom of Choice: Report to the President and Congress on Housing Needs of Handicapped Individuals* at 52 (1976); the Congressional finding is in the White House Conference on Handicapped Individuals Act (Act of December 7,

1974, Title III of Pub. L. 93–516, 88 Stat. 1631–1634,
at 29 U.S.C.A. §701 note (1975)).

4. Section 504 is at 29 U.S.C.A. §794 (1975) but note the
1978 amendments discussed later and found in the 1979
U.S.C.A. Supplement [All citations to federal statute will
be to the version printed in United States Code Anno-
tated]; the Title VI provision is at 42 U.S.C.A. §2000 d
(1974); the Title IX provision is 20 U.S.C.A. §1681
(1974); on the legislative history of §504 see, for example, 4 U.S. Code Cong. & Admin. News 6388–6391 (1974)
and *Lloyd v. Regional Transportation Authority,* 548 F.2d
1277, 1285 (7th Cir. 1977); §503 is at 29 U.S.C.A. §793
(1975).

5. The *Lloyd* case is at 548 F.2d 1277 (7th Cir. 1977); the
Supreme Court Title VI case is *Lau v. Nichols,* 414 U.S.
563 (1974); the quoted language from *Lloyd* is at 548
F.2d at 1284; the Title VI regulations are at 45 C.F.R.
§80.3; the HEW §504 regulations are §§84.4(b)(1)(iv),
84.11(a)(3), and 84.22(b); the examples of state legislation are Ill. Rev. Stat., ch. 48, §§851, 853(a)(b)(c), 854,
Indiana Code §22-9-1-2, *New York Human Rights Law*
18 Consol. Laws N.Y. §296.2-a, Revised Code of Washington §49.60.180.

6. *State ex rel. Beattie v. Bd. of Educ. of City of Antigo,* 172
N.W. 153 (Wis. 1919) is the Wisconsin case; older
statutes and ordinances are collected in Comment, *Abroad
in the Land: Legal Strategies to Effectuate the Rights of
the Physically Disabled,* 61 Georgetown L.J. 1501, 1503
(1973) and in Burgdorf and Burgdorf, *A History of Un-
equal Treatment: The Qualifications of Handicapped Persons as "Suspect Class" under the Equal Protection
Clause,* 15 Santa Clara Lawyer 855, 863 (1975); the social
outcast statement is made by Leonard Kriegel in *Uncle
Tom and Tiny Tim: Some Reflections on the Cripple as
Negro,* 38 American Scholar 412, 416 (1969).

7. For the categorical class judgment problem see Safilios-
Rothschild, *The Sociology and Social Psychology of Disability and Rehabilitation* at 4 (1970); the United Nations
statement is in *Barrier Free Design: Report of a United
Nations Expert Group Meeting* at 3 (1975); the Bogdan
and Biklen statement is in "Handicapism," *Social Policy*
at 14, 15 (March–April, 1977); *Hairston v. Drosick,* 423
F. Supp. 180, 183 (S.D.W. Va. 1976); the Jack McCallister statement is in the Foreword, *The Legal Rights of
Persons with Epilepsy: A Survey of State Laws and Ad-

ministrative Policies Relating to Persons with Epilepsy with a Special Section on Model Legislation (1976); the blind school teacher applicant case is *Gurmankin v. Costanzo,* 556 F.2d 184 (3rd Cir. 1977), affirming 411 F. Supp. 982 (E.D. Pa. 1976), and for the lower court language see 411 F. Supp. at 986, 987–988; the final paragraph is adapted from my paper presented to a session of the Section on Individual Rights and Responsibilities of the American Bar Association's August, 1977, Annual Meeting, the paper entitled "The Civil Rights of Physically Handicapped People: Four Issues for Lawyers."

8. See generally, Beatrice Wright, *Physical Disability—A Psychological Approach* at 254–260 (1960); Yuker, Block and Campbell, *A Scale to Measure Attitudes toward Disabled Persons* (1960); "Reactions to the Handicapped—Sweaty Palms and Saccharine Words," *Psychology Today* (November, 1975), 122.

9. The testimony before the Compliance Board is in its *First Report to the Congress* at 27 (1974); *Building Design for the Physically Handicapped . . . Hearings before the Subcommittee on Public Buildings and Grounds of the Committee on Public Works on H.R. 6589 and S. 222,* 90th Cong., 2nd Sess. at 40 (1968); the statement by Max Starkloff is in the Compliance Board's report, *Freedom of Choice* at 21, 22.

10. Goffman, *Stigma: Notes on the Management of Spoiled Identity* at 3, 5, 6, 13 (1963); the statement by Justice Douglas is in his autobiography, *Go East, Young Man: The Early Years—The Autobiography of William O. Douglas* at 34–35 (1974); the second quotation is from Leonard Kriegel's article, *Uncle Tom and Tiny Tim: Reflections of the Cripple as Negro,* 38 American Scholar 412, 414 (1969).

11. The Compliance Board Statistics are in the First Report to the Congress at 1 (1974); the GAO report is in Comptroller-General of the United States, *Report to the Congress: Further Action Needed to Make All Public Buildings Accessible to the Physically Handicapped* at 1 (1975); the EFL statement is in Educational Facilities Laboratories and the National Endowment for the Arts, *Arts and the Handicapped: An Issue of Access* at 6 (1975).

12. The HEW §504 regulations were published at 42 *Fed. Reg.* 22,676 (May 4, 1977) (45 C.F.R. Part 84), and the HEW Executive Order Guidelines regulations were published at 43 *Fed. Reg.* 2132 (January 13, 1978) (45

C.F.R. Part 85); the statement about UMTA is in Comptroller-General of the United States, *Mass Transit for Elderly and Handicapped Persons: Urban Mass Transportation Administration's Actions* at (i) (1977); on criticism of the Architectural Barriers Act, see Farber, *The Handicapped Plead for Entrance—Will Anyone Answer?* 64 Ky. L.J. 99, 112 (1975) which is the source of the quoted statement on the A.B. Act, the 1978 Amendments to the Rehabilitation Act are Rehabilitation, Comprehensive Services and Developmental Disabilities Amendments of 1978, Pub. L. 95–602, 92 Stat. 2855, §118; the change in the effective date of Transbus is at 44 *Fed. Reg.* 47,343 (August 13, 1979).

13. The economic impact statement is from O'Neill, *Discrimination against Handicapped Persons: The Costs Benefits and Inflation—Any Impact of Implementing §504 of the Rehabilitation Act of 1973 Covering Recipients of HEW Financial Assistance* (February 14, 1977) available from the Department of Health, Education and Welfare at 7 (my pagination—document not paginated); the quoted statement is from the HEW §504 regulation §84.22(b); see chapter III for some examples of federal funding to remove barriers.

II

A Primer on Rights

One of the most important public events for handicapped people in 1977 was the issuance of final regulations by the Department of Health, Education and Welfare to implement §504 of the Rehabilitation Act of 1973. For several years after enactment of the law, Congress had conducted periodic hearings to determine why regulatory agencies were not issuing regulations as speedily as Congress had expected. A federal district court had ordered the Secretary of HEW to issue the regulations, but without requiring that it be done within a specific time period. Handicapped people had demonstrated for weeks in the early spring of 1977 at HEW headquarters and regional HEW offices throughout the nation.

Behind the demand that HEW issue the regulations were two desires: that this major civil rights law be enforced, and that the federal executive branch signify its commitment to equal rights for handicapped people. Apart from the substantive importance of the regulations was an equally important, and perhaps farther-reaching, symbolic significance. Because programs assisted by HEW affected the lives of many handicapped persons, the implementation of the regulations would provide a test of the success of §504 in the achievement of equal rights for handicapped persons.

The HEW §504 regulations do not, by any means, constitute all of the federal law pertaining to the civil rights of handicapped persons. Each executive department and agency is required to implement §504 for programs which receive federal financial assistance from it. Amendments in 1978 applied §504 to the federal executive agencies and the U.S. Postal Service. Other sections of the Rehabilitation Act establish legal protection for handicapped persons. Statutes such as the Architectural Barriers Act, the Education of All Handicapped Children Act, and provisions of the revenue sharing amendments of 1976 contain important provisions protecting the civil rights of handicapped persons. Many state laws and local ordinances also contain provisions that establish equal rights for handicapped persons (which sometimes reach more deeply into the private sector than do federal laws).

Nevertheless, the HEW regulations are important as an example of the practical application of fundamental concepts intended to implement the nondiscrimination mandate. The purpose of this chapter is to examine the HEW §504 regulations and to consider the concepts, principles, and examples provided there in order to obtain a general introduction to the implementation of civil rights for handicapped persons.[1]

What is the scope of the HEW §504 regulations?

The regulations are intended primarily to implement the requirements of §504 for HEW programs. Section 504 provided, as originally enacted:

No otherwise qualified handicapped individual in the United States, as defined in [29 U.S.C. §706(6)], shall, solely by reason of his handicap, be excluded from the participation in, be denied the benefits of, or be subjected to discrimination under any program or activity receiving Federal financial assistance.

Amendments in 1978 expanded §504 to cover the federal executive agencies.

The regulations also give, as a statutory basis for authority, §606 of the Education for All Handicapped Children Act, which provides:

The Secretary shall assure that each recipient of assistance under this chapter shall make positive efforts to employ and advance in employment qualified handicapped individuals in programs assisted under this chapter.

The regulations are also intended to implement parts of the Comprehensive Alcohol Abuse and Alcoholism Prevention Treatment and Rehabilitation Act of 1970, and of the Drug Abuse Office and Treatment Act of 1972; both these laws are beyond the scope of this book.

There will be a continuing question of what "programs or activities" the statute and regulations include and what constitutes "federal financial assistance." The regulations define "federal financial assistance" as "any grant, loan, contract (other than a procurement contract or a contract of insurance or guaranty), or any other arrangement by which the Department provides or otherwise makes available assistance in the form of" funds, services of federal personnel, or property. One federal court has already noted the need for administrative agencies to draw a distinction between the terms "federal contracts" (as used in the §503 affirmative action employment provision) and federal grants, while another district court has limited the scope of §504 to certain types of federal grants:

> [§504] appears to be limited to entities which receive federal grants in the nature of gifts to support activities deemed to be in the public interest or for the public welfare. The term "federal financial assistance" as used in [§504] does not comprehend government procurement contracts but rather refers to the form of grant assistance that goes primarily to public entities.

The exclusion of contracts "of insurance or guaranty" from coverage by the act's provision should not be confused with the requirement in the employment part of the regulations that programs or activities may not discriminate in the provision of "fringe benefits available by virtue of employment, whether or not administered by the recipient" (which could include health, disability, and life insurance programs). HEW's stated reason for excluding procurement contracts was that such contracts are already covered by the provisions of §503. Its rationale for excluding contracts of insurance or guaranty is that since Title VI of the Civil Rights Acts of 1964 and Title IX of the Education Amendments of 1972 explicitly exclude such contracts, then §504 (a statute modeled on the other two titles) should be interpreted to provide a similar exclusion. The regulations set forth a somewhat confusing explanation as to when §504 applies to recipients under Medicaid and Medicare programs, a rather complex matter deserving careful attention if discrimination occurs in these programs.

Included within the scope of the HEW §504 regulations are many programs whereby HEW provides assistance—including education, health, and social welfare programs and activities—to many different types of "recipients," including states and political subdivisions of states, public and private agencies, institutions, and organizations. The term "recipient" is defined to include those entities that receive the assistance from HEW, not the persons served by the programs who are called "beneficiaries." Whether recipients receive assistance directly or through another recipient, §504 applies.[2]

Who is considered handicapped within the meaning of the HEW §504 regulations?

The definition of the term "handicapped person" in the Rehabilitation Act and in the HEW implementing regulations has been one of the more controversial aspects of recent federal policy toward handicapped persons. The act provides a definition (limited in application to the civil rights provisions and one other title of the act) which has three criteria, any one of which may result in an individual being considered handicapped for the purpose of §504. A "handicapped person" within the meaning of the Act is any person who:

1. has a physical or mental impairment which substantially limits one or more major life activities, or
2. has a record of such an impairment, or
3. is regarded as having such an impairment.

Neither the Act nor the regulations provide a list of specific handicaps covered, but the regulations do specify broad categories of disorders and conditions which will be considered "impairments." Among these conditions are physiological disorders or conditions involving the neurological, musculoskeletal, cardiovascular, and respiratory (including speech) systems, in addition to special sense organs. Additionally, such mental or psychological disorders as mental retardation, organic brain syndrome, emotional or mental illness, and specific learning disabilities are included within the meaning of "physical or mental impairment." Moreover, if a "cosmetic disfigurement" or "anatomical loss" affects the specified body systems, such a condition constitutes an "impairment." The regulations list additional systems and parts of the body included in these definitions.

While neither the Rehabilitation Act nor the regulations list specific conditions considered to be handicaps, the departmental Analysis accompanying the regulations notes that clearly included are such diseases and conditions as orthopedic, visual, speech and hearing impairments, cerebral palsy, epilepsy, muscular dystrophy, multiple sclerosis, cancer, heart disease, diabetes, mental retardation, and emotional illness. HEW also included drug addiction and alcoholism, two conditions which this book will not discuss as such and matters which prompted amendments in 1978 to the Act with respect to the civil rights coverage of those groups.

It is not enough for an individual to have one of these conditions in order to be considered handicapped; the condition must be such that it "substantially limits one or more major life activities." "Major life activities" have been defined as "functions such as caring for one's self, performing manual tasks, walking, seeing, hearing, speaking, breathing, learning, and working." HEW rejected the suggestion that it should limit the coverage of the regulations to more common "traditional" handicaps. Its position has been that the statutory language of §504 requires the expansive approach taken. The departmental Analysis accompanying the final regulations does state that HEW intends "to give particular attention to its enforcement of §504 to eliminating discrimination against persons with the severe handicaps that were the focus of concern in the Rehabilitation Act of 1973." In this statement HEW seems to indicate that it will give priority to enforcing §504 in those cases involving discrimination against persons with substantial and serious handicaps; HEW may also be indicating that it will act to fulfill the purpose underlying 1974 amendments to the Rehabilitation Act mandating that state vocational rehabilitation agencies give priorities in their services to severely handicapped people (who, the Congress found, had been neglected by such agencies). The regulations also include "specific learning disabilities" such as dyslexia and developmental aphasia (a subject also beyond the scope of this book).

(2) *A Record of a Physical or Mental Impairment that Substantially Limits One or More Major Life Activities.*

The second part of the definition is intended to include persons who have a history of a handicapping condition, but no longer have the condition, as well as persons who were once incorrectly classified as having a handicap. Examples of persons with a history of a handicap are individuals with histories of mental illness, heart disease, or cancer. These persons may very well have recovered, but the record of their earlier problems continues to provoke discrimination against them. In the second category of "the misclassified" are persons such as those who have been classified as mentally retarded, not on the basis of accurate criteria, but for such reasons as racial or cultural bias. However, it should be noted that environmental, cultural, or economic disadvantages are not in themselves considered handicaps within the meaning of §504. Neither are such characteristics as a prison record, age, or homosexuality considered, in and of themselves, handicaps. Only if an individual with one of these characteristics also meets one of the three definitions for handicapped persons will the individual qualify for protection under §504.

(3) *Regarded as Having a Physical or Mental Handicap that Substantially Limits One or More Major Life Activities.*

This part of the definition is intended to encompass persons who may not have a handicap, as defined in the statute and regulations, or a record of such a handicap, but who nevertheless encounter discrimination which indicates that they are considered to be handicapped. The examples given, in the Analysis accompanying the regulations, are individuals with limps or disfiguring scars. Such conditions may not in fact constitute an impairment for the individuals involved, but the individuals may encounter prejudice because of the conditions. This part of the definitions is perhaps the least precise in defining the class of handicapped persons protected.

The original statutory definition was provided by 1974 amendments to the Rehabilitation Act to expand the class of persons included within the protection of §504 and the other civil rights provisions of the Rehabilitation Act. As noted, changes limited to alcoholics and drug abusers were made in 1978.[8]

Is the §504 definition of handicapped persons the only one used in statutes establishing civil rights for handicapped persons?

No. In other federal statutes and in state and local laws, other definitions with different emphases are used.

For example, the Education for All Handicapped Children Act gives this definition for children entitled to the law's protection:

> "handicapped children" means mentally retarded, hard of hearing, deaf, speech impaired, visually handicapped, seriously emotionally disturbed, orthopedically impaired, or other health impaired children, or children with specific learning disabilities, who by reason thereof require special education and related services.

The Urban Mass Transportation Act provides this definition of handicapped persons within that statute's coverage:

> For purposes of this chapter, the term "handicapped person" means any individual who, by reason of illness, injury, age, congenital malfunction, or other permanent or temporary incapacity or disability, is unable without special facilities or special planning or design to utilize mass transportation fa-

cilities and services as effectively as persons who are not so affected.

The State of Michigan, in its "Michigan Handicappers' Civil Rights Act," defines "handicap" in this manner:

As used in this act . . .
(b) "Handicap" means a determinable physical or mental characteristic of an individual or the history of the characteristic which may result from disease, injury, congenital condition of birth, or functional disorder which characteristic:
    (i) for purpose of [the section related to employment], is unrelated to the individual's ability to perform the duties of a particular job or position, or is unrelated to the individual's qualifications for employment or promotion.
    (ii) for purposes of [the section related to public accommodations] is unrelated to the individual's ability to utilize and benefit from a place of public accommodation or public service.
    (iii) for purposes of [the section related to education] is unrelated to the individual's ability to utilize and benefit from educational opportunities, programs and facilities at an educational institution.
    (iv) for purposes of [the section related to housing] is unrelated to the individual's ability to acquire, rent or maintain property.
(c) "Handicapper" means an individual who has a handicap.

These examples indicate the different emphases separate statutes may have in their definitions of who is considered handicapped. There is controversy over what constitutes a good definition, just as there is controversy over use of the term "handicapped" and "disabled." In a case interpreting a Washington employment discrimination statute that included sensorily, mentally, or physically handicapped persons with other protected classes, the state supreme court upheld use of the word "handicap" in the statute despite the lack of a definition of that term in the statute. An employer had argued that the statute was unconstitutionally vague and indefinite. The court rejected that argument:

> the statute provides fair notice of what is required. . . .
> Men of common intelligence need not guess at the meaning of handicap because it has a well defined usage measured by common practice and understanding. "Handicap" commonly connotes a condition that prevents normal functioning in some way. A person with a handicap does not enjoy, in some manner, the full and normal use of his sensory, mental, or physical faculties. A handicap is: ". . . a disadvantage that makes achievement unusually difficult; *esp:* a physical disability that limits the capacity to work. . . ." It is obvious that "handicap" has a well understood, common meaning. Men of ordinary intelligence can understand what constitutes a "handicap" within the context of [the statute under review] and, consequently, the statute is not void for vagueness. . . . [4]

What does the term "otherwise qualified handicapped person" mean in the HEW §504 regulations?

§504 prohibits discrimination against "otherwise qualified handicapped persons." The regulations provide examples of a "qualified handicapped person":

1. With respect to employment, a handicapped person who, with reasonable accommodation, can perform the essential functions of the job in question.
2. With respect to public preschool, elementary, secondary, or adult education services, the handicapped person be:
   a. of an age during which nonhandicapped persons are provided such services;
   b. of any age during which it is mandatory un-

der state law to provide such services, or to whom a state is required to provide a free appropriate education under the mandate of the federal legislation pertaining to education of handicapped persons; and

3. With respect to postsecondary and vocational education services, a handicapped person who meets the academic and technical standards requisite to admission or participation in the recipient's education program or activity;

4. With respect to other services, a handicapped person who meets the essential eligibility requirements for receipt of such services.

The qualifying conditions illustrate, in different settings, both the responsibilities of handicapped persons and the obligations of recipients. In postsecondary and vocational education programs, handicapped persons must meet "academic and technical" standards requisite to admission and participation, but that is the prime requirement. As we will see in the chapter on postsecondary education, postsecondary and vocational institutions must make sure that their standards and methods of testing accurately measure the abilities of handicapped persons, and they must also make accommodations for handicapped persons in their programs. How the Supreme Court decision in *Southeastern Community College v. Davis* affects their requirement is discussed in the chapter on postsecondary education. Likewise, handicapped persons employed or seeking employment with recipients covered under §504 must be able to perform "the essential functions of the job in question" (which must be defined accurately and fairly), but employers must make "reasonable accommodations" to the known physical or mental limitations of those handicapped persons. The rights and responsibilities are a balance between those obligations imposed on recipients and those imposed on handicapped individuals.

By contrast, the rights of handicapped students to receive appropriate public education services in preschool, elementary, and secondary programs is conditioned primarily on one qualification: age. If a handicapped child meets the age requirement, then that child is entitled to a free, appropriate public education. There is no requirement that the child be "qualified" in any sense, regardless of the nature or severity of the handicap. Rather the obligations to meet this mandate are imposed on the public school systems. HEW rejected arguments that the obligation to provide services for handicapped students should depend upon those students' abilities to enjoy a "substantial benefit" from education. Moreover, the age limit qualifications are subject to modification if a school is ordered to provide services that were formerly denied because of a recipient's violation of §504.[5]

Do the HEW §504 regulations establish general categories of prohibited discriminatory action or suggest broad principles to evaluate whether specific actions are discriminatory?

Yes. The HEW regulations provide a list of several prohibited discriminatory actions that serve as guideposts in identifying acts or policies that would violate §504. First, a recipient may not deny a qualified handicapped person, on the basis of handicap, the opportunity to participate in or benefit from an aid, benefit, or service. Second, recipients may not afford an opportunity to qualified handicapped persons to participate in or benefit from an aid, benefit or service on a basis not equal to that afforded others. Third, recipients are prohibited from providing aid, benefit, or service "not as effective as those provided to others." Fourth, the provision of different or separate aid, benefits, or services is prohibited "unless such action is necessary to provide qualified handicapped persons with aid, benefits, or services that are as effective as those provided to others."

The initial statement of general principles concludes with a prohibition of limitations of a qualified handicapped person's enjoyments of "any right, privilege, advantage, or opportunity enjoyed by others" benefiting from the program. The regulations emphasize the rights of qualified handicapped persons to participate as members of planning or advisory boards of recipients. They further prohibit recipients from providing "significant assistance" to an agency, organization, or person that discriminates on the basis of handicap in providing aid, benefits, or services to persons (beneficiaries) in the recipient's program. The discriminatory actions prohibited apply to direct actions by recipients or through such indirect actions as contractual, licensing, or other arrangements.

A basic principle emerges from the listing of prohibited discriminatory acts—the right to equally effective benefits and participation, all provided in an integrated setting. But the regulations further explain the application of this principle. The critically important term "equally effective" is interpreted as

> not required to produce the identical results or level of achievement for handicapped and nonhandicapped persons, but must afford handicapped persons equal opportunity to obtain the same result, to gain the same benefit, or to reach the same level of achievement, in the most integrated setting appropriate to the person's needs.

The fundamental premise is one of equivalent, not identical, services. The thrust of this requirement is to emphasize that adjustments to regular programs or provisions of different programs may be necessary to meet the individual needs of handicapped persons to the same extent that the corresponding needs of nonhandicapped persons are met. The Analysis accompanying the regulations illustrates this requirement by the example of a welfare office that uses the telephone to communicate with clients now being required to provide alternative modes of communicating with deaf clients. In support of this interpretation, HEW cites the decision of the U.S. Supreme Court in *Lau v. Nichols,* which held that, under the provisions of the Civil Rights Act of 1964 against discrimination on the basis of race, color, or national origin, the San Francisco public schools could not refuse to conduct programs for non-English-speaking Chinese students. At stake, HEW contends, is "an equal opportunity to achieve equal results."

In those situations where separate or different programs are permitted to exist, recipients must still give qualified handicapped persons the option of participating in regular programs. Additionally, the prohibition against indirect support to entities or persons that discriminate prohibits acts such as a contribution by a recipient to a professional or social organization that discriminates.[6]

Do the HEW §504 regulations require "special treatment" for handicapped persons?

The answer depends upon how we define the term "special treatment." The preamble to the regulations states:

> In drafting a regulation to prohibit exclusion and discrimination, it became clear that different or special treatment of handicapped persons, because of their handicaps, may be necessary in a number of contexts in order to ensure equal opportunity. Thus, for example, it is meaningless to "admit" a handicapped person in a wheelchair to a program if the program is offered only on the third floor of a walk-up building. Nor is one providing equal educational opportunity to a deaf child by admitting him or her to a classroom but providing no means for the child to understand the teacher or receive instruction.

This statement pertains to the obligation to take "special" action in the sense of providing accessibility to programs or appropriate educational services. To this category we could add the requirement that employers make "reasonable accommodation" for handicapped employees or the requirement that recipient hospitals that provide health services or benefits establish a procedure for effective communication with hearing-impaired persons needing emergency health care.

But apart from these actions necessary to accomplish the fundamental goal of opening the doors to equal opportunity, the regulations also speak of "remedial action, voluntary action, and self-evaluation."

§84.6(a) of the regulations provides that where the Director of the Office for Civil Rights of HEW finds that a recipient has discriminated on the basis of handicap, "the recipient shall take such remedial action as the Director deems necessary to overcome the effects of the discrimination." The Director may require remedial action to be taken toward persons who are no longer part of a program but were part of the program when the discrimination occurred or toward persons who would have been participants in the program if the discrimination had not occurred. Additionally, §84.6(b) provides that recipients "may take steps," on a voluntary basis, "to overcome the effects of conditions that resulted in limited participation in the recipient's program or activity by qualified handicapped persons."

In the proposed regulations, what is now called "voluntary action" was termed "affirmative action." The action to be taken was essentially the same as that now provided for in the final regulations, except that the proposed regulations allowed such action "in the absense of a finding of discrimination" in violation of §504, where the final regulation allows the action "in addition to any action that is required." It should be noted that, in the legislative history of §504, Congressional committee reports state, "Where applicable, section 504 is intended to include a requirement of affirmative action as well as a prohibition against discrimination." The Analysis accompanying the final regulations offers this explanation of the purpose of the present language:

> . . . the term "voluntary action" has been substituted for the term "affirmative action" because the use of the latter term led to some confusion. We believe the term "voluntary action" more accurately reflects the purpose of the paragraph. This provision allows action, beyond that required by the regulation, to overcome conditions that led to limited participation by handicapped persons, whether or not the limited participation was caused by any discriminatory actions on the part of the recipient.

§84.6(c) also requires that within one year of the effective date of the regulations, recipients undertake "self-evaluation" of their current policies and practices as to the effects on qualified handicapped persons, modify such policies and practices that do not meet the requirements of §504, and take "appropriate remedial steps to eliminate the effects of any discrimination that resulted from adherence to these policies and practices." Those sections also require that handicapped persons and organizations representing the handicapped be consulted in the self-evaluation process. Recipients that employ 15 or more persons must also keep written records of the self-evaluation.

These §504 requirements may be contrasted to a 1972 statute passed by Congress prohibiting discrimination against blind persons by institutions of higher education in any course of study, but not requiring any accommodations to the needs of blind persons and to a 1975 provision of the Education for All Handicapped Children Act, which requires the Secretary of HEW to assure that "positive efforts" are made in the employment and advancement of qualified handicapped persons in programs funded under that law. How §504 will be interpreted in relation to these other statutes remains to be seen. Legal commentators have expressed the concern that, unless administered carefully, affirmative action could result in "creaming," or the choice by recipients of only those handicapped persons with minimal handicaps, thereby giving the appearance that the law is fulfilled, but in reality excluding many handicapped persons.

Therefore, the term "special treatment" must be examined from two viewpoints. In terms of specific "quotas" or "goals" to serve or hire handicapped persons, the requirement is somewhat unclear. But there is a clear requirement with respect to the obligation to make reasonable accommodations to the needs of handicapped persons. The essence of what this second "affirmative action" concept means for different handicapped groups, particularly in employment, was well-expressed by one legal writer, commenting on §503:

> The general principles underlying the affirmative action concept suggest that analysis should begin with a consideration of how handicapped individuals differ from the majority. For example, the blind cannot be dependent upon visual communications, the deaf cannot be dependent upon aural communication, the one-armed person cannot be dependent on two

levers which must be moved simultaneously, the wheelchair passenger cannot be dependent on traversals of near-vertical planes or narrow passageways, and the mentally retarded cannot be dependent on certain mental reflexes. Removing such dependencies from his work environment may be part of a contractor's affirmative action obligation.[7]

The Supreme Court's ruling in the *Davis* case, discussed in the chapter on postsecondary education, obviously raises questions about this obligation. The precise effect remains unclear at present.

Does the possible expense a recipient might incur in complying with §504 have a bearing on enforcement?
§504 makes no reference to the factor of expense in implementation of the statute. In the introduction to its final §504 regulations, HEW makes this statement about the significance of cost:

. . . ending discriminatory practices and providing equal access to programs may involve major burdens on some recipients. Those burdens and costs, to be sure, provide no basis for exemption from Section 504 or this regulation: Congress' mandate to end discrimination is clear. But it is also clear that factors of burden and cost had to be taken into account in the regulation in prescribing the actions necessary to end discrimination and to bring handicapped persons into full participation in federally financed programs and activities.

The application of this policy is illustrated in the section of the HEW §504 regulations dealing with the reasonable accommodation requirement in employment practices. Under this section, employers must make reasonable accommodations to the known physical or mental limitations of otherwise qualified handicapped applicants or employees unless "the recipient can demonstrate that the accommodation would impose an undue hardship on the operation of its program." In determining whether an accommodation would impose an undue hardship, the regulations allow consideration for the overall size of the program, the type of operation, and the nature and cost of the accommodations needed. The Analysis accompanying this section emphasizes that "reasonable accommodations" may include such changes as modification of work schedules, job restructuring and, in some cases, physical modifications or relocation of particular offices or jobs so that they are in accessible facilities. To what extent the "undue hardship" principle would affect the "reasonable accommodation" requirement varies with individual cases. The Analysis accompanying the section distinguishes the situation of a small day-care center (which might be required to make only such minimal accommodations as equipping a telephone to enable a hearing impaired secretary to use a telephone) from the case of a large school district (which might be required to provide a teacher's aide to a blind teacher). Moreover, the Analysis suggests, while it might be reasonable to require a state welfare agency to provide an interpreter for a deaf employee, such a requirement would constitute an undue hardship for a provider of foster home care.

The reasonable accommodation cost principle in employment should be compared to regulatory requirements in architectural barriers and education. A recipient must operate a program or activity so that, when viewed in its entirety, it is "readily accessible to handicapped persons," although the regulations do not require that each existing facility or every part of a facility be accessible. In meeting the accessibility requirement, recipients may use a variety of methods (including reassignment of classes or services to accessible buildings, assignment of aides to handicapped persons, and home visits, in addition to structural changes) to meet the accessibility requirement. However, carrying of handicapped persons is generally prohibited. The program "must be accessible when viewed in its entirety," and, in choosing available methods, the recipient must give priority to those methods that offer programs and activities in the most integrated setting appropriate. Unlike the reasonable accommodations requirement in employment, which is flexible in its application to recipients in terms of what they may be required to do, the program accessibility requirement is strict in its basic mandate, i.e., recipients must provide programs which, when viewed in their entirety, are accessible. The flexibility of this requirement is in what recipients may *choose* to do. In both employment and program accessibility, recipients are constrained in their choices by the integration requirements. But the regulations evidently recognize cost explicitly as a factor only in the area of employment. While the Analysis accompanying the regulations acknowledges cost as a factor for small health, welfare, or other social service providers and grants them a special privilege, the basic accessibility requirement remains the same for all recipients. While cost may turn out to be a factor in determining what alternatives a recipient chooses, and while the size and nature of a program may partially determine whether the program "on the whole" is accessible, the basic requirement does not vary.

In further contrast to the flexibility of the reasonable accommodation requirement and the choices permitted to meet the accessibility requirement, at least two aspects of the preschool, elementary, and secondary education part permits no flexibility due to costs. There is no suspension of the requirement that *each* qualified handicapped person in a recipient's jurisdiction is entitled to a free appropriate public education, regardless of the severity of the handicap. One of the consequences is that all school-age handicapped children, as discussed more fully in Chapter V, are entitled to a free appropriate public education.

A second aspect of the education mandate which does not permit avoidance because of cost is the provision pertaining to those handicapped persons who, in order to receive appropriate public education, must be placed in a public or private residential program. While the basic thrust of the §504 education requirement (and of the related requirement under the Education for All Handicapped Children Act) is that handicapped students must be educated "with persons who are not handicapped to the maximum extent appropriate to the needs of the handicapped person," the regulations provide for those persons who will need residential placement:

If placement in a public or private residential program is necessary to provide a free appropriate public
education because of his or her handicap, the
program, including non-medical care and room and
board, shall be provided at no cost to the person or
his or her parents or guardian.

The placement requirement is absolute. Compliance
does not depend on the cost of the placement or the ability of the parents to pay. If such placement is necessary
(as opposed to simply being desired by the parents or
guardian), it must be made at public expense.

Cost may be a determining factor in some situations,
merely a relevant factor in others, and irrelevant to yet
other situations. Again, the *Davis* decision may have some
influence on this question. Moreover, the 1978 Amendments to the Rehabilitation Act recognizes the problem of
cost and authorizes some assistance for this purpose.[8]

Are regulations such as the HEW §504 regulations the final word on what §504 will mean?

Not necessarily. It is clear from the legislative
history of §504 that Congress intended to look to the executive departments for an important role in developing
the substantive requirements of §504. Courts are also inclined to show deference to the interpretations of administrative agencies charged with enforcing laws.

Yet the statute has an existence distinct from the regulations. The regulations are subject to evaluation in terms
of their conformity with the underlying statute, among
other grounds. There will be continuing debate about
whether the regulations meet the full Congressional mandate. There has been a debate about whether regulations
adopted by the Urban Mass Transportation Administration, partially on the basis of §504, measure up to the
statutory requirements. While Congress did not provide
as much guidance in the implementation of §504 as some
would like, policies and standards were established in the
legislative history and may be inferred by virtue of the
relationship of §504 to Title VI and Title IX.

In this context, it is worth noting the effective date
of the HEW §504 regulations, June 3, 1977. §504

was enacted in 1973, and courts were enforcing §504 directly before the regulations took effect. While the enforcement of §504 is discussed in Chapter VIII, one should not assume that violation of §504 which occurred before the effective date of the regulations cannot be challenged. The legal issues are complicated, but there can be enforcement of §504, in some cases, apart from the effective date of the regulations.

To the extent the §504 regulations do not meet the intent of §504, they may be subject to judicial scrutiny. Note also that judicial scrutiny may result in limitations on administrative enforcement. This is one reading of the *Davis* case.

NOTES

1. Examples of the Congressional hearings are *Hearings before the Subcommittee on the Handicapped of the Committee on Labor and Public Welfare on S.3108 and H.R. 14225*, 93rd Cong., 2nd Sess. (1974) and *Hearings before the Subcommittee on the Handicapped of the Committee on Labor and Public Welfare on Oversight Hearings on the Rehabilitation of the Handicapped Program and the Implementation of Same by Agencies under the Rehabilitation Act of 1973*, 94th Cong., 2nd Sess. (1976); the federal court case is *Cherry v. Mathews*, 419 F. Supp. 922 (D.D.C. 1976); the Architectural Barriers Act, as amended, is at 42 U.S.C.A. §§4151–57 (1977); the Education for All Handicapped Children Act is at 20 U.S.C.A. §§1401–61 (Supp. 1977), and see Chapter V of this book; the revenue sharing provision is at 31 U.S.C.A. §1242 (1976); an example of a state statute is that of Washington, R.C.W. Chapter 49.60 and see Chapter III for a discussion of the architectural barriers ordinance of Prince George's County, Maryland (cities and localities may also have general civil rights provisions pertaining to handicapped persons); HEW published regulations to implement its responsibilities under Executive Order 11914 at 43 *Fed. Reg.* 2132 (January 13, 1978) (45 C.F.R. Part 85); the 1978 Amendments are Rehabilitations, Comprehensive Services, and Developmental Disabilities Amend-

ments of 1978, Pub. L. 95–602, 92 Stat. 2955 §119, 29 U.S.C. 11 §794 (Supp. 1979).

2. §504 is codified at 29 U.S.C.A. §794 (1975); §606 is at 20 U.S.C.A. §1405 (Supp. 1977); the two federal cases are, respectively, *Drennon v. Philadelphia General Hospital,* 428 F. Supp. 809, 818 (E.D. Pa. 1977), and *Rogers v. Frito-Lay, Inc.,* 433 F. Supp. 200, 204 (N.D. Tex. 1977, *appeal docketed,* No. 77–2443, 5th Cir. July 13, 1977); fringe benefits for handicapped persons are covered by §84.11(b)(6), and see also Analysis at 42 *Fed. Reg.* at 22,689; on contracts of insurance and guaranty see §84.3(h) and 42 *Fed. Reg.* at 22,685; the definition of "recipients" is at §84.3(f).

3. The statutory definition is at 29 U.S.C.A. §706(6) (1975); the regulatory definitions are at §84.3(j), with Analysis at 42 *Fed. Reg.* at 22,685–22,686, see also *Id.* at 22,676, the 1978 Amendments are Pub. L. 95–602, §122(6), *supra,* note 1.

4. The Education for All Handicapped Children Act definition is at 20 U.S.C.A. §1401(1) (1978); the UMT Act definition is at 49 U.S.C.A. §1612(d) (1976); the Michigan law is MICH. COMP. LAWS ANN. §37.1103 (Pocket Part 1977–78); the state supreme court case is *Chicago, Milwaukee, St. Paul, & Pacific Railroad Company v. Washington State Human Rights Commission,* 557 F.2d 307, 310 (Wash. 1976).

5. The HEW §504 regulatory provision is §84.3(k); see Chapters V, VI, and VII on the qualifications in the context of their respective subject matter, *Southeastern Community College v. Davis,* 1355 99 S. Ct. (1979).

6. The general categories of discrimination prohibited are in §84.4 with Analysis at 42 *Fed. Reg.* 22,687; *Lau v. Nichols,* 414 U.S. 563 (1974).

7. The Preamble is at 42 *Fed. Reg.* at 22,676; the "reasonable accommodation" provision is §84.12; the Analysis of §84.6 is at 42 *Fed. Reg.* at 22,687; the "affirmative action" requirement is referred to in legislative history, *e.g.* the report of the Senate Labor and Public Welfare Committee, 4 U.S. CODE CONG. & ADMIN. NEWS at 6390 (1974), and see *Lloyd v. Regional Transportation Authority,* 548 F.2d 1277, 1285 (7th Cir. 1977); the provision on blind persons is at 20 U.S.C.A. §1684 (1978); the provision on the Education for All Handicapped Children Act is 20 U.S.C.A. §1405 (Supp. 1978); the legal commentary is Note, *Affirmative Action toward Hir-*

ing *Qualified Handicapped Individuals,* 49 S. Cal. L. Rev. 785, 809 (1976); *Southeastern Community College v. Davis, supra,* note 5.

8. For the HEW comments see 42 *Fed. Reg.* at 22,676; see also the respective chapters on the subject matter areas discussed; Analysis on the employment regulations is at 42 *Fed. Reg.* at 22,688; for the HEW policy on carrying handicapped persons, see 43 *Fed. Reg.* 36,035 (August 14, 1978); *Southeastern Community College v. Davis, supra,* note 5; examples of the congressional concerns about cost are 29 U.S.C.A. §794(b) and §§777(d) and (e) (Supp. 1979).

9. *Southeastern Community College v. Davis, supra,* note 5.

III

The Right to Access:
Architectural Barriers

The demand for access to the structures and transportation services of our society has been a cornerstone of the handicapped rights movement. A generation ago, the "Model White Cane Law" (which came to have a significance beyond the needs of blind persons alone) addressed the right of handicapped persons to have freedom of movement and use of public accommodations and common carriers (particularly when accompanied by guide dogs). More recently, the passage of the Architectural Barriers Act by Congress in 1968 marked a new era in federal policy toward handicapped persons.

In its 1967 report *Design for All Americans*, the National Commission on Architectural Barriers to Rehabilitation of the Handicapped concluded, "The greatest single obstacle to employment for the handicapped is the physical design of the buildings and facilities they must use." Not only in employment, but in such matters as education and access to government agencies and services, architectural barriers must be eliminated in order for handicapped persons to enjoy full citizenship. Apart from the practical problems presented by architectural barriers, those obstacles also convey to handicapped persons a message as symbols. As clearly as "No Irish Allowed" and "White Only," the stairways, narrow doors, and sidewalk curbs of our society indicate to handicapped persons their exclusion from the centers of our social life. For many handicapped persons—not just those with ambulatory handicaps, but also blind persons and deaf persons (who face barriers when appropriate stimuli such as brailled elevator buttons and visual public announcement systems are absent)—the existence of architectural barriers is a fact that cannot be discarded by public declarations in favor of equality for handicapped persons.

Elimination of architectural barriers is very much consistent with our national policy to protect and improve our environment. As Rita McGaughey, of the National Easter Seal Society for Crippled Children and Adults, has written, "It is obvious . . . that . . . improving our environment means much more than cleaning up the air." Moreover, the improvements to be made by barrier-free design affect not only the environment of handicapped persons, but also result in easier and safer movement for many other persons. The statement in *Design for All Americans* that "The modern man-made environment is designed for the young and healthy," is reinforced by a conclusion of the United Nations Expert Group Meeting on Barrier-Free Design:

> Buildings, roads, open spaces cater to a fictitious model of the human being—exclusively for a man (not a woman) in the prime of life and the peak of his physical fitness.
>
> Statistically speaking, only a small minority of the population can fall into this category, even among the fit. Naturally, there is no thought of the handicapped.

Fundamental to the demand for accessibility is the premise that the present structural arrangements of our society which exclude physically handicapped persons are not inevitable or immutable. We can change things. Moreover, as one legal writer has argued in the *Georgetown Law Journal,* the rejection by government of the barrier-free alternative in building its facilities (particularly when the cost of accessible features is minimal) constitutes an official act of purposeful discrimination which courts may deem an infringement of the basic rights of handicapped persons.

This chapter considers some of the policies underlying the legal mandate for barrier-free design and outlines the broad scheme of legal rights to an accessible society.[1]

What were some of the social and political considerations which led to passage of the Architectural Barriers Act?

When Congress considered proposals for architectural barriers legislation in the late 1960s and early 1970s, supporters of the legislation expressed their belief that progress toward removing barriers would occur with education of the public and a heightened awareness among design professionals about the advantages of barrier-free design. Senator E. L. Bartlett of Alaska, a sponsor of the proposed legislation, told a subcommittee of the House of Representatives that architectural barriers resulted from "simple thoughtlessness. . . . Certainly, no calculated effort to create obstacles for the handicapped has created these difficulties." A spokesman for the National Commission on Architectural Barriers told the subcommittee, *"It is primarily a matter of oversight."*

In retrospect, the view that architectural barriers were the result of thoughtlessness and oversight, and the hope that the problem would be solved by education and awareness, may appear somewhat naïve. The reaction of some recipients of HEW funds to the accessibility mandate of the §504 regulations, and the policies of agencies such as the Urban Mass Transportation Administration toward achieving accessibility, may indicate that the exclusion of handicapped persons was the result of some deliberate decisions.

A prominent concern in the formative stages of the legislation was that the public investment in rehabilitation of handicapped persons was doomed to diminishing returns because of barriers. But probably the most basic reason for the architectural barriers legislation was the practical acknowledgment reflected in a 1975 report by the General Accounting Office on the implementation of the Architectural Barriers Act:

If the handicapped cannot enter and use public buildings, they cannot easily vote, obtain government services, conduct business, or become independent and self-supporting. Efforts to enhance talents and market job skills become meaningless when the job site and usual place of business are inaccessible.[2]

What are the major provisions of the Architectural Barriers Act?

The mandate of the act is that:

> Every building designed, constructed, or altered after the effective date of a standard issued under this chapter which is applicable to such building, shall be designed, constructed, or altered in accordance with such standard.

As amended in 1976, the Act, which became law in 1968, applies to buildings or facilities:

1. to be constructed or altered by or on behalf of the United States.
2. to be leased in whole or in part by the United States after August 12, 1968 [see discussion below];
3. to be financed in whole or in part by a grant or a loan made by the United States after August 12, 1968, if such building or facility is subject to standards for design, construction, or alteration issued under authority of the law authorizing the grant or loan;
4. to be constructed [under legislation providing for the construction of the Washington, D.C., Metro public transportation system].

The second provision concerning leases originally included a limitation applying to "construction or alteration in accordance with plans and specifications of the United States." That language was dropped in the 1976 amendments. The amendment, which does not apply to leases entered into before January 1, 1977, now applies to leases entered into on or after that date, as well as renewal of leases entered into before January 1, 1977 but renewed after that date. The fourth provision, pertaining to the Washington, D.C., Metro public transportation system, was added by a 1970 amendment to the Architectural Barriers Act, intended to insure that the subway system then being constructed would be accessible. The Metro amendment provided the basis for an early accessibility lawsuit which will be discussed later. The first and second provisions of this section, pertaining to construction, alteration, and leasing arrangements by the United States government (particularly leasing arrangements after January 1, 1977) are comparatively clear, while the third section, pertaining to the coverage of certain grants and loans, may have applications that are difficult to define; it should also be noted that this third section is one point at which §504 may intersect with the Architectural Barriers Act.

The act's definition of "building" excludes privately owned residential structures not leased by the government for subsidized housing programs and any building or facility on a military installation designed and constructed primarily for use by able-bodied military personnel. Included within the definition of "building" is "any building or facility . . . the intended use for which either will require that such building or facility be accessible to the public, or may result in the employment or residence therein of physically handicapped persons," and which meets one of the four requirements set out above.

Amendments enacted in 1976, to the act, had the effect of broadening the coverage of the act to more Government-leased buildings and facilities, removing what had been an exemption of the United States Postal Service from the act's coverage, and mandating a system of continuing surveys and investigations to monitor implementation of the act. Furthermore, subsidized housing programs were included within the definition of "building." But, perhaps most importantly, the act now contains a clear statutory mandate that federal agencies insure that buildings are made accessible to physically handicapped persons.[3]

What does the Act direct that federal departments and agencies do to overcome architectural barriers?

As the act was amended in 1976, it provides that the Administrator of General Services, in consultation with the Secretary of Health, Education and Welfare, shall prescribe standards for the design, construction, and alteration of buildings to insure "whenever possible" that physically handicapped persons will have ready access to, and use of, the buildings covered by the act. The Administrator's authority does not extend to all federal buildings and facilities. The responsibility for prescribing standards for residential structures covered by the act rests with the Secretary of Housing and Urban Development, for Defense Department facilities with the secretary of that department, and for postal service buildings with the Postal Service, all of which must consult with the Secretary of Health, Education and Welfare in the establishment of their standards.

The act also provides that the Administrator of the General Services Administration, or the three other executive authorities, may "modify or waive" the accessibility standards established "on a case by case basis." An application for such a waiver may be made by the head of the government department, agency, or instrumentality concerned. The modification or waiver may be allowed upon a determination that the action is "clearly necessary." The act also requires a system of continuing surveys and investigation to insure compliance with standards prescribed under the act and annual reports to Congress by the Administrator of General Services and the Architectural and Transportation Barriers Compliance Board on their enforcement activities.

Since its enactment in 1968, Congress had amended the act twice: first, in 1970 to specify that the Metro subway system under construction in Washington, D.C., meet the requirements of the act and again in 1976. The 1976 amendments were largely the result of a report in 1975 to Congress by the General Accounting Office evaluating the act's implementation. A major change brought about in 1976 was to make the law more clearly mandatory. Before the amendments, for example, the act provided that the Administrator of General Services, and the heads of other executive departments were "authorized to prescribe" accessibility standards. The act now provides that they "shall prescribe" the standards, eliminating what may have appeared to be discretionary power to fulfill the law. Additionally, as now written, the act provides that the standards should be sufficient "to insure wherever possible" access and use of buildings, wherever the previous standard of sufficiency was "as may be necessary to insure." Further changes were to expand the coverage of the act to more government-leased buildings (as well as privately owned buildings leased to the government for public housing), and bring the Postal Service within the law's coverage.

Pursuant to the act, agencies adopted regulations to implement the law. The General Services Administration did so in its "Accommodation for the Physically Handicapped" provision as part of the Federal Property Management Regulations. Those regulations adopted the ANSI Standard for buildings constructed, designed, or altered after September 2, 1969, but also established certain exceptions to the Standard. The exceptions are the design, construction, or alteration of any portion of a building "which need not, because of its intended use, be made accessible to, or usable by, the public or physically handicapped persons"; the alteration of an existing building if the alteration does not involve installation of, or work on, such features as "existing stairs, doors, elevators, toilets, entrances, drinking fountains, floors, telephone locations, curbs, parking areas" or any other facilities susceptible of installation or improvements to accommodate the physically handicapped; the alteration of an existing building or such portion of the building to which application of the standards is not structurally possible; and, finally, the construction or alteration of a building for which bids have been solicited or plans and specifications have been completed or substantially completed on or before September 2, 1969. (This last provision pertaining to the September 2 date does not apply to projects under the Metro system.) Regulations announced in April, 1978, by GSA provide another exception in the leasing of buildings, and also allow departures from the ANSI Standard by the use of "other methods . . . when it is clearly evident that equivalent accessibility and usability of the facility is thereby provided." The GSA regulations provide a procedure whereby the Administrator of General Services Administration may waive, on a case-by-case basis, the applicability of the standards of the regulation. Record-keeping requirements are set forth.

The Department of Housing and Urban Development has adopted the ANSI Standard (issued September 24, 1969) with modifications for purposes of the Architectural Barriers Act, as has the Department of Health, Education and Welfare. The Department of Defense had adopted the ANSI Standard before the act.

The regulations adopted by the departments, and their implementation of the Act, have been criticized extensively, particularly in the GAO Report to Congress on implementation of the Architectural Barriers Act. Of particular controversy may be the exceptions in the GSA regulations and the question of whether those provisions are adequately defined, as well as whether they are consistent with the act.[4]

What significance do the "American National Standards Institute's Specifications for Making Buildings and Facilities Accessible to, and Usable by, the Physically Handicapped" (the ANSI Standard) have in the implementation of the Architectural Barriers Act?

In 1961, as the result of work by such groups as the President's Committee on Employment of the Handicapped and the National Easter Seals Society for Crippled Children and Adults, the American National Standards Institute issued a standard designed to provide criteria in the design and construction of some buildings. The so-called "ANSI Standard" became a basic guide for early accessibility efforts at the federal and state levels, although the ANSI Standard has met considerable criticism and is not the only set of building criteria addressing accessibility questions. In the implementation of the Architectural Barriers Act, the agencies generally followed the ANSI Standard, with modification of the Standard by some departments.

The announced purpose of the Standard is "to make all buildings and facilities used by the public accessible to, and functional for, the physically handicapped to, through, and within their doors, without loss of function, space, or facility where the general public is concerned." The Standard purports to include the needs of a wide range of handicapped persons, including persons with nonambulatory, sight, and hearing disabilities, as well as problems faced by persons who encounter barriers as a result of aging. It addresses such features of construction as parking lots, ramps, doors and doorways, toilet facilities, and warning signals.[5]

What are some criticisms which have been directed toward the ANSI Standard?

Since its announcement in 1961 (and its reaffirmation in 1971), the ANSI Standard has met criticism from many persons concerned about accessibility. The 1975 GAO Report to Congress on the implementation of the Architectural Barriers Act listed four deficiencies in the Standard:

1. While it defines various categories of accessibility, it lacks specificity in certain important areas, which results in varying interpretations of its specification.
2. It does not specify what facilities are to be covered and to what extent its specifications should be followed.
3. It does not cover residential housing.
4. It contains very few descriptive drawings.

A 1974 Report by the Iowa Chapter of the American Institute of Architects, directed principally toward measuring compliance with the Act in Iowa, also considered deficiencies in the ANSI Standard. Among the problems identified by the Iowa report were the need for more clarity and precision in the use of terms and some indication of the "degree of disability" which the Standard intends to accommodate.

Because of such criticism, a project has been underway at Syracuse University to revise the Standard. Some states have chosen to implement barrier-free legislation by means other than the ANSI Standard, and the final version of the HEW §504 regulation provides that compliance with the "New Construction" accessibility section may be effectuated by design, construction, or alteration of facilities in conformance with the ANSI Standard, although departure from the Standard is permitted when it is "clearly evident that equivalent access" will be provided. Both state accessibility laws and the HEW §504 accessibility requirements will be discussed later. It is worth noting that codes developed by other groups also address accessibility, such as the Basic Building Code of the Building Officials Conference of America.[6]

What are some of the criticisms, apart from those concerned with the ANSI Standard, which have been directed toward the Architectural Barriers Act?

Major criticisms, discussed earlier, were the definitional questions, discretionary aspects, and other weaknesses addressed by the 1976 amendments to the act.

However, a number of other criticisms have focused on the agencies charged with implementation of the act. In an article published in the *Kentucky Law Journal,* Alan J. Farber discussed some of the administrative problems. Farber expressed concern that regulations adopted by the Administrator of the General Services Administration included an overly broad waiver provision. The regulations enumerate a series of structural features that are clearly important to access (such as stairs, doors, elevators, toilets, and telephone location) but may slight the significance of other features that are important for use of buildings. (Farber suggests that office furniture design, for example, clearly affects the utility of a facility, but may not be covered by the GSA provision.) Moreover, Farber pointed out, the same GSA regulation exempts from the regulation's coverage those circumstances where the "application of the standards is not structurally possible," a vague standard that may be difficult to observe in practice because of the question of whether a review would be required. Farber raised questions about the appropriateness of the ANSI Standards to achieving the intent of the act and questioned the legislative policy of delegation to administrative agencies of the power to set standards under the act.

Further criticism of the act has concerned a possible conflict of interest created by the statute in that the General Services Administration is given the dual functions of regulating the agencies and building the facilities it regulates. GSA further met criticism because of its delay in incorporating the ANSI Standard in handbooks used by architects and engineers in designing buildings, as well as the charge in the 1975 General Accounting Office report to Congress that adequate design-review procedures and systems of surveys and investigations were yet to be established.

The Department of Housing and Urban Development

adopted the ANSI Standard, despite the fact that the Standard does not address accessibility in residential facilities. Moreover, for those housing programs to which HUD applied the Standard, it interpreted its own regulations so that the primary emphasis of accessibility requirement should be on buildings intended for use by the handicapped; in some cases, HUD staff interpreted the accessibility requirement as applicable in only a certain percentage of housing units for the elderly, thereby effectively excluding handicapped persons with families who required larger accommodations. The GAO Report found conflicts between the ANSI Standard and other HUD standards of design, in addition to inadequate design-review procedures to insure compliance with the act.

Criticism of the Department of Health, Education and Welfare followed the same lines. HEW supplemented its adoption of the ANSI Standard with additional criteria. HEW's construction responsibilities are twofold: programs for such HEW agencies as the Social Security Administration and the Indian Health Service and, on the other hand, construction assistance, through such HEW divisions as the Office of Education and the Public Health Service, for specialized buildings like hospitals, research laboratories, and higher education buildings. Inadequate design-review procedures, policies toward the granting of waivers by lower-echelon officials, and inadequate documentation of certifications of compliance with the act were other deficiencies noted in the GAO Report to the Congress.

While this discussion does not cover all the deficiencies in the act's administration, it does outline some major concerns: the reliance by the administrative agencies on the ANSI Standard in situations where that criteria may not meet the needs for barrier-free design, the uncertain and unclear policies toward waivers of the requirements, the concern that compliance review and oversight of the accessibility requirements is inadequate, and the question of whether administrative policies meet the full intent of the Congressional mandate. To what extent the 1976 amendments to the act and the increased activity and reorganization of the Architectural and Transportation

Barriers Compliance Board will affect these problems are questions which await resolution.[7]

What is the function of the Architectural and Transportation Barriers Compliance Board in the enforcement of the Architectural Barriers Act?

The Compliance Board was created by §502 of the Rehabilitation Act of 1973, to insure compliance with the Architectural Barriers Act. Prior to creation of the Compliance Board, there was no single agency charged with enforcement of the act. The Compliance Board also is charged with a wide range of research and information gathering responsibilities with respect to such accessibility problems as barriers in housing and transportation. The Board originally was made up of high-ranking representatives from several Cabinet departments and the General Services Administration, the Postal Service, and the Veteran's Administration.

In the 1974 amendments to the Rehabilitation Act, Congress made several changes in the Board's authority and makeup. The Secretary of Health, Education and Welfare was designated as permanent Chairman of the Board and a Consumer Advisory Panel (a majority of which had to be handicapped individuals) was created "to provide guidance, advice and recommendations to the Board in carrying out its functions." The law created a position on the Board for the Department of Defense and authorized the appointment of an Executive Director and other personnel necessary to carry out the Board's functions. Perhaps most important in terms of the Board's enforcement authority was the power given by a 1974 amendment to issue binding final orders to federal departments, agencies, or instrumentalities, which may include the withholding or suspension of Federal funds with respect to any building found not to be in compliance with standards to implement the act.

In the 1978 amendments to the Rehabilitation Act, Congress made further changes in the structure and function of the Compliance Board. The President now appoints eleven additional public members (of whom five must be handicapped individuals) and the Department of Justice has a representative. The President is to appoint the first chairman of the reorganized board, who serves for a term of not more than two years, and thereafter the chairman is elected by a vote of the majority of the Board for a term of one year. Terms of office for each appointed member are three years, except that the members first taking office shall serve, as designated, four for a term of one year, four for a term of two years, and three for a term of three years, and any member appointed to fill a vacancy shall serve for a remainder of the term for which his predecessor was appointed.

The Board is to ensure compliance with the standards prescribed pursuant to the Architectural Barriers Act (which applies to the United States Postal Service) including but not limited to enforcing standards under the act. Additionally, the Board is to ensure that all waivers and modifications of standards are based upon findings of fact and are not inconsistent with provisions of the Architectural Barriers Act and §502 of the Rehabilitation Act as amended.

The executive director of the Board is authorized, at the direction of the Board, to bring a civil law suit in any appropriate federal district court to enforce any final order of the Board to compel compliance with the Architectural Barriers Act. Moreover, the executive director may intervene, appear, participate, or appear as *amicus curiae,* in any court of the United States or in any state court in civil cases related to the Architectural Barriers Act or §502 of the Rehabilitation Act.

The Board is also able to establish minimum guidelines in requirements for the standards issued pursuant to the Architectural Barriers Act and for ensuring that public conveyances, including rolling stock, are readily accessible to and usable by physically handicapped persons. The Board is given large responsibilities to provide technical assistance and to develop standards for any public or private activity, persons, or entity affected by regulations prescribed pursuant to the civil rights provisions of the Rehabilitation Act with respect to overcoming architectural, transportation, and communications barriers. An additional important responsibility imposed by the 1978 amendments is to submit to the President and Congress, within one year following enactment of the Rehabilitation

Act amendments, a report containing an assessment of the amount required to be expended by states and political subdivisions to provide handicapped individuals full access to all programs and activities receiving federal assistance.

In December, 1976, the Compliance Board issued final procedural regulations to handle complaints. The Board has begun the administrative enforcement process with respect to several complaints. The Board's procedures will be discussed in chapter VIII.[8]

What is the Washington, D.C. "Metro case" brought to enforce the Architectural Barriers Act?

In October, 1973, a federal district judge issued an injunction against the Washington Metropolitan Area Transit Authority prohibiting the Transit Authority:

> from commercially operating any station of the Metro Railway transportation system until [the Transit Authority] installs and makes operational all those facilities, including elevators, as may be necessary to ensure that physically handicapped persons will have ready access to, and use of, such Metro railway systems station in compliance with [the Architectural Barriers Act and the General Service Administration regulations promulgated].

The suit was addressed principally to the issue of accessibility of the stations in the Metro system, focusing on the Gallery Place station. The relief granted by the court —an order requiring the installation of elevators—was an early landmark in the enforcement of accessibility rights on behalf of handicapped persons.

In 1976, the federal court again had occasion to consider accessibility of the Metro stations. The court rejected a request by city business groups that the Gallery Place station (which had been ordered closed until it met the accessibility order of the court) be opened to the public despite continued inaccessibility. The court was not persuaded that the alleged inconvenience to the non-handicapped public (who could use another station two blocks from Gallery Place) and the possible loss of business by establishments located near that station were sufficient reasons to lift the injunction. The court stated in forceful language its reasons for keeping the station closed until the requirements of the order were met:

> The history of defendant's repeated refusal to comply with the obligations imposed by the Act, a history that has required two separate actions by Congress [the original Architectural Barriers Act in 1968 and the special amendment pertaining to the Metro system] and this Court's injunction to rectify leaves the Court with little recourse but to continue its injunction. There is simply no other way apparent to the Court to ensure that the defendant, once and for all, will accept and carry out its obligations under the Act, not only with regard to Gallery Place but with regard to the remainder of the stations in its system. To now set a precedent to the contrary would in this Court's view lead to repeated excuses by defendant that elevator construction has been delayed for any number of facially valid reasons, e.g., lack of funds, construction delays, etc., with a concomitant request to operate the station in violation of the law. The Act has imposed obligations upon defendant, those obligations must be enforced and this Court believes that the present use of its equity power is the proper—and only—manner for enforcement.

In its opinion, the court did suggest that, under the Architectural Barriers Act, the defendant could apply to the Administrator of GSA for a waiver of the act's requirements, subject to any attack the plaintiffs might make on the waiver. A waiver was subsequently granted by GSA, but a consent decree ended the lawsuit with the station made accessible in 1978.[9]

What is the scope of the HEW §504 regulations in terms of program accessibility?

The fundamental prohibition of the regulations is that no qualified handicapped person shall, "because a recipient's facilities are inaccessible to or unusable by handicapped persons," be denied benefits, be excluded from participation, or otherwise be subjected to discrimination as prohibited under §504. The regulations cover existing facilities and the issue of program accessibility; methods

for achieving program accessibility; problems of small
health, welfare, or other social service providers; and the
issues of time periods, transition plans, and notice to
interested persons about the existence and location of
accessible services, activities, and facilities. Design, construction, and alteration of new construction by recipients
is covered, as well as the role of the ANSI Standards in
complying with the program accessibility regulations.[10]

**What are the requirements for program accessibility in
existing facilities and what are some of the methods by
which the regulations permit these requirements to be met?**

In existing facilities, the HEW §504 regulations require
recipients to operate "each program or activity" to which
the HEW regulations apply so that the program or activity
"when viewed in its entirety is readily accessible to handicapped persons." The existing-facilities regulations are
explicit in not requiring a recipient to make "each of its
existing facilities or every part of a facility accessible to
and usable by handicapped persons."

The regulations suggest a variety of methods to meet
the existing-facilities requirements, including redesign of
equipment, reassignment of classes or other services to
accessible buildings, assignment of aides to handicapped
persons (although carrying is generally prohibited, with
limited exceptions), delivery of health, welfare, or other
social services at alternate accessible sites, alteration of
existing facilities or construction of new facilities in conformance wth the "new construction" section, "or any
other methods that result in making [a recipient's] program or activity accessible to handicapped persons." The
regulations state that a recipient is not required to make
structural changes in existing facilities "where other methods are effective in achieving compliance" with the
program-accessibility requirement for existing facilities.
However, in choosing among available methods to achieve
compliance, recipients must give priority to those methods
that offer programs and activities in the most integrated
setting appropriate.

The program-accessibility requirement for existing
facilities was quite controversial in the policy-making
stage of the HEW §504 regulations, and the Analysis ac-

companying the regulations reflects this controversy. The
HEW position in the Analysis is that "Structural changes
in existing facilities are required only where there is no
other feasible way to make the recipient's program accessible." HEW was particularly concerned about problems which universities would have in implementing
program accessibility for existing facilities and, in the view
of many handicapped persons, HEW made too many con-
cessions to the higher education institutions. One example
of the department's attitude is seen in this statement from
the Analysis:

> . . . a university does not have to make all of its ex-
> isting classroom buildings accessible to handicapped
> students if some of its buildings are already acces-
> sible and if it is possible to reschedule or relocate
> enough classes so as to offer all required courses and
> a reasonable selection of elective courses in acces-
> sible facilities. If sufficient relocation of classes is not
> possible using existing facilities, enough alterations
> to ensure program accessibility are required. A uni-
> versity may not exclude a handicapped student from
> a specifically requested course offering because it is
> not offered in an accessible location, but it need not
> make every section of that course accessible.

HEW rejected the concept of allowing several institutions of higher education to form a consortium, whereby
one postsecondary institution in a geographical area would
be made accessible to handicapped persons and other
schools would participate in that school's program. HEW
rejected this approach because the consortium concept restricted the choices of handicapped persons in selecting institutions of higher education and would have been, in the
department's view, discriminatory and inconsistent with
the objectives of §504. Colleges are not prohibited from
establishing consortia for the benefits of *all* students, but
would be prohibited from doing so if a consortium was
established for the purposes of meeting the accessibility
requirement and the arrangement required handicapped
students (but not other students) to attend the accessible
college. The Analysis also states that while public school
districts need not make each building completely acces-

sible, neither may a district "make only one facility or part of a facility accessible if the result is to segregate handicapped students in a single setting."

The regulations make a special accommodation for providers of small health, welfare, or other social services. Those recipients with fewer than fifteen employees may, as an alternative, refer a handicapped person to other providers that are accessible if, after consultation with a handicapped person seeking service, the provider finds that there is no method of complying with the accessibility requirement without making a significant alteration in its existing facilities. The Analysis also states that "all recipients that provide health, welfare, or other social services may also comply with [the existing-facilities requirement] by delivering services at alternative accessible sites or making home visits." The implications of this statement in the overall context of the regulations and the program accessibility provision is unclear and raises questions about the scope and coverage of the purported exceptions.[11]

How long do recipients have to meet existing-facilities program-accessibility requirements?

The regulations state that recipients must come into compliance within sixty days of June 3, 1977, except that where structural changes are necessary, the changes must be made within three years of that date. In any event, the regulations state, recipients must comply as expeditiously as possible. In this connection, the department states in its Analysis accompanying the regulations that since outside ramps can be built quickly and at relatively low cost, "it will be expected that such structural additions will be made promptly" to comply with the time period requirement. Moreover, HEW emphasizes that the three year period is allowed only in the case of structural changes, and that the period is not to be construed as a waiting period.[12]

What is the requirement of the HEW §504 regulations for a transition plan affecting structural changes?

Where it is necessary for a recipient to make structural changes in order to meet the existing-facilities program-accessibility requirements, recipients must have developed, within six months of June 3, 1977, a transition plan setting forth the steps necessary to complete the changes. Interested persons, including handicapped individuals and organizations representing handicapped persons, must be given the opportunity to help develop the transition plan, and the plan must be made available for public inspection. The regulations specify the minimum requirements for the plan:

1. It must identify physical obstacles in the recipient's facilities that limit the accessibility of the program or activity to handicapped persons.
2. It must describe in detail the methods that will be used to make the facilities accessible.
3. It must specify the schedule for taking the steps necessary to achieve full program accessibility. If it will take longer than one year, the plan must identify steps that will be taken each year of the transition period.
4. The plan must identify the person responsible for implementating the plan.

Also, recipients must adopt and use procedures that insure that persons with hearing and visual handicaps (as well as other interested persons) can obtain information about the existence and location of accessible services, activities, and facilities.[18]

What do the HEW §504 regulations require for new construction?

The regulations state that each facility or part of a facility constructed by, on behalf of, or for the use of a recipient must be designed and constructed so as to be readily accessible and usable by handicapped persons if the construction was commenced after June 3, 1977. Likewise, alterations to facilities or parts of a facility after the same date must "to the maximum extent feasible" be made so that the altered portion is readily accessible and usable if the alteration is in a manner that affects or could affect the usability of the facility.

The new construction provision specifies that for design, construction, and alteration, conformance with the

ANSI Standard will serve to satisfy the regulations. However, the regulations permit departures from the ANSI Standard "when it is clearly evident that equivalent access" will be provided. Reference to the ANSI Standard may raise a question: while the §504 regulations speak only in terms of program or activity accessibility, the Standard addresses building accessibility and, some commentators suggest, may imply a higher degree of accessability than the regulations purport to require.

The application of this section carries, along with other parts of the regulations, the question of when §504 will be interpreted to require what the regulations specify. The statute became law in 1973, yet we see it not being applied to new construction or alterations until 1977. This may be a question that courts will consider in the future.

The Analysis of the new construction section goes on to provide that commencement of construction means groundbreaking, and that recipients will not be required to alter the design of a facility for which ground was broken before June 3, 1977. Additionally, the alteration requirement is applicable to such projects as doorway or wall alteration, but not, the Analysis states, to altering ceilings. The test seems to be that if the alteration is undertaken to a feature which could affect accessibility to the building by the manner of construction, then the alteration must be made so as to increase accessibility.[14]

Can there be situations in which both the Office for Civil Rights and the Architectural and Transportation Barriers Compliance Board both have jurisdiction?

Yes. There could be situations where HEW recipients also are subject to the Architectural Barriers Act of 1968 and, hence, to the jurisdiction of the Compliance Board. In proposed regulations to implement §504, HEW had proposed to require OCR to defer to the Compliance Board for a limited period when such cases arose. However, the final regulations rejected that concept. The procedures to follow, the substantive requirements of the two laws, and the effective dates for compliance could be complex questions in the enforcement of the laws and regulations.[15]

Are architectural barriers regulated at the state and local level?

Yes. States and local governments have dealt with the problem of architectural barriers, and these provisions may affect facilities which the federal legislation does not reach. Therefore, in dealing with architectural barriers, state and local provisions should also be considered as bases for legal rights. The state and local legislation may be separate provisions dealing specifically with architectural barriers, as well as other general legislation protecting the civil rights of handicapped persons.

What are some of the buildings and facilities covered by state architectural barriers laws?

State provisions may cover a variety of buildings and facilities, including structures utilized for education, employment, transportation, recreation, the provision of goods or services, and, in some cases, certain types of housing. Such improved areas as parking lots, harbors, parks, beaches, public telephones, and drinking fountains may also be covered. Many of these structures and facilities are privately owned and, hence, often would not be affected by federal architectural barriers legislation. Thus one of the most important aspects of state legislation is that it reaches into the private sector to regulate barriers in buildings which are frequently used by handicapped persons.

At the same time, state legislation may affect many public buildings which are owned by the state or political subdivisions. These public facilities may be those owned by or on behalf of the state or its political subdivisions, leased or rented by those branches of government, or financed in whole or in part by government money.[16]

What types of features do state accessibility requirements often cover?

In some cases the state legislation applies to a wide range of features which may prevent barriers to movement by handicapped persons. Among these are:

—Such site conditions as disembarking areas, grading, ramps, and sidewalks.

—Entrances, doors, and doorways.
—Stairs—including treads and handrails.
—Floors—including nonslip surfaces and carpeting.
—Public toilet rooms—including lavatories and toilet
    stalls.
—Elevators—including door features, car size, and
    car controls.
—Drinking fountains and public telephones.

Moreover, special features needed to overcome barriers
for blind persons may be covered, such as the design and
location of apartment room numbers, toilet rooms, and
elevators. Warning signals that are both audible and visual
are sometimes included to help both blind persons and
those with hearing impairments.

Legislation may address special problems in such government facilities as libraries, courthouses, police stations,
townhalls, and polling booths. Shopping center stores may
be required to have aisles and checkout lanes of certain
dimensions, as well as alternative entrances apart from
turnstiles.

In some cases, lodging and residential facilities and
hotels and motels must have a certain percentage of facilities accessible for handicapped persons. There may be a
requirement that the units designed must be proportion-
ately distributed in the number of bedrooms, size, quality,
and price as all other units in the facility.[17]

**What concepts guide reconstruction, renovation, or al-
teration of buildings and facilities in state architectural
barriers legislation?**

Changes and alterations of structures are frequently
regulated by state architectural barriers laws. These
changes offer an opportunity to incorporate barrier-free
features, just as new construction enables changes to be
made easily. One fact which legislation sometimes looks to
is the amount or percentage of floor area which the
change or alteration involves. Thus, if it involves a relatively small amount of the floor area which could be
used by the public or employees, only the area affected
and areas necessary to provide continuous and unob-
structed travel to and from these areas must meet the

barrier-free design requirements. If a substantial portion of the building or facility is to be renovated, then the state law may require the entire facility to meet barrier-free design requirements. Requirements can vary where the facility is leased by the state. In some cases, the operative requirement may be the cost in relation to the value of the building. The degree of accessibility required in renovation may vary with the percentage.[18]

How do enforcement boards function in the implementation of state architectural barriers legislation?

In some states, enforcement of architectural barriers legislation is vested in a board. These boards have been created to allow more active public participation in enforcement, particularly by handicapped persons and representatives of interested groups (such as the construction industry) which are closely affected by the architectural barriers legislation. These boards may have several functions:

—They may establish rules and regulations to make buildings accessible.
—They may have enforcement authority to institute and prosecute court proceedings to compel compliance with the law.
—They may have authority to modify or substitute or waive rules and regulations if compliance is not practicable in a particular case.
—They may serve as the agency which receives complaints of noncompliance with the laws, investigates those complaints, and makes determinations about their validity.[19]

What are some of the considerations which could influence a board to grant a variance?

Where literal application of some requirements is impractical (a standard that may vary and may be too imprecise for many persons), a board may grant a variance. Variances may also be granted where nonpublic areas are affected. In some cases, alternatives may be allowed—such as allowing a service performed on upper stories to be provided to handicapped persons below.[20]

Is barrier-free design expensive?

Not necessarily. The GAO Report to Congress concluded:

Government, private contractor and design personnel agree that the cost of accessibility features is negligible when such items are incorporated in the design phase; sometimes, they may even result in cost savings. In addition, although the cost of altering existing inaccessible buildings is more than that of initial barrier-free construction, it is relatively small when compared to the total construction cost. . . . Government estimators provided us with the current cost of converting selected buildings to conform to the ANSI Standard, as well as the added cost (that amount which represents cost for accessibility features over and above nonaccessible original construction) if the buildings had originally complied with the Standard.

When compared to total project cost, the current cost of altering buildings is relatively small. The percentage ranged from 2.4 percent to .06 of the project cost. However, the cost is even less when accessibility features are incorporated into the original construction program. In all instances they amounted to less than one percent of the total project cost.

It is necessary, as some design experts emphasize, to evaluate projects on an individual basis. An Inflationary Impact Statement prepared to assess §504 suggests some of the factors which may have a bearing on cost, particularly in higher education.[21]

Is there federal legislation designed to help some recipients meet the cost of barrier-free design?

Yes. Both the Education for All Handicapped Children Act and the 1976 legislation pertaining to Higher Education authorize grants or loans for this purpose. Additionally, the 1978 Amendments to the Rehabilitation Act open the door to future financial assistance in removing barriers. However, that law mandates that a prior study be made to justify the assistance.[22]

Has the problem of accessibility of polling places been given special attention?

Yes. Legislation is being considered to require accessibility to polling places.

Additionally, a case before the United States Court of Appeals for the Ninth Circuit challenged the failure of a city to locate its polling places in facilities accessible to handicapped persons, but was dismissed on procedural grounds. This case was brought on the basis of federal constitutional, as well as state law grounds, and was lost in the district court by the plaintiff. That court held, among other points, that the availability of the absentee ballot to handicapped voters (a mechanism challenged by the plaintiff as inadequate and stigmatizing) was an adequate alternative to accessible polling places.[23]

What is the federal income tax deduction allowed for expenditures to remove architectural and transportation barriers to the handicapped and elderly?

A provision of the Tax Reform Act of 1976 provides that a taxpayer may elect to deduct certain amounts paid or incurred by the taxpayer in any taxable year beginning after December 31, 1976 and before January 1, 1980 for qualified architectural and transportation barrier removal expenses. Certain expenses for the purpose of making any facility, or public transportation vehicle, owned or leased by the taxpayer for use in connection with his trade or business more accessible to and usable by handicapped or elderly individuals may be deducted. For an expense to qualify as a removal expense under this provision; the taxpayer must satisfy the requirements of regulations adopted by the government setting forth additional criteria and incorporating design standards based on the ANSI Standard. The deduction may not exceed $25,000 for any taxable year. The statute defines the term "handicapped individual" as any individual who has a physical or mental disability (including, but not limited to, blindness or deafness) which for that individual constitutes or results in a functional limitation to employment, or who has a physical or mental impairment (including, but not limited to, a sight or hearing impairment) which "substantially limits one or more major life activities" of the individual.

For a complete understanding of the application of this provision in specific situations it is necessary to review the regulations promulgated pursuant to the statute. The terms "facility" and "public transportation vehicle" are defined, and among other requirements established in the regulation, is one that only expenses specifically attributable to removal of existing architectural or transportation barriers qualify as expenses in this context. At press time, there was a question as to whether the statute would be extended but efforts were underway to extend the law.[24]

Do the provisions implementing the handicapped anti-discrimination provision of the revenue sharing program have a limitation on construction projects?

Yes. The regulations prohibiting discrimination in revenue sharing programs and listing discriminatory acts prohibited provide an exception to construction projects commenced prior to January 1, 1977. A construction project is deemed to have commenced when the government unit receiving revenue sharing assistance has obligated itself by contract for the physical construction of the project or any portion of the project. However, the revenue sharing regulations do not include handicapped persons as a class to be considered in the selection of sites and locations of facilities and the exclusion from, denial of the benefits of, or the subjection to discrimination in the use of facilities. At press time revised regulations were being prepared.[25]

Is there a special "curb accessibility" program in federal law?

Yes. A provision of federal highway act legislation requires that in the state highway safety legislation, the Secretary must not approve any program which does not include among its features a provision for adequate and reasonable access for the safe and convenient movement of physically handicapped persons, including those in wheelchairs, across curbs constructed or replaced on or after July 1, 1976 at all pedestrian crosswalks throughout the state. Curb cuts may also be regulated by state and local law.[26]

Is the problem of architectural barriers sometimes addressed by local legislation?

Yes. Cities and counties sometimes regulate barriers, and these local legal sources should always be considered in determining rights. One local law that has received favorable comment is that of Prince George's County, Maryland. The Building Code of that county has been amended to require barrier-free design in certain circumstances and to enhance accessibility for handicapped persons. The law explicitly acknowledges the importance of barrier-free design, and then goes on to spell out the requirements in varying circumstances. The ordinance establishes specific design standards.[27]

NOTES

1. Professor ten Broek discusses the model White Cane Law in his article, *The Right to Live in the World: The Disabled in the Law of Torts,* 54 CALIF. L. REV. 841 (1966); the AB Act is at 42 U.S.C.A. §§4151–57 (1977); NATIONAL COMMISSION ON ARCHITECTURAL BARRIERS TO REHABILITATION OF THE HANDICAPPED, DESIGN FOR ALL AMERICANS 3 (1967); McGaughey, *From Problem to Solution: The New Focus in Fighting Environmental Barriers to the Handicapped,* 37 REHABILITATION LITERATURE at 10 (1976); DESIGN FOR ALL AMERICANS, 2; *Barrier Free Design: Report of a United Nations Expert Group Meeting* at 4; Comment, *Abroad in the Land: Legal Strategies to Effectuate the Rights of the Physically Disabled,* 61 Geo. L.J. 1501, 1511, 1512 (1973).

2. Senator Bartlett's statement is in *Building Design for the Physically Handicapped: Hearings before the Subcommittee on Public Buildings and Grounds of the Committee on Public Works on H.R. 6589 and S.222,* 90th Cong., 2nd Sess. at 3 with the statement of the National Commission at 48–49, emphasis in the original; COMPTROLLER-GENERAL OF THE UNITED STATES, REPORT TO THE CONGRESS: FURTHER ACTION TO MAKE ALL PUBLIC BUILDINGS ACCESSIBLE TO THE PHYSICALLY HANDICAPPED 1 (1975).

3. 42 U.S.C.A. §4151 (1977).

4. 42 U.S.C.A. §§4151–57 (1977) is the Act; the GSA regulations are at 41 C.F.R. 101–96 *et seq*; the HUD regulations are at 24 C.F.R. 40.1 *et seq*; the GAO report is that of the Comptroller-General cited *supra* note 2; the revised GSA regulations are at 43 *Fed. Reg.* 16,478 (April 16, 1978) and now incorporated in 41 C.F.R. 101–19.6, with a revision on reporting requirements at 44 *Fed. Reg.* 39,392 (July 6, 1979).

5. The Standard is reprinted in ACCESSIBILITY: THE LAW AND THE REALITY, *A Survey to Test the Application and Effectiveness of Public Law 90–480 in Iowa* 21–31 (1974).

6. COMPTROLLER-GENERAL, REPORT TO THE CONGRESS, *supra* note 2, at 30; ACCESSIBILITY: THE LAW AND THE REALITY, *supra* note 5, at 15; see the discussion of the North Carolina approach in the Comptroller-General's REPORT TO THE CONGRESS at 30–33; the HEW §504 regulation is §84.23,42 *Fed. Reg.* 22,681 (May 4, 1977).

7. Farber, *The Handicapped Plead for Entrance—Will Anyone Answer?* 64 Ky. L.J. 99; other criticisms are throughout the Comptroller-General's REPORT TO THE CONGRESS, *supra* note 2.

8. 29 U.S.C.A. §792 (Supp. 1979).

9. *Washington Urban League, Inc. v. Washington Metropolitan Area Transit Authority,* Civil Action No. 776–72 (October 23, 1973, and September 1, 1976, Consent Decree, September 28, 1978).

10. §§84.21–84.23.

11. §84.22; Analysis at 42 *Fed. Reg.* 22,689 (May 4, 1977); on carrying, see the Policy Interpretation at 43 Fed. Reg. 36,0305 (August 14, 1978).

12. §84.22(d); Analysis at 42 *Fed. Reg.* 22,690 (May 4, 1977).

13. §84.22 (e).

14. §84.23; Analysis at 42 *Fed. Reg.* 22,690 (May 4, 1977).

15. Analysis at 42 *Fed. Reg.* 22,690 (May 4, 1977).

16. Discussion of state laws in this and the next four questions is not cited to specific state laws, but is a synopsis of various provisions. The reader may want to review the statutes of Michigan, §§125.1351–.1354 M.C.L.A. (1976 and Supp. 1978–1979), and Massachusetts, whose Architectural Barrier Board has published *Rules and Regulations.* Because of continual review of these new statutes, one should be alert to changes and amendments.

17. *Id.*

18. *Id.*

19. *Id.*
20. *Id.*
21. COMPTROLLER-GENERAL, REPORT TO THE CONGRESS, *supra*, note 2 at 87–88; the inflationary impact statement is O'Neill, *Discrimination against Handicapped Persons* . . . (Part V), cited in note 13, chapter 1.
22. 20 U.S.C.A. §1406 (1978); 20 U.S.C.A. §1132d–11(b) (3) (1978); 29 U.S.C. 11 §794(b) (Supp. 1979).
23. *Selph v. The Council of the City of Los Angeles*, 390 F. Supp. 58 (C.D. Cal. 1975, *appeal* dismissed, No. 75–2757, 9th Circuit, March 22, 1979); the legislation is S. 392, 125 Cong. Rec. 51,372 (February 8, 1979).
24. The statutory provision is §2122 of the Tax Reform Act of 1976, adding §190 to the Internal Revenue Code; interim regulations were published at 42 *Fed. Reg.* 17,870 (April 4, 1977); with final regulation at 44 *Fed. Reg.* 43,269 (July 24, 1979), to be at 26 C.F.R. §1.190–1, –2, –3.
25. §51.56(c)(2), 42 *Fed. Reg.* at 18,366 (April 6, 1977).
26. 23 U.S.C.A. §402(b)(1)(F)(Supp. 1977); 23 C.F.R. §625.7.
27. See Appendix C, where part of the ordinance is set out.

IV

The Right to Access:
Transportation

**What were some of the early court decisions involving
accessibility of public transportation, and what rationales
do these early cases reflect?**

The early transportation cases reflected an uneasiness
on the part of courts about the issue of civil rights for
handicapped persons and a strong inclination to defer to
the position of administrators, particularly on technological matters.

In *Snowden v. Birmingham—Jefferson County Transit
Authority*,[1] a wheelchair-user brought suit against local
and federal transportation officials, contending that the
development and operation of the federally assisted
public mass transportation system so that the system
was not accessible to persons in wheelchairs violated her
rights (and the rights of other handicapped persons)
under §504, a provision of federal transportation legislation, and the Constitution. She sought an injunction stop-
ping the purchase of the inaccessible buses" until adequate
and effective public mass transportation" had been made
available.

The local transit authority was planning to purchase
twenty-two new forty-five-passenger diesel buses. The
buses were not accessible to wheelchair-users, but the
defendants claimed that such items as stanchions, grabrails, step-well lighting, and powered doors interlocking
with the brakes would make the buses more readily and
safely usable by elderly and physically handicapped
persons not confined to wheelchairs. The Court accepted

that view. It stated in its opinion that accessible standard-size buses designed for "safe and convenient use by passengers confined to wheelchairs" were not in production (a conclusion hotly disputed by many persons). And smaller buses that would be accessible to wheelchair-users had not been proven effective for use in regular line haul urban mass transportation service. The court further pointed to ongoing research and demonstration efforts of the Urban Mass Transportation Administration (particularly the "Transbus" project, which we will discuss later).

The court examined this situation in light of a provision of federal transportation legislation:

It is hereby declared to be the national policy that elderly and handicapped persons have the same right as other persons to utilize mass transportation facilities and services; that special efforts shall be made in the planning and design of mass transportation facilities and services so that the availability to elderly and handicapped persons of mass transportation which they can effectively utilize will be assured; and that all Federal programs offering assistance in the field of mass transportation (including programs under this chapter) should contain provisions implementing this policy.[3]

The court concluded that the special equipment and features noted earlier were "special efforts" as envisioned under the statute. Further, "Modern technology has not progressed to the point of doing any more for those persons confined to a wheelchair than is already being done by" the local transit authority and that "it would seem inherently unreasonable to bring all new bus procurement to a halt while new equipment is being designed, developed, tested and produced."

As to the plaintiff's claim under §504, the court stated that persons "confined to wheelchairs are permitted to ride [the transit authority's] vehicles":

Although it is necessary for persons handicapped in this manner to arrange for someone to help them board and alight from the bus, these persons are allowed to use the transportation vehicles in question. Thus, it cannot be said that persons who ambulate by wheelchair are excluded from using the defendant's transportation system. For this reason, the court finds no violation of the Rehabilitation Act of 1973 on the part of [the defendant], and hence that act provides plaintiff and the class she represents with no cause of action.[3]

The court rejected the argument that the plaintiff's right to equal protection under the Constitution had been denied. It held that the Constitution did not require provisions of any special class or type of physical facilities to accommodate any special class or type of citizen in the absence of a statute imposing such requirements. The court further found that the actions of the defendant had a rational basis, and that the plaintiff did not have a "fundamental right" to transportation. The judgment was affirmed by an appellate court.

In a second federal case, *United Handicapped Federation v. Andre*,[4] the district court in Minnesota followed the reasoning of the *Snowden* court closely. There the initial purchase was for 309 standard-size transit buses (with 10 vans specifically equipped to transport persons confined to wheelchairs), later supplemented by a request for 29 standard-size transit buses and for small buses that were specially equipped to transport persons in wheelchairs. The court noted research by UMTA (particularly Transbus) and such minor features as nonskid floors, special grabrails, improved lighting, safety rear doors, and improved destination signs. This court also took the view that "No bus manufacturer in the United States presently produces a standard-size transit bus that is specially designed for total accessibility by the wheelchair handicapped with features providing safety for the handicapped and all other passengers." The court noted the 10 small buses to be purchased as "special efforts," and concluded further that "The court is not persuaded that the statute requires that every standard-size transit bus be specially equipped to transport the wheelchair handicapped." The *Andre* court adopted the view of the *Snowden* court that §504 was not violated as long as the transit authorities permitted handicapped persons to ride the vehicles (albeit the structure of the vehicles required wheelchair users to arrange for someone to assist them) and further held that "this laudable statement of Congressional policy [§504]" [did not require] that all regular route standard-size transit buses be totally accessible to those whose physical disabilities confined them to wheelchairs and that failure to make them accessible was not an act of discrimination in violation of the statute.[5] It agreed with the holding of the *Snowden* case that the inaccessible buses did not violate constitutional rights. The *Andre* case was reversed, and remanded for the lower court to consider DOT regulations.

In a third case, *Martin v. Municipality of Metropolitan Seattle*,[6] the plaintiff sued under a state antidiscrimination law that included handicapped persons within the protected classes. The plaintiff challenged a transit-system policy which had one accessible bus (available only to residents of a special handicapped housing unit) out of a fleet of over 600 vehicles, with plans to acquire 145 new vehicles, 5 of which would be accessible to persons in wheelchairs. However, the 5 accessible units were to be operated only through organizations that served handicapped persons and would be available only to members of those organizations.

The court again adopted the attitude evident in *Snowden* and *Andre* that the exclusion of handicapped persons from public transportation systems did not result from defendants' "actively refusing to provide service or charging onerous or increased fares":

> The sole reason that the plaintiff is unable to use Metro transit services is the physical problem inherent in a step-entry vehicle in view of the plaintiff's wheelchair bound condition. . . . [The defendant transit authority] does not in any affirmative way distinguish between the handicapped and other persons or refuse or withhold admission to handicapped persons to the buses of its system. With the exception of the physical limitations on accessibility inherent in presently available heavy-duty transit coaches already set forth, [the defendant transit authority]

has not taken any direct or indirect action causing handicapped persons to be treated as not welcome, accepted, desired, or solicited as users of the . . . transit system, nor has [it] done anything which directly or indirectly results in any discrimination or the refusing or withholding of admission to the plaintiff or any other handicapped person.

This court also emphasized some of the benefits of minor features to enhance buses for some persons, the technological developments, and the need to weigh the overall public interest. Subsequently, in an appeal, the Supreme Court of Washington did not reach the merits of the case because of procedural issues.

What do these cases indicate about the attitude of courts towards civil rights of handicapped persons in general and the issue of accessibility in particular?
They indicate, first, a misdirected and perhaps naive view toward the question of civil rights for handicapped persons. To hold that inaccessible vehicles do not deny handicapped persons the right to ride the vehicles because those persons may board and alight by arranging for assistance is more than just misguided; the attitude reflects a misunderstanding of the handicapped rights issue that distorts the question before the courts. The issue is not the right to ride a bus, by one means or another, but the right to have access to public transportation services so that handicapped persons can move throughout their communities. If the plaintiffs in these cases were interested only in the right to ride buses, with assisting persons accompanying them, that is a right often secured for them by old legal cases.

The acts of discrimination charged against public transportation agencies must be evaluated in terms of the effect of transit policies in preventing the independent and self-sufficient movement of handicapped persons which national policy supports. A "right" to access to public transit which requires the laborious assistance of a handicapped person's acquaintances is no "right" in reality. The achievement of the antidiscrimination goal of §504 requires accommodation to the needs of handicapped

persons. An effective answer to the position of the courts
on the nondiscrimination issue is that found in the intro-
ductory statement of the HEW §504 regulations:

> There is overwhelming evidence that in the past
> many handicapped persons have been excluded
> from programs entirely, or denied equal treatment,
> simply because they are handicapped. But eliminat-
> ing such gross exclusions and denials of equal
> treatment is not sufficient to assure genuine equal
> opportunity. In drafting a regulation to prohibit
> exclusion and discrimination, it became clear that
> different or special treatment of handicapped persons,
> because of their handicaps, may be necessary in a
> number of contexts in order to ensure equal oppor-
> tunity. Thus, for example, it is meaningless to "admit"
> a handicapped person in a wheelchair to a program
> if the program is offered only on the third floor of a
> walk-up building. Nor is one providing an equal edu-
> cational opportunity to a deaf child by admitting
> him or her to a classroom but providing no means
> for the child to understand the teacher or receive
> instruction.[7]

This statement is a succinct rebuttal to the position of
the courts on the antidiscrimination issue. The HEW
statement does not ignore the issue of costs and financial
burden which concerned the courts (and it permits taking
such factors into consideration in remedying problems),
but the statement emphasizes, "Those burdens and costs,
to be sure, provide no basis for exemption from §504
of this regulation: Congress' mandate to end discrimination is clear."

The decisions, secondly, indicate a willingness by
the courts to show deference to both the judgments and
testimony of administrators in matters pertaining to
transportation policy. This judicial deference may have
stemmed from inexperience with technological considerations related to accessible public transportation, unfamil-
iarity with the significance of transportation to handicapped persons, and discomfort about applying notions
of equal treatment to handicapped persons. The state
of technology and the capacity of transit authorities

to provide some degree of accessible service are matters
in which the courts seemed to defer too much to
administrators. These courts considered the matter of bus
design and system planning as best left to administrators
charged with the responsibility of these functions, and
would have been reluctant to substitute an opinion on
these issues (even if they had been willing to carry the
cases far enough to form an opinion) for that of the public
officials. This judicial deference is all the more questionable in light of a 1977 General Accounting Office report
concluding, among other statements, "Before 1975 the
Urban Mass Transportation Administration was passive
in carrying out this law. As a result, mass transit grants
awarded to local transit officials seldom addressed the
needs of elderly and handicapped persons." The report
specifically criticized UMTA for making "only minimal
efforts" to see that its instructions to grant applicants
on accessibility were carried out.[8]

Thirdly, the courts seemed unwilling to recognize the
delay in efforts to provide accessible public transportation
and the meagerness of those efforts. The federal legislation
requiring "special efforts" in public transportation policies
toward accessibility had been enacted in 1970; §504
had been enacted in 1973. The accomplishments of
public transportation agencies, particularly, in the research and demonstration field, should have been assessed
against the fact that, by the mid-1970s, the efforts had
resulted in very little actual, accessible transportation
services. The urgency of the situation was evident, and
the need of handicapped persons for accessible transportation was clear. Yet the courts seemed content with
generally vague and indefinite commitments from public
agencies for future action.

Moreover, the courts were misguided in their approval
of such features as grabrails, nonskid surfaces, and step-
well lighting as the kind of "special efforts" envisioned by
the statute. The plaintiffs in these cases were wheelchair-
users. The features listed by the courts not only failed to
make the vehicles more accessible to those plaintiffs, but
in fact seem designed more to enhance safety and ease of
nonhandicapped persons. While some of the features may
have benefited some ambulatory persons who were handi-

capped, they were of little help to the more severely
handicapped persons who have been a major concern of
Congress in establishing civil rights.

How did the Bartels and Lloyd cases differ in their holdings toward accessible public transportation?

In *Bartels v. Biernat*,[9] handicapped plaintiffs brought
suit to gain greater access to the public transportation
system, seeking to prevent the execution of contracts
for the purchase of 100 buses, none of which would be
accessible. The court examined the interests of handicapped persons in the context of the public policies
underlying accessible public transportation. It recognized
the need for "the most modern and efficient public
transit system that money can buy; the evils of mass
transportation by means of the privately owned and
operated automobile are manifest." [10] But the court noted
another significant interest:

> On the other hand, society has a distinct interest in
> utilizing every possible source of human skill and
> ingenuity, including the skills and talents of mobility-
> handicapped individuals. When effectively confined
> to a single floor, building or city block, not only are
> the handicapped deprived of the myriad benefits of
> society, but society is deprived of the valuable con-
> tributions of these otherwise normal human beings.
> And this deprivation is compounded by the fact that,
> when unable to fend for themselves, the handicapped
> must depend upon the public purse for their suste-
> nance. This is a burden that should be inflicted
> upon neither the mobility handicapped nor society
> in general.[11]

The court observed that the public interest "stands
behind each position that has been asserted." However,
the court concluded that, after due consideration of the
public interest and the position of each party, justice
would be best served by the granting of a preliminary
injunction, providing the relief requested by the mobility-
handicapped plaintiffs. The court noted the requirements
of §504 and the "special efforts" public transportation
legislation and concluded that, while the plaintiffs (at

that stage of the litigation) had not demonstrated a substantial likelihood of success on the merits, neither had the defendants demonstrated that they had met the requirements of the statutes. The court commented on what it considered "the rather strict language" of the statutes, emphasizing that "*no* handicapped person" suffer exclusion from, be denied the benefits of, or be subjected to discrimination under "*any* program receiving federal financial aid," and further noted that the statute mandated that special efforts "*must* be made in the planning and design of mass transportation facilities and services so that their effective availability to elderly and handicapped persons *will be assured.*" [12]

The preliminary injunction restrained the defendants from accepting any bids then outstanding on the buses, or from taking any action that would result in binding contracts was to remain in effect pending final determination of the case by the court.

While the *Bartels* court considered its final order, the U.S. Court of Appeals for the Seventh Circuit (in Chicago) had before it the case of *Lloyd v. Regional Transportation Authority.*[18] In this transportation-accessibility case, the plaintiffs had been unsuccessful before the lower federal district court. But unlike the other unsuccessful federal cases, the district court had held that the principal statutes upon which plaintiffs relied failed to provide a "private cause of action" (a right of private individuals to bring a lawsuit seeking enforcement of a statute). The question decided by the Court of Appeals was whether the private cause of action under §504 existed (the court held that plaintiffs did have a cause of action), but in its opinion suggested the contours of the rights under §504. Construing §504 and regulations promulgated by the Urban Mass Transportation Administration (together with what were then the proposed HEW §504 regulations), the court identified affirmative rights created by §504. Paraphrasing a Supreme Court decision involving the obligations of public school officials to educate non-English-speaking Chinese students, the Court of Appeals in *Lloyd* stated that there was no equality of treatment of handicapped persons merely by providing to them the same facilities

as ambulatory persons. Handicapped persons who could
not gain access to the facilities were effectively foreclosed
from any meaningful public transportation. While the
court reserved judgment on the ultimate merits of the
case and suggested that existing and future regulations
would merit the lower court's consideration, it did suggest
broad parameters of the right to accessible transportation.
The case was then remanded to the lower court for
further proceedings.

**Did the Lloyd decision have an effect on the further
development of the Bartels case?**

Yes. After the Seventh Circuit ruling in *Lloyd,* the
Bartels court issued a second opinion.[14] The second
Bartels opinion took note of the existence of transportation provided by private corporations and nonprofit
groups, and observed that while such systems do provide
transportation on a demand responsive basis to handicapped persons, the service seemed quite expensive. The
court also noted the reasons given for not initiating new
operations: transit officials hoped to stabilize and preserve
the existing system while improving the level of service
and lowering the fares, and they believed that more data
on the needs and travel patterns of handicapped persons
was necessary before making any plan for adding new
services. The court then pointed to the inaccessibility of
the existing fleet and the lack of plans for providing
transit services to handicapped persons either by means
of regular route service or by an alternative system of
service. The transit agency did not indicate plans "to
make available vehicles or services which could be effectively and readily used by the mobility handicapped."

The court then declared that the local transit officials
had violated §504 "by attempting to purchase one
hundred new effectively inaccessible buses so as to know-
ingly exclude mobility-handicapped individuals from participating in the benefits of the federally assisted mass
transit program." Furthermore, the court held that
federal transportation officials had violated §504 by
approving the local transit authority's application for
federal financial assistance with the full knowledge that
existing buses and the new buses to be purchased would

be effectively inaccessible to handicapped individuals and by their corresponding failure to require the local transit agency to give assurances that "appropriate mass transit services so as not to exclude such individuals from the federally assisted mass transit program" would be provided.

The court granted judgment in favor of plaintiffs and proceeded to fashion a remedy. In granting relief to the plaintiffs, the court recognized the problem of transit agencies. Section 504, the court said, did not allow the local government to wait "until the perfect solution is found." The court considered the technology "necessary to implement some of the proposed solutions to the problem . . . not fully advanced," and the court noted that it had not been presented with any study of the particular problems facing that community. The local government operated a transit system with buses almost 15 years old, on the average, and the court warned of the importance of "provid[ing] some access to the transit system for the plaintiff class and assur[ing] that additional improvements will be made without placing restrictions on the defendants that will necessarily result in collapse of the transit system." Turning to regulations promulgated by the UMTA in part under §504 (and the same regulations pointed to by the *Lloyd* court), the court considered the "regulations and accompanying guidelines . . . an appropriate point of reference in drafting the remedy":

> The regulations do not require a full and immediate solution to the problem. What they do require is that the planning process show that special efforts are being taken to ensure that the mobility handicapped will be provided with services equivalent to the rest of the community.[15]

It then issued a permanent injunction against local and federal defendants. The local defendants were permanently enjoined from acquiring, leasing, renting, or in any way operating any mass transit vehicles (other than those already owned and operated by the local government) that were not designed for:

accessibility and effective utilization by mobility-handicapped individuals until such time as defendants can demonstrate to the satisfaction of the Court that mass transportation facilities and services which can be effectively utilized by mobility-handicapped individuals have been planned, designed and are being made available to such individuals in a nondiscriminatory manner.

The federal defendants were ordered not to release any federal funds to the local defendants for any mass transit vehicles which did not meet the requirements imposed on the local defendants.

The court did add the proviso that any mass transit vehicles not designed to meet the stated requirements might be acquired with federal funds if it was demonstrated that there was "a compelling necessity for immediate purchase of such vehicles such that a failure of the system would result without their purchase and that all diligence is being used to plan, design, and implement facilities and services which can be effectively utilized by mobility-handicapped individuals." The court also retained jurisdiction of the case until all requirements of the court and its judgment had been satisfied.

What are some of the major provisions of the interim regulations promulgated by the Urban Mass Transportation Administration for accessible public transportation?

The regulations to which these courts referred provide that UMTA will grant approval for projects under the assistance program involved only if:

(a) The urban transportation planning process exhibits satisfactory special efforts in planning public mass transportation facilities and services that can be utilized by elderly and handicapped persons; and

(b) The annual element of the transportation improvements program . . . submitted after September 30, 1976, contains projects or project elements designed to benefit elderly and handicapped persons, specifically including wheelchair users and those with semiambulatory capabilities; and

(c) After September 30, 1977, reasonable progress

has been demonstrated in implementing previously programmed projects.[16]

The following discussion is provided as background to the next question concerning the final DOT §504 regulations. With the regulations, UMTA issued an "advisory information" appendix to the regulations, setting forth general guidance on the meaning of "special efforts" in planning. "Special efforts" refers both to service for elderly and handicapped persons in general and specifically to service for wheelchair users and semiambulatory persons. For wheelchair users and other persons who cannot negotiate steps, special efforts in planning means genuine, good-faith progress in planning service for wheelchair users and semiambulatory handicapped persons that is reasonable by comparison with the service provided to the general public and that meets a significant fraction of the actual transportation needs of such persons within a reasonable time period.

The regulatory material gives examples of a "level of effort" sufficient for the special-efforts requirement. One example is a program for wheelchair users and semiambulatory persons that expends a specified amount of funds according to a formula spelled out by UMTA. A second example is the purchase of "only wheelchair-accessible new fixed route equipment until one-half of the fleet is accessible" or, as an alternative to that approach, "provison of a substitute service that would provide comparable coverage and service levels." The third example is a system of any design

that would assure that every wheelchair user or semiambulatory person in the urbanized area would have public transportation available if requested for 10 round-trips per week at fares comparable to those which are charged on standard transit buses for trips of similar length, within the service area of the public transportation authority.

This third alternative would permit issuing trip coupons to individuals who could then purchase the necessary services.[17] The guidelines do not purport to be regulatory minimum standards, but they do describe qualitative boundaries of the special-efforts concept.

The regulations continued to recognize the validity of paratransit services whereby private nonprofit corporations and associations receive grants for the special transportation needs of elderly and handicapped persons. To qualify as special efforts which meet the needs of wheelchair users and semiambulatory persons under this program, four conditions must be met:

1. The service and vehicles must serve wheelchair users and semiambulatory persons.
2. The service must meet a priority need identified in the planning process.
3. The service must not be restricted to a particular organizational or institutional clientele.
4. Any fares charged must be comparable to those charged on standard transit buses for trips of similar length.[18]

Moreover, the UMTA regulations also required the "wheelchair accessibility option" for standard full-sized urban transit buses. Solicitations for procurement must provide for a design that permits the addition of this option and must require an assurance from each bidder that it offers the option for its buses. A "wheelchair accessibility option" means a level-change mechanism such as a lift or ramp, sufficient clearance to permit a wheelchair user to reach a securement location, and at least one wheelchair securement device.[19] The option is for procurement solicitations issued on or before September 30, 1979.

Other important provisions require that recipients under §5 of the Urban Mass Transportation Act must charge fares to elderly and handicapped persons during nonpeak hours which do not exceed one-half of the rates generally applicable to other persons at peak hours (a requirement mandated by the act itself where the facilities and equipment utilized are financed under §504 whether the operation of the facilities and equipment is by the applicant for UMTA assistance or by another entity); accessibility for fixed facilities, such as stations and terminals, and for such features on the buses as

priority seating for elderly and handicapped persons,
floor surfaces, and handrails; that consumers be represented in the planning process for public transportation;
and provisions for rapid rail and light rail vehicles.

The regulations also allow the UMTA Adminstrator to
grant waivers or modifications where "clearly necessary"
and consistent with the laws underlying the regulations.
Waiver requests for facilities covered by the Architectural
Barriers Act must also be presented to the Administrator
of General Services. A request for a waiver has to be
presented at the public hearing which is required of
applicants before they submit proposals to UMTA.[20]

Has the Department of Transportation issued final regulations to implement §504?

On July 2, 1979, the final regulations issued by DOT
became effective. Public transit buses for which solicitations are issued after that date must be wheelchair
accessible. DOT states that it still contemplates that
Transbus will ultimately become the core of public bus
systems. Within ten years, half the buses used in peak-
hour service must be accessible to wheelchair users, and
these buses must be utilized before inaccessible vehicles
in off-peak hours in order to maximize the number of
accessible buses in service.

Program accessibility for a fixed route bus system is
defined as:

1. when the system is accessible to handicapped persons who can use steps, and,
2. when the system, viewed in its entirety, is accessible
   to wheelchair users. This is where the peak-hour
   bus service provision comes into play.

The regulations state that fixed route bus systems shall
achieve program accessibility as soon as practicable but
no later than three years after July 2, 1979. That time
limit is extended to ten years for extraordinarily expensive structural changes to, or replacement of, existing
facilities, including vehicles, necessary to achieve program
accessibility. The regulations do not require recipients to
install a lift on any bus for which a solicitation was
issued on or before February 15, 1977.

For rapid rail, commuter rail, and light rail (trolley and street car) systems, the regulations introduced a concept of "key stations." For example, all existing rapid rail systems must be made accessible to handicapped people over time, subject only to a limited waiver provision. The systems are given thirty years to make key stations accessible if station accessibility involves extraordinary costs. Less costly changes must be made in three years. Key stations include stations where passenger boardings exceed average station boardings by fifteen percent, transfer points on a rail line or between rail lines, end stations (unless near another accessible station), stations serving major activity centers (e.g., employment centers, hospitals), stations that are special trip generators for sizable numbers of handicapped persons, and stations that are major exchange points with other modes of transportation. Similar concepts, but different time periods, are applied to commuter rail and light rail systems.

Paratransit systems must be operated so that the system, when viewed in its entirety, is accessible to handicapped persons, including wheelchair users. The system must operate a number of vehicles sufficient to provide generally equal service to handicapped people who need such vehicles as is provided to other persons. Where it is necessary to purchase new vehicles or to make structural changes to meet this requirement, the purchase or changes must be made as soon as practicable but no later than three years after July 2, 1979. New paratransit vehicles for which solicitations are issued after July 2, 1979, must be accessible unless the paratransit system will be in compliance with the general accessibility requirement without the new vehicles which are accessible.

Within three years after July 2, 1979, each recipient whose transit system has not achieved program accessibility must provide or assure the provision of interim accessible transportation for handicapped people who could otherwise use the system if it were accessible. This interim service must be provided until program accessibility has been achieved. Standards for the interim service must be developed in consultation with local handicapped groups and individuals, and recipients are required to spend a minimum amount of the financial assistance on this transportation.

Subject to this expenditure limitation, some general standards are established in the regulations for the interim service. The service must be available within the recipient's normal service area and during normal service hours and, to the extent feasible:

1. have no restrictions on trip purpose;
2. combined wait and travel time, transfer frequency, and fares must be comparable to that of the regular fixed route system;
3. service must be available to all handicapped people who could otherwise use the system if it was accessible, including wheelchair users who cannot transfer from a wheelchair and those who use powered wheelchairs;
4. there can be no waiting list such that handicapped persons who have qualified or registered for the service are consistently excluded because of low capacity.

Other important provisions require accessibility in new airport terminals, new rest area facilities along federally assisted highways, and new railroad stations. Existing facilities of these types must be made accessible within certain time periods. Additional requirements apply to accessibility of existing fixed facilities in mass transportation with changes generally required as soon as practicable but not less than three years after July 2, 1979. The regulations also contain important provisions pertaining to accessibility in and services to handicapped passengers at airports and railroads.

The DOT §504 regulations were generally met by disappointment among handicapped people. Of particular concern has been the policy of granting long years of compliance periods to meet the requirements.

It is not altogether clear what the relationship will be between the final DOT §504 regulations and the previous interim regulations. While the final regulations are intended to supplant the interim regulations, it is also clear that the earlier rule will have some effect on administrative regulatory policy.[21]

Apart from the decision in Lloyd and Bartels, have other judicial opinions reflected the influence of the interim regulations?

Yes. In *United Handicapped Federation v. Andre,* the Court of Appeals for the Eighth Circuit reversed the district court's decision and remanded the case for reconsideration. The issuance of the regulations, and the Seventh Circuit's ruling in *Lloyd* intervened between the lower court ruling discussed in the first question in this chapter and the appellate reversal in *Andre.* The Eighth Circuit, as did the Seventh Circuit, pointed to both the UMTA regulations and the HEW regulations. The *Andre* court then reached this conclusion:

> On the basis of the record before the district court, if it were not for the subsequent promulgation of the administrative guidelines and regulations, we would agree with the district court's result. However, we feel that the denial of relief to the plaintiffs cannot be justified in light of these recent definitions and guidelines. Although the buses in question here have been purchased and placed in service, because of the recent developments the defendants now have the burden to take affirmative action to conform to the regulations and guidelines. It is difficult to assess the record and the statutes in any other light. . . . The district court, upon receiving further evidence, should reappraise defendants' compliance with the statutes, regulations and guidelines, and fashion whatever equitable relief it deems necessary.[22]

In a second case, *Vanko v. Finley,*[23] a federal district court considered a case brought by a wheelchair user seeking changes to make the public transportation system usable by handicapped persons. The court refused to hold that all transit rolling stock and facilites must be usable by all mobility-handicapped and elderly people, and it further held that "Congress did not create immediate rights of access for all handicapped individuals to all mass transit facilities." The court recognized "the psychological and rehabilitative benefits to be gained from integrating wheelchair users into the regular transit system," but it held that local transit authorities could continue their basic approach to the "special efforts" compliance requirements of the operation of "a separate paratransport system parallel to the main bus and rapid systems." Two issues concerned the court in *Vanko*: whether the local transit agency was required to provide service for elderly and handicapped individuals "that is reasonable by comparison with the service provided to the general public" (a requirement taken from the UMTA regulations) and whether the transit authority was, in fact, meeting that requirement. The court reiterated these issues with respect to what §504 would require in public transportation and held that §504 did not require the defendants to make all buses accessible. The court also rejected constitutional arguments that a different result was dictated.

In response to the question about service "reasonable by comparison with the service provided to the general public," the court held that "comparability is, in fact, required by applicable federal law, but that local transit authorities have an interim time period in which to design, plan for, and effectuate such a comparable system of mass transit for the mobility handicapped." The court would not consider "vague plans for the indefinite future and second-rate transit for the mobility handicapped" as sufficient for compliance with federal law, but neither would it require "instantaneous conversion to a transportation system that is comparable in every minute detail." Moreover the court held that "the same substantial good faith progress in both the planning and implementation of transit programs for the mobility handicapped" was sufficient for §504 and the special efforts legislation and regulations under the special efforts law. It then examined the program actually being planned for transportation of handicapped persons and found that the transit authority was in full compliance with their statutory and regulatory obligations. The approved system included a door-to-door service, with a priority system for scheduling trips.

What is the "Transbus mandate"?

On May 19, 1977, Secretary of Transportation Brock Adams issued a decision on the vehicle known as "Transbus." Transbus is a low-floor, ramped bus intended to be a mainline bus. A subsequent modification allowed the use of a lift as an alternative to the ramp. It had been a part of UMTA research efforts for several years. The decision to mandate Transbus required the use of a Transbus specification for all standard-size buses acquired with UMTA assistance in procurements issued for bids after September 30, 1979.

Prior to Adams' decision the previous administration had decided against Transbus in favor of another type of vehicle called the "advanced design bus." This reconsideration of the earlier Transbus decision was the result of considerable public controversy. The advanced design bus was regarded by many handicapped persons as unsatisfactory. Transbus itself was the goal of a lawsuit filed by a large group of handicapped individuals and groups.

In the decision announcing the Transbus mandate, the Secretary of Transportation pointed to the requirements of §504 and the special efforts statute, in addition to other legal and policy reasons. However, the Secretary announced that until the Transbus decision became effective, the regulations previously announced would serve as an existing policy for the interim. As this book went to press, renewed concern was arising over whether the mandate would be implemented, particularly in light of the recent lifting of the September 30 date.[24]

Do federal statutes other than §504 and the special efforts statute address the issue of accessible transportation?

Yes. There is legislation other than the two statutes, notably concerning federal aid to highways. But courts have devoted most of their attention to §504 and the special efforts statute of the urban mass transportation legislation.[25]

Are there differing views of the intent of Congress in enacting accessible transit legislation?

Yes. Although members of Congress made strong statements during consideration of some transit legislation, generally, courts have not been persuaded that such statements mandate a high degree of accessibility on the basis of those statutes alone, although one court has commented, "The legislative history in this record shows that individuals in the Congress have been unhappy with the Department of Transportation and its failure to achieve the prescribed goal of equal access. Various proposals for additional legislation have been suggested." [26]

Does state law have a bearing on rights to accessible public transportation?

Yes. We have already discussed the *Martin* case and the use of a state civil rights statute. Other state laws might be used in some states. California, for example, has legislation which addresses public transit. This legislation has served as a basis for litigation, although in one case it did not result in the degree of accessibility that plaintiffs wanted. [27]

Is the right of access to airlines addressed by administrative regulations?

Yes. The Federal Aviation Administration has adopted regulations pertaining to the transportation of persons who may need assistance. These regulations provide that a passenger may not be refused transportation on the basis that his transportation might be inimical to safety unless the carrier (referred to in the regulations as a certificate holder) has established procedures, including reasonable notice requirements for passengers who may need assistance to move expeditiously to an exit in case of emergency. A carrier who has these procedures may not refuse to carry the passenger unless the passenger fails to comply with the notice requirements in the procedures or unless the passenger cannot be carried in accordance with the procedure. Furthermore, the Civil Aeronautics Board is now considering changes in existing policies.

The Administrator of the FAA may require changes in the procedures, and a copy of the procedures must be provided to the FAA district office charged with overall inspection of the carrier. An advisory circular has also been prepared by the FAA for training airline personnel to help handicapped travelers. The regulations also address seating of persons who cannot sit erect. They require airline personnel to brief handicapped persons about the best emergency exit procedures and to ask each handicapped passenger how best to help them without causing pain or injury. The FAA rejected a proposed regulation that would require the storage of canes and crutches to ensure that each would be readily accessible in the event of an emergency if those items had been carried aboard by the passengers. The regulations described cover various commercial flights but not travel clubs using large airplanes. Some modifications of the regulations apply to small aircraft.

Additionally, the recently promulgated DOT §504 regulations have important provisions pertaining to airport accessibility and service to handicapped people. Important provisions apply to boarding (which cannot be by means of lifts ordinarily used to move freight), information systems, and assistance in moving through airports.[28]

Do any regulations cover transportation of handicapped persons in interstate buses?

Yes. The Interstate Commerce Commission (ICC) has regulations prohibiting carriers from denying transportation to any person on the basis of a handicap, physical disability, or blindness, or because that person cannot board a bus without assistance. A guide dog, a seeing-eye dog, or other guide dog specially trained for that purpose must be provided free passage when accompanied by a blind person. Carriers must, whenever possible, provide assistance in boarding buses, including advanced boarding and seating. They must also offer help in the use of terminal accommodations and baggage service, and all terminals must prominently display a notice stating how to obtain such assistance. Terminal accommodations must be accessible to handicapped, disabled, blind, and elderly passengers. All terminals newly built or substantially renovated after January 1, 1978, must conform to the ANSI Standard. It is unclear whether the regulation incorporates only the 1971 version or subsequent versions approved by the American National Standards Institute. The regulation also incorporates a waiver provision under which carriers may seek relief from the regulation, but which also requires public notice of the filing of such petitions.[29]

What is the federal statute pertaining to the Amtrak Corporation and railroad service for elderly and handicapped persons?

A federal law authorizes the Amtrak Corporation to take "all steps necessary to insure that no elderly or handicapped individual is denied intercity transportation on any passenger train operated" by or on behalf of Amtrak. These steps are authorized to include, but not be limited to, acquiring special equipment and devices and giving special training to employees; designing and acquiring new equipment and facilities, and eliminating barriers in existing equipment and facilities, all to comply with the "highest standards" for design, construction, and alteration of property for the accommodation of elderly and handicapped individuals; and providing special assistance while boarding and alighting and in terminal areas to elderly and handicapped individuals.

Additionally, the final DOT §504 regulations effective July 2, 1979, have important provisions affecting station accessibility and passenger services.

In some cases, it may be necessary for a handicapped person to give notice of intention to travel by train. Some individuals may also be required to have an attendant. However, train personnel are required to provide a wide variety of assistance in moving in and about the train. Additionally, standards are set for the development of accessible railroad cars.[30]

NOTES

1. 407 F. Supp. 394 (N.D. Ala. 1975), aff'd per curiam, 551 F.2d 862 (5th Cir. 1977), rehearing den., 554 F.2d 475 (5th Cir. 1977).
2. 49 U.S.C.A. §1612 (a) (1976).
3. 407 F. Supp. at 397.
4. 409 F. Supp. 1297 (D. Minn. 1976), vacated and remanded, 558 F.2d 413 (8th Cir. 1977).

5. 409 F. Supp. at 1301.
6. *Martin v. Municipality of Metro. Seattle,* No. 795806 (Superior Court for King County, Wash., November 25, 1975), *aff'd on other grounds,* 90 Wn.2d 39, 578 P.2d 525 (May 4, 1978).
7. 42 *Fed. Reg.* 22,676 (May 4, 1977).
8. COMPTROLLER-GENERAL OF THE UNITED STATES, MASS TRANSIT FOR ELDERLY AND HANDICAPPED PERSONS: URBAN MASS TRANSPORTATION ADMINISTRATION'S POLICY ACTIONS (i), (ii) (1977).
9. 405 F. Supp. 1012 (E.D. Wis. 1975), 427 F. Supp. 226 (E.D. Wis. 1977).
10. 405 F. Supp. at 1017.
11. 405 F. Supp. at 1017–18.
12. 405 F. Supp. at 1018; emphasis in original.
13. 548 F.2d 1277 (7th Cir. 1977).
14. 427 F. Supp 226 (E.D. Wis. 1977).
15. 427 F. Supp. at 233.
16. 49 C.F.R. §613.204, 41 *Fed. Reg.* 18,234 (April 30, 1976).
17. Appendix to 49 C.F.R. §613.204, 41 *Fed. Reg.* 18,234 (April 30, 1976); Appendix to 20 C.F.R. §450.120, 41 *Fed. Reg.* 18,236 (April 30, 1976).
18. *Ibid.*
19. 49 C.F.R. §609.15(c).
20. 49 C.F.R. §609.1–.25; Appendix to 23 C.F.R. §450.120, 41 *Fed. Reg.* 18,235 (April 30, 1976); *see also* 49 C.F.R. §613.204.
21. 49 C.F.R. Part 27.
22. 558 F.2d 416.
23. 440 F. Supp. 656 (N.D. Ohio 1977).
24. The Transbus Mandate is entitled, "Decision of Brock Adams, Secretary of Transportation, to Mandate Transbus" (May 19, 1977); the case was *Disabled in Action of Pennsylvania, Inc. v. Coleman,* No. 76–1913 (March 17, 1978, dismissing the complaint as moot and denying plaintiff's motion for summary judgment, the transbus lift modification was at 43 *Fed. Reg.* 41,987, with the change in effective date at 44 *Fed. Reg.* 47,344 (August 13, 1979).
25. 23 U.S.C. §142 note.
26. *Atlantis Community, Inc. v. Adams,* Civil Action No. 77M707 (November 9, 1977), *but compare* the court's subsequent Memorandum Opinion and Order of June 30, 1978, 453 F. Supp. 825 (D. Col. 1978), *appeal docketed,* No. 78–1963 (9th Cir., Dec. 14, 1978); the 1975 booklet by Raggio, et al., *Equal Access to Public Transportation:*

The Disabled and the Elderly, discusses some of this legislative history.

27. *E.g.,* CAL. GOV'T CODE §4450; *Center for Independent Living v. Alameda-Contra Costa Transit Dist.* (Superior Court No. 496609–8) and *Roberts v. Alameda-Contra Costa Transit Dist.* (Superior Court No. 496705–5) (August 29, 1977), *appeal pending* 1 Civil 42362 (Court of Appeal of California, 1st Appellate District); Michigan Enrolled Senate Bill 1157 (79th Legislature, Regular Session of 1978).

28. See 42 14 C.F.R. *Fed. Reg.* 18,392 (April 7, 1977), 49 C.F.R. §27.71. See also proposed regulations by the Civil Aeronautics Board, 44 *Fed. Reg.* 32401 (June 6, 1979).

29. 42 *Fed. Reg.* 29,309 (June 8, 1977), to become 49 C.F.R. §1063 revised regulations are being contemplated.

30. 45 U.S.C.A. §545(c) (Supp. 1978); 49 C.F.R. §27.73.

V

The Right to Education: Preschool, Elementary, and Secondary

Just as accessibility—the right of access to structures and public transportation systems—is one cornerstone of the civil-rights movement among handicapped persons, the right to education has been another basic concern. In the United States, education has been for many "outsiders" the means for movement from one part of our society to another. For immigrants learning the ways of a strange land, for women gaining access to professions, for blacks seeking an end to separate and inferior schooling, or for poor people wanting new opportunities—for many groups the right to education was essential to better lives. Education has been important not only because of the technical skills and information it provides (essential in a complex society), but important also as a symbol of well-being and as a "door opener" for those who have met the system's requirements.

Physically handicapped people have sought education for the reasons other groups have sought it. The difficulties encountered by physically handicapped people in securing education exemplify the problems they have encountered as they have attempted to secure legal equality in other areas. They have, in some situations, been excluded from public schools. When they were admitted, it was often to segregated classrooms or buildings set aside for handicapped persons; in some cases they were sent away to distant state schools for students with particular handicaps. When they were able to gain some education, they were often denied the opportunity to pursue certain goals or to train for certain careers because of stereotyped prejudices about the abilities of handicapped persons. These three issues—exclusion, segregation, and denial of choices—have characterized the existence of handicapped people for decades and are common to the experiences of other minorities.

The legal rights of physically handicapped persons to education are perhaps clearer than other legal rights discussed. Presently the dominant federal legal sources are two statutes—§504 of the Rehabilitation Act of 1973 and the Education for All Handicapped Children Act of 1975. The §504 antidiscrimination principles provide protection to handicapped students in many preschool, elementary, secondary, vocational, and college programs. The Education for All Handicapped Children Act (which builds on earlier federal legislation pertaining to education for handicapped persons) [1] combines a federal financial commitment to the states for purposes of education with requirements on the conduct of the educational programs (allowing room, however, for states to regulate many questions, thereby establishing the importance of state law as a source of legal rights). Under the act, a cutoff of federal funds is possible if the act is not followed. Regulations detail application of the federal and state statutes. Court decisions interpreting these statutes and the implementing regulations are appearing and will be an important source of law in the future. And constitutional provisions (particularly the equal protection and due-process clauses of the 14th Amendment) that were important in early cases involving education of handicapped children may continue to be important, although the importance of constitutional arguments may be displaced by increased reliance on statutes and regulations. In connection with the constitutional aspects of the right to education, it is significant to note that in enacting the Education for All Handicapped Children Act, Congress declared that "it is in the national interest that the Federal Government assist State and local efforts to provide programs to meet the educational needs of handicapped children in order to assure equal protection of the law." [2]

NOTE: For purposes of the Education for All Handicapped Children Act, the term "parent" includes also a guardian, a person acting as a parent of a child, or a surrogate parent (a term discussed later), but not the state if the child is a ward of the state.

What major concepts underlie the federal requirements for a "free appropriate public education"?

The Education for All Handicapped Children Act provides four basic requirements in its definition of the term. It includes "special education and related services" which:

1. Have been provided at public expense, under public supervision and direction, and without charge,
2. Meet standards established by the state educational agency,
3. Include an appropriate preschool, elementary, or secondary education in the state involved,
4. Are provided in conformity with an "individualized education program," a requirement of the act discussed later.[3]

Both the terms "special education" and "related services" are defined more fully in the act. "Special education" is defined as "specially designed instruction, at no cost to parents or guardians, to meet the unique needs of a handicapped child." Included in the act's definition of special education are classroom instruction, instruction in physical education, home instruction, and instruction in hospitals and institutions.[4] "Related services" include a long list of services designed to assist a handicapped child to benefit from special education. Among the enumerated services are transportation, speech pathology and audiology, psychological services, physical and occupational therapy, counseling, and medical services for the purpose of diagnosis and evaluation.[5]

How does the §504 concept of a "free appropriate public education" compare with the Education for All Handicapped Children Act?

§504 applies to school systems receiving federal assistance, and the HEW §504 regulations include a requirement for a free appropriate public education. The §504 regulations emphasize that each qualified handicapped person (defined generally in terms of age—during which nonhandicapped persons are provided services or during which it is mandatory under state law to provide services to handicapped persons, or persons to whom a state is required to provide education under other federal legislation requiring education for handicapped children)[6] in a recipient's jurisdiction, "regardless of the nature or severity of the person's handicap," [7] must be provided a free appropriate public education.

The §504 concept of "appropriateness" in education is defined in part as "the provision of regular or special education and related aids and services"; thus §504 protects also those handicapped students who do not need any special education, but can be served in regular programs. The services must be designed to meet individual educational needs of handicapped persons "as adequately as the needs of nonhandicapped persons are met," as well as meeting other provisions of the §504 regulations which apply to these educational programs. The §504 regulations refer to the "individualized education programs" provided for under the Education for All Handicapped Children Act (discussed later) as one way to meet the §504 requirement of providing education to a handicapped child. Additionally, the §504 regulations provide that if a recipient refers a handicapped child to another program, the recipient remains responsible for ensuring compliance of the second program with the HEW §504 preschool, elementary, and secondary regulations.

The §504 regulations emphasize that there can be no cost to a handicapped person or to parents or guardians, except for fees applied also to nonhandicapped persons. If a recipient cannot provide the free services directly, but must refer a handicapped person to another program, then the recipient must pay the costs of the program, including transportation to and from the program at a cost no greater than would be incurred if the person were in the responsible recipient's program. When it is necessary to place a handicapped student in a residential setting, the responsible recipient must also pay for the placement (including nonmedical care and room and board). The Education for All Handicapped Children Act regulations have a similar provision pertaining to residential placement.[8] However, if the residential placement is made at the choice of a parent or guardian (as opposed to having been made because residential placement is necessary to furnish an appropriate education) the recipient is not required to pay for these services. If there is a disagreement between parents and recipients about whether residential placement is appropriate, the due process hearing mechanism (discussed later) is available to resolve these disputes.[9]

Does the definition of the term "handicapped children" in the Education for All Handicapped Children Act differ from the term "handicapped individual" in the §504 regulations?

Yes, in certain ways. The Education for All Handicapped Children Act provides a listing of specific handicapping conditions that are encompassed in that law. The act applies to children within these groups who, by reason of their handicaps, need special education and related services.[10] Included as handicaps are such broad categories as hearing or speech impairments, visual handicaps, and orthopedic impairments; regulations promulgated under the act define the handicaps in great detail.[11] These definitions are more detailed than the broader, less specific provisions of the Rehabilitation Act and its regulations. Moreover, the Rehabilitation Act does not confine its protection to the apparently limited class of the Education for All Handicapped Children Act (those handicapped children who, because of their handicaps, need special education and related services).

What is the function of the State Annual Program Plans?

The Education for All Handicapped Children Act establishes certain eligibility requirements as a condition of states' receiving funds under the act. One requirement is the State Annual Program Plan, a document a state must submit to the federal Commissioner of Education to receive federal funds, indicating how it will meet the act's requirement. The act and its regulations set forth detailed requirements for what the plan must contain. The plan must have public participation in its development, and must be available to the public subsequent to approval.

Among the information a state must provide is the state policy that insures the rights of all handicapped children to a free appropriate public education, including data about the handicapped children who are receiving or need special education and related services. Other parts of the plan must indicate how the state will meet the substantive requirements of the act. Additionally, the plan must indicate administrative procedures for handling funds and distribution to local education agencies. The regulations also contain provisions pertaining to the application local education agencies must submit to the state agencies for funds.[12]

Does the Education for All Handicapped Children Act pay for all of the cost schools incur in educating handicapped children?

No. The federal money is to be used to meet "excess costs" in providing special education and related services. Local education agencies are required to spend a minimum amount of money for handicapped students, apart from the money received under the act. The computation of these amounts is by means of formulas in the regulations. The federal funds are not intended to supplant state and local funds for the education of handicapped children. This funding arrangement is not related to the requirement that the education provided to handicapped children is to be free to them or their parents.

At what ages must handicapped children be offered a free appropriate public education?

The Education for All Handicapped Children Act provides that by September 1, 1978, a free appropriate public education must be available to all handicapped children between the ages of 3 and 18. By September 1, 1980, all handicapped children between the age of 3 and 21 must have available a free appropriate public education. However, the statute also provides that for those handicapped children aged 3 to 5 and for those aged 18 to 21 inclusive, the requirements of the statute are not to be applied in a state where application of the requirements would be inconsistent with state law or practice, or a court order, respecting public education of those age groups in the state.[14] The regulations spell out more precisely when a state must provide education to persons within these age groups.[15]

It should be noted that the age requirements pertain to implementation of the 1975 law. States may have already established ages at which education is to be provided, and these laws should be checked both for their conformity with federal law and for their application in years preceding the federal law. The HEW §504 regulations contain a requirement that the free appropriate public education requirement is to be met "at the earliest practicable time and in no event later than September 1, 1978," [16] although exclusion of handicapped persons is prohibited after the effective date of the HEW §504 regulations. However, a decision by a federal district court in Mississippi indicated that the requirements of §504 and the Education of the Handicapped Act (which preceded the 1975 education legislation) were immediately enforceable.[17] Moreover, §504 has served as the basis for at least one successful suit for education of a physically handicapped child before the regulations went into effect.[18] Therefore, for disputes over education before the dates in the regulations, there may be controversy as to what is required and when.

Are services and programs other than traditional classroom education to be provided to handicapped children?

Yes. Handicapped children must have available to them "the variety of educational programs and services available to non-handicapped children in the area served by" local public agencies, including (but not limited to) art, music, industrial arts, consumer and homemaking education, and vocational education. Additionally, steps must be taken to provide nonacademic and extracurricular services and activities. Included within these services and activities are counseling services, athletics, transportation, health services, recreational activities, special-interest groups or clubs sponsored by the public agencies, referrals to agencies that provide assistance to handicapped persons, and both employment of students by the public agency and assistance in making outside employment available.

Physical education must be provided. The integrationist principle also applies here unless a child is enrolled full time in a separate facility or the child's needs are such that special physical education is appropriate. Otherwise, handicapped children must be afforded an opportunity for participation in the regular program.

The requirements above are taken from the regulations to implement the Education for All Handicapped Children Act. The §504 HEW regulations pertaining to nonacademic services in preschool, elementary, and secondary education generally follow the other regulations. Analysis accompanying the §504 regulations notes that in provisions of physical education and athletic activities, the integrationist principle could mean that a student in a wheelchair might be able to participate in a regular archery course, or a deaf student in a wrestling course. The §504 regulations also provide that recipients must ensure that qualified handicapped students are not counseled toward "more restrictive career objectives than are nonhandicapped students with similar interest and abilities." The emphasis of the §504 regulations is on equal opportunity for participation in services and activities; thus the provision on counseling reflects a concern that handicapped persons not be pigeonholed into limited professional goals. The physical education requirements of both sets of regulations, and the extracurricular activites sections, reflect a concern for equal opportunity, integration, and appropriate services.[19]

Have courts considered the right of handicapped students to participate in athletics?

Yes. In *Kampmeier v. Nyquist,* the United States Court of Appeals for the Second Circuit considered the rights of two visually handicapped New York students to participate in school athletics. The case deserves extended comment not only because of the court decision but also because it reveals mistaken assumptions and misguided approaches courts may take in handicapped rights cases. The school districts prohibited participation in school athletics by students with sight in only one eye. One student had a congenital cataract in one eye, wore glasses with industrial quality safety lenses, and wore mesh side shields and extended ear pieces. The student was in the seventh grade in 1975. Her parents were willing to release the school and its employees from liability for any athletic injuries to the student's good eye.

The second student, one year ahead of the girl, had been virtually blind in one eye since age six. He had been allowed, prior to the 1975–76 school year, to participate in all school sports, including interscholastic basketball, community-association football league, and the school's regular physical education program.

A school physician had recommended that the children be prohibited from participating in any contact sport at school, solely because of lack of vision in one eye. The New York Commissioner of Education had promulgated regulations requiring approval of the school medical officer before any student could be allowed to participate in any interscholastic athletics, and in advisory information to school officials had listed blindness in one eye as a disqualifying condition for contact sports, but not for noncontact sports. However, the commissioner's guidelines stressed that the guidelines were advisory and were not "absolute mandates for the school physician." The guidelines recognized that such factors as anticipated risks, athletic fitness of the candidate otherwise, special protective preventive measures that might be utilized, and the nature of the supervisory control had a bearing on the decision.

Physicians who examined the students were divided in their opinions on the matter. As reported in the decision of the court, two of the girl's doctors felt that her lack of vision should not hinder her "full participation in school athletic activities," while a third doctor wrote that with special protective eye wear, the risk to either eye was remote although there would be a risk and the protective eye wear would by no means guarantee the safety of her eyes. A doctor for the boy concluded that the disadvantages of participating in contact sports "far outweigh any possible advantages."

A federal district court denied a request for a preliminary injunction on behalf of the students. The Court of

Appeals first recognized that §504 permitted a lawsuit by the students and their parents to challenge the school policy. However, the court interpreted §504 to mean that "exclusion of handicapped children from a school activity is not improper if there exists a substantial justification for the school's policy." The court held that §504 prohibits only the exclusion of handicapped persons who are "otherwise qualified," and pointed to the school's reliance "on medical opinion that children with sight in only one eye are not qualified to play in contact sports because of the high risk of eye injury." The court viewed the evidence presented by the plaintiffs as not sufficient to "cast doubts on the substantiality of this rationale."

The court viewed its task as balancing the possibility of irreparable injury to both sides. It recognized the importance of athletics in the lives of teenage students and acknowledged that the students would be deprived "of the freedom to participate in sports of their choice." Against that interest the court recognized what it characterized as "a parens patriae interest in protecting the well-being of their students" on the part of public school officials, as evidenced by their reliance on medical opinion about the risk of injury to a child's one good eye. Further concerns of the school were fears that athletes lacking depth perception and peripheral vision may be a "special hazard to their fellow competitors" (although the Court of Appeals found that the district court record showed no evidence to support that claim) and a fear of negligence liability should a child with vision in only one eye be injured in contact sports (although the parents of the girl, after unsuccessfully trying to insure their daughter, had been willing to release the school and its employees from liability for any athletic injury to her). The court distinguished the situation of the plaintiffs from a case in which a federal district court granted a preliminary injunction to allow a university student with limited vision to play intercollegiate basketball, stating that the cases differed in that the university student "was old enough to weigh the risks and make the decision for himself."

The *Kampmeier* case is troubling, and questionable, for several reasons. First, it was decided before the final

HEW §504 regulations had been announced. The court's holding that exclusion of handicapped children from a school activity is not improper if there exists a "substantial justification" for the school's policy contradicts the regulations and does not have the precision mandated for such decisions by §504. Although the final HEW §504 regulations had not yet been issued, it is clear that the requirement of §504 is stricter than the court's concept of "substantial justification." The regulatory requirement for nonacademic settings provides that "a recipient shall ensure that handicapped persons participate with nonhandicapped persons in such activities and services to the maximum extent appropriate to the needs of the handicapped person in question." A balancing process is necessary, but the justification for exclusion under the regulations probably has to be more than the simply "substantial." The standard used by the court is unclear and may reflect the limited medical opinion counseling against participation together with the fears and reluctance of the school officials. On a quantitative basis only, it would appear from the opinion of the Court of Appeals that there was also a "substantial justification" for allowing the student to participate in the activities. There were medical opinions supporting one student, the willingness of one child's parents to waive liability associated with athletic activities, the past athletic participation by the boy, and the desire of the students to participate in the athletic programs. The evidence in favor of the students seems substantial. The opinion, of course, may not reflect all of the material facts in the case, but it suggests that school officials may not have to meet a very strict standard in terms of the "substantial justification" test. The court's result is subject to criticism that, even accepting the criteria applied to evaluate the school's action, the opinion indicates substantial evidence in favor of the students.

But the opinion is also subject to criticism because it departs from the policy (included in the regulations for both §504 and the Education for All Handicapped Children Act) of precision in the evaluation of handicapped students and their abilities to participate in certain activities. The §504 regulations speak of "validated" testing in the initial placement of a handicapped person in a regular

or special education program, of tests and other evaluation material tailored to assess specific areas of educational
need, and of tests selected and administered to best ensure that, in the administration of tests to a student
with impaired sensory, manual, or speaking skills, the test
results accurately reflect "the student's aptitude or achievement level or whatever other factor the test purports to
measure. . . ." The philosophy underlying these rules is
that substantial effort must be taken to avoid the mistakes
and stereotyped judgments that have, in the past, been
so characteristic of the evaluation of handicapped children.

The regulations under the Education for All Handicapped Children Act reiterate the policy of the §504 regulations on this point. They emphasize trained personnel
for the evaluation tasks and a multicriteria approach in
determining an appropriate program by a team which
assesses a child in a number of areas. While evaluation
of handicapped students for purposes of athletic competi-
tion may not lend itself to as much precision as evaluation
for academic purposes, the need is for more precision
than the court's rough "substantial justification" standard.

The court's decision, by suggesting that the students
were not otherwise qualified, attempts to refute their
claim based upon §504. But, to the extent that the court's
assumption on the issue of qualification is questionable,
the decision is open to criticism and the rights of the
students to equal treatment and integration denied.

A further issue complicating the decision is the procedural posture of the case. The Court of Appeals was
called upon to review a lower court's denial of a preliminary injunction, not a permanent injunction or other final
order. To some extent, this situation may have influenced
the Court of Appeals in that it felt that the preliminary
action taken by the lower court should be upheld. If the
case had been brought to the court at a different point in
the litigation, the result might have been different.

In a subsequent state court proceeding involving the
girl, the court noted "sweeping changes" at the federal
and state levels affecting the substantive and procedural
rights of handicapped persons, particularly the Rehabilitation Act of 1973, the Education for All Handicapped

Children Act, and New York legislation in response to the federal mandate. The court found that her participation in contact sports with protective eye wear would be reasonably safe within the meaning of state law. However, the court also was concerned that there had not been a proper determination that the girl was in fact properly classified as handicapped. Because of this concern, the state court refused to enter a final determination of the girl's rights, but, pending "any legally valid identification, evaluation or classification of the petitioner as physically handicapped and in need of special education or related services," enjoined her exclusion, on account of her visual handicap, from contact sports.[20]

Does the Education for All Handicapped Children Act establish priorities for the expenditure of funds granted by the Act?

Yes. "First priority children" are handicapped children who are in an age group to which the state must make a free appropriate education available and are not receiving any education. "Second priority children" are those with the most severe handicaps who are receiving an inadequate education. Use of funds for purposes of the second priority children is outlined by the regulations.[21] After September 1, 1978, there should be no second priority children, since states will have to insure that all children have a free appropriate education.

What is the "Individualized Education Program" required by the Education for All Handicapped Children Act?

The "Individual Education Program" (IEP) is a written statement required by the act for *each* handicapped child developed in a meeting consisting of a qualified representative of the local educational agency, the teacher of the child, the parents or guardian of the child, and, whenever appropriate, the child. The act lists five requirements which the IEP must contain:

1. A statement of the child's present level of educational performance.

2. A statement of annual goals, including short term instructional objectives.
3. A statement of specific educational services to be provided to the child, and indicating the extent to which the child will be able to participate in regular educational programs.
4. The projected date for the initiation and the anticipated duration of these services.
5. "Appropriate objective criteria and evaluation procedures and schedules for determining, on at least an annual basis, whether the short term instructional objectives are being achieved."

Each public agency must have in effect on October 1, 1977 (and at the beginning of each school year, thereafter) an IEP for every handicapped child who is receiving special education from the agency. The IEP must be in effect before special education and related services are provided to the child and must be implemented as soon as possible after a series of required meetings.

The public agency is responsible for initiating and conducting meetings associated with the IEP. For those children determined to need special education during the school year 1977–78, the meeting was required to have been held early enough so that the IEP would be developed by October 1, 1977. For other children, the IEP meeting must be held within thirty calendar days of a determination that the child needs special education and related services. Besides these meetings to develop the IEP, a meeting must be held at least once a year to review each child's IEP and, if appropriate, to revise it. The Education for All Handicapped Children Act regulations provide that the participants at each meeting are to be:

A representative of the public agency, other than the child's teacher, who is qualified to provide, or supervise the provision of, special education; the child's teacher; one or both of the child's parents, as provided for in a separate regulation pertaining to parent participation; the child, where appropriate; and additionally, other persons at the discretion of the parent or agency, particularly someone knowledgeable about evaluation procedures used in evaluating the child, if the child has been evaluated for the first time.

Parent participation is an essential part of the IEP process. The public agency has the responsibility to insure that one or both parents are present at each meeting (or at least afforded the opportunity to be present). The agency must notify the parents of the meeting early enough so that the parents can attend, and must schedule it at a mutually agreed-upon time and place. Notice to the parent must indicate the purpose, time, and location of the meeting, and who will attend the meeting. If neither parent can attend the meeting, the agency must use other means to insure their participation in the IEP process—including records of phone calls, correspondence, and visits to the parents. The public agency has an obligation to insure that the parents understand the proceedings at an IEP meeting, including providing an interpreter for persons who are deaf or whose native language is not English. The parents are entitled to a copy of the IEP.

The IEP requirement also applies in situations where private school is necessary, or where the child is enrolled in a parochial or other private school and the child receives special education or related services from a public agency. The public agency must still initiate the IEP meeting as it would if the child had been in the public agency. However, a representative of the private facility must attend the IEP meeting or otherwise be involved in the IEP process. Once the child is placed in the private facility, then it may, at the discretion of the public agency, conduct IEP meetings. But the public agency remains responsible for parental involvement in the review process and must have an agency representative also involved in the process. The public agency must insure that the parents and public agency representative agree to changes in the program before they are implemented. The public agency also remains responsible for insuring compliance with the Education for All Handicapped Children Act. Where a child had been placed in a private school or facility before the effective date of the regulations under the act, the public agency must develop an IEP for each such child. A separate regulation applies where a child is in a private or parochial school and receives special education services from a public school.

It is important to note that the educational services may not be limited to those already provided; in some cases public agencies may have to develop new appropriate programs. The §504 regulations state that implementation of an IEP is one way to meet the requirements of a free appropriate public education, and the §504 requirements may be met by "full implementation" of the IEP.[22]

Do parents have a right to an independent educational evaluation of their child?

Yes. Under the Education for All Handicapped Children Act and implementing regulations, parents have the right to an evaluation conducted by a qualified examiner not employed by the public agency responsible for the child's education. This evaluation is to be provided at public expense, and the public agency must provide information about where an independent evaluation can be obtained.

The parents may request such an evaluation if they disagree with the evaluation obtained by the public agency. However, the agency may respond to the parents' request for an independent evaluation with a request for a hearing before an impartial hearing officer on the issue of the agency's evaluation. If the determination at the hearing is that the agency's evaluation is correct, the parent are still entitled to an independent evaluation, but the evaluation will no longer be provided at public expense.

The evaluation, whether done at public or private expense, must be considered by the public agency in decisions made with respect to the provision of a free appropriate public education to the child, and may be presented as evidence at a due process hearing. If a hearing officer in a due process hearing requests an independent evaluation of a child, then the evaluation is to be at public expense. Whenever an independent evaluation is at public expense, the criteria under which the evaluation is obtained, including location of the evaluation and the qualifications of the examiner, must be the same ones used by the public agency when it initiates an evaluation.[23]

Must the public agency give notice to parents and seek their consent for certain actions affecting a handicapped child?

Yes. When the public agency proposes to initiate or change the identification, evaluation, or educational placement of a handicapped child or the provision of a free appropriate public education to the child, or when it refuses to take any of these actions, parents must be given written notice.

Parental consent must be obtained before the following actions can be taken:

1. preplacement evaluation
2. initial placement of a handicapped child in a program providing special education and related services.

Only in these two matters can consent be required as a condition of any benefit to the parent or child. When a parent refuses consent, two alternatives are available. If state law requires parental consent before a handicapped child is evaluated or first given special education services, the state procedures will govern the agency in an attempt to override the parent's refusal. If no state law requires parental consent, the agency may use the due-process hearing mechanism to seek a determination of whether the child may be evaluated or first given special education and related services without parental consent. If the hearing officer upholds the agency, it may evaluate or initially provide special education and related services without parental consent. However, the hearing officer's decision is subject to the parent's right to administrative appeal and a lawsuit challenging that decision.

A notice to the parents must meet certain requirements. It must explain procedural safeguards available to the parent, describe the action taken or refused, explain the agency's action, and describe the options con-

sidered by the agency and rejected. In this notice the
agency must describe the tests, reports, records, and evaluation procedures relied on by the agency, and any other
relevant factors. The Education for All Handicapped
Children Act regulations require that the notice must be
written in language understandable to the general public,
and they specify what must be done when a foreign language or other mode of communication is used.[24]

What is the function of the due process hearing in the education of handicapped children?

The due process hearing is intended to provide a forum
for disputes over the identification, evaluation, or educational placement of a handicapped child or the provision
of a free appropriate public education to the child. Proposals to initiate or change these procedures or refusal
to initiate or change them justify a due process hearing,
and a parent or a public educational agency may initiate
a hearing. A hearing must be conducted by the state
education agency or the public agency, depending upon
the requirements of the state in its statutes, regulations,
or a written policy of a state educational agency. The
due process hearing is not intended to bar mediation
efforts to resolve disputes short of a hearing, but those
efforts may not be used to delay or deny a parent's right
to a hearing.

The requirements for the hearing are detailed in the
regulations implementing the Education for All Handicapped Children Act. The HEW §504 regulations also
address the issue of procedural safeguards in preschool,
elementary, and secondary education. The §504 regulations list several requirements for the procedural safeguards framework:

1. Notice.
2. An opportunity for parents or guardians of the handicapped person to examine relevant records.
3. An impartial hearing with opportunity for participation by the person's parents or guardians and to
   be represented by counsel.
4. A review procedure.

The §504 regulations state that compliance with the Education for All Handicapped Children Act is one means of meeting the requirements, and, in the Analysis accompanying the regulations, the act is offered as a model. The §504 regulations, according to the Analysis, specify "minimum necessary procedures" because "the due process procedures [of the Education for All Handicapped Children Act] are inappropriate for some recipients not subject to that act." These §504 regulations apply to recipients who operate preschool, elementary, or secondary education programs and require the system of procedural safeguards with respect to actions regarding the identification, evaluation, or educational placement of persons who, because of a handicap, need or are believed to need special instruction or related services.[25] State laws may also apply to due process hearings and should of course be consulted.

Who conducts the due process hearing?

The Education for All Handicapped Children Act and its regulations require an impartial hearing officer. The act states that a due process hearing may not be conducted by an employee of the "agency or unit involved in the education or care of the child." The regulations also exclude "any person having a personal or professional interest which would conflict with his or her objectivity in the hearing." (However, a person otherwise qualified to serve as a hearing officer is not considered an employee of the agency because the person is paid to serve as a hearing officer.) Public agencies must keep a list of the persons who serve as hearing officers, stating the qualifications of each of them.

In the Analysis accompanying the regulations, the regulations writers considered comments that panels of several persons be designated to conduct hearings, and that parents and school-board members be allowed to serve as hearing officers. In the regulations published in the August 23, 1977, *Federal Register,* the Analysis approves of the use of panels if the impartiality standards of the regulations are met, but disapproves of the use of parents or school-board members.[26]

What are some of the rights which parties to due process hearings have at the local school level or in review of local decisions by state educational agencies?

The Education for All Handicapped Children Act enumerates several rights accorded to any parties. These are:

1. The right to be accompanied and advised by counsel and by individuals with special knowledge or training with respect to the problems of handicapped children.
2. The right to present evidence and confront, cross-examine, and compel the attendance of witnesses.
3. The right to a written or electronic verbatim record of the hearing.
4. The right to written findings of fact and decisions.

Regulations implementing the act reiterate these rights, and add to the list the rights of parents to have the affected child present at the hearing and to open the hearing to the public. The regulations also prohibit introducing evidence at the hearing that has not been disclosed to a party at least five days before the hearing. The Analysis provides that any party has the right "to prohibit the introduction of evidence not previously disclosed to the other party." Additionally, public agencies must have informed parents of any free or low-cost legal or other relevant services available in the area.[27]

Can a decision made in a due process hearing be appealed?

Yes. A decision made in a due process hearing is final unless appealed by a party to the hearing. The Education for All Handicapped Children Act provides that, for hearings conducted at the local level, "any party aggrieved by the findings and decision rendered" may appeal to the State educational agency which shall conduct "an impartial review of such hearing." The act states that the officer conducting the review "shall make an independent decision upon completion of such review."

Regulations implementing the act expand the requirements for a review conducted at the state level. The reviewing officer must:

1. Examine the entire hearing record.
2. Insure that the procedures at the hearing were consistent with due process.
3. Seek additional evidence if necessary. If the officer conducts a hearing to receive the evidence, that hearing must follow the previously discussed procedural requirements of due process hearings.
4. Afford the parties an opportunity for oral or written argument, or both, at the discretion of the reviewing officer.
5. Make an "independent decision" upon completion of review.
6. Give a copy of written findings and the decision to the parties.

Again, the decision of the reviewing officer is final, unless a party brings a lawsuit to challenge the decision.[28]

Can a party bring a lawsuit under the Education for All Handicapped Children Act if dissatisfied with the administrative review?

Yes. A party aggrieved by the findings and decision of the reviewing officer, or a party who does not have a right to administrative review of the original due process hearing, may bring a civil action with respect to the complaint presented in any state court of competent jurisdiction or in a federal district court, without having to meet the federal "amount in controversy" requirement. In a lawsuit brought for judicial review of procedural due process action under the Education for All Handicapped Children Act, the court must receive the records of the administrative hearing, hear additional evidence at the request of a party, and, basing its decision on "the preponderance of the evidence," grant such relief "as the court determines is appropriate." Additionally, there may be other bases for a lawsuit, including §504 and state law provisions.[29]

Are there time periods within which hearings and reviews in the administrative process must be conducted?

Yes. The regulations implementing the Education for All Handicapped Children Act provide that the local public agency shall insure that a final decision is rendered in a hearing and a copy of the decision mailed to each party not later than forty-five days after the receipt of a request for a hearing. In a review conducted by the state education agency, the final decision must be reached and a copy of the decision mailed to each party not later than thirty days after the receipt of a request for review. The appropriate time periods for filing a lawsuit is a question deserving careful attention from an attorney. State law provisions may have a bearing on time periods at the judicial and the administrative levels and should be checked for variations from the federal law. The regulations of August 23, 1977, provide that a hearing officer or a reviewing officer may grant specific extensions of time at the request of either party.[30]

Is there a requirement that hearings and reviews be conducted at a convenient time and place?

Yes. The regulations to implement the Education for All Handicapped Children Act state that each hearing and each review involving oral argument must be conducted at a time and place which is reasonably convenient to the parents and child involved.[31]

What is the status of the child pending the outcome of administrative or judicial proceedings?

Unless the parents and the public agency agree otherwise, the child must remain in his or her present educational placement. However, if the complaint at issue involves an application for initial admission to a public school, then the child (with the consent of the parents) must be placed in the public school until the completion of all the proceedings.[32]

Is there a provision for surrogate parents?

Yes. This provision of the Education for All Handicapped Children Act applies to protect the rights of a child where the parent or guardian of the child is not known, is unavailable, or the child is a ward of the state. The regulatory Analysis published under the act explains the statutory term "unavailable" as a situation where, after reasonable efforts, the public agency cannot discover the whereabouts of the parent. Moreover, "ward of the state" is qualified as wardship under the laws of that state.

The public agency must assign an individual to act as surrogate for the parents, and it must have a method for determining whether a child needs a surrogate and for assigning a surrogate.

Selection of the surrogate parent by the public agency may be in any way permitted by state law. Public agencies must insure that a person selected as a surrogate has no interest that conflicts with the interests of the child represented and that the surrogate has knowledge and skills that insure adequate representation of the child. The act prohibits any person from acting as a surrogate who is an employee of a state, local, or intermediate educational unit involved in the education or care of the child, but the regulations interpret the requirement as not disqualifying persons solely because they are paid by an agency to act as surrogates.

The fundamental responsibility of the surrogate parent is to represent the child in all matters relating to the identification, evaluation, and educational placement of the child and in matters pertaining to provision of a free appropriate public education for the child. The Analysis accompanying the regulations emphasizes that appointment of surrogate parents is appropriate only when the conditions set forth in the regulations exist, and not in situations where the parents are uncooperative or nonresponsive.[33]

Can the administrative procedures of the §504 HEW regulations also be used with respect to actions affecting the identification, evaluation, or educational placement of handicapped persons?

The answer is uncertain. The §504 HEW regulations require recipients to establish and implement a system of procedural safeguards, which must include certain elements, discussed earlier. The HEW regulations refer to compliance with the Education for All Handicapped Children Act as one means to meet the due process requirement. However, in the Analysis accompanying the regulations, HEW makes this statement:

It is not the intention of the Department, except in extraordinary circumstances, to review the result of individual placement and other educational decisions, so long as the school district complies with the "process" requirements of [the HEW regulations concerning identification and location, evaluation, and due process procedures]. However, the Department will place a high priority on investigating cases which may involve exclusion of a child from the education system or a pattern or practice of discriminatory placements or education.

How the implementation of the regulatory systems under §504, the Education for All Handicapped Children Act, and state laws will be coordinated remains a question. Among the factors determining the answer will be the policies of the administrative agencies involved, the attitudes of courts, and the understanding of administrators and courts about the requirements of the relevant legislation.[84]

Do regulations address the problem of testing and evaluating materials and procedures used to evaluate and place handicapped children?

Yes. The Education for All Handicapped Children Act requires that such material must be selected and administered so as not to be racially or culturally discriminatory, and that these materials or procedures shall be provided and administered in the child's native language or other mode of communication, unless it clearly is not feasible to do so. Additionally, the Act provides that "no single procedure shall be the sole criterion for determining an appropriate educational program for a child."

Regulations implementing the act require that before any action is taken to place a handicapped child in a special education program, a full and individual evaluation of the child must be conducted in accordance with the pertinent regulatory provisions.

The state and local educational agencies are required to insure, at a minimum, that tests and other evaluation materials meet the "native language or other mode of communication" requirement of the statute, that they have been "validated for the specific purpose for which they are used," that they are administered "by trained personnel in conformance with the instructions provided by their producer," and that they "include those tailored to assess specific areas of educational need and not merely those which are designed to provide a single general intelligence quotient." Moreover, at a minimum, the state and local education agencies must meet the requirements, described earlier, that tests which require sensory, manual, or speaking skills must be selected and administered to children with impairment in those skills so as not to reflect the impaired skills, except where those skills are the factors the test purports to measure.

Other minimum requirements imposed on the state and local education agencies are that "no single procedure [be] used as the sole criterion" in determining an appropriate educational program, a requirement for evaluation by a "multidisciplinary team" (including at least one teacher or other specialist with knowledge in the area of suspected disability), and all areas related to the suspected disability be assessed (enumerating subjects deserving consideration). A comment to the regulations notes that children with speech impairment as their primary handicap may not need a complete battery of assessments, including psychological, physical, or adaptive behavior, but suggests how a qualified speech pathologist would conduct an evaluation.

The regulations also require public agencies to follow certain procedures in interpreting the evaluation data and in making placement decisions. The evaluations must draw upon a variety of sources (including aptitude and achievement tests, teacher recommendations, and consideration of physical condition, social and cultural background, and adaptive behavior). The information thus obtained must be "documented and carefully considered," and the placement decision must be made by a group of persons knowledgeable about the child, about the meaning of the evaluation data, and about placement options.

The "least restrictive environment" requirement (discussed later) must be followed in the placement decision. Once a determination is made that a child needs special education and related services, an IEP must be developed. In addition to the annual review requirements of the IEP, the evaluation of the child described above must be conducted every three years (or more frequently if "conditions warrant or if the child's parent or teacher requests an evaluation").

The regulations implementing the Education for All Handicapped Children Act are designed to conform with the §504 HEW regulations pertaining to evaluation and placement of handicapped children (or those believed to need special education or related services) in a regular or special education program. An individual evaluation is required before the initial placement of a child or any subsequent significant change in the program, but comments to the §504 regulations state, "A full reevaluation is not required every time an adjustment in placement is made." The HEW §504 regulations incorporate the reevaluation requirements of the Education for All Handicapped Children Act regulations.[35]

What are some of the concepts underlying the "least restrictive alternative" requirement?

The Education for All Handicapped Children Act requires that states adopt procedures to assure that

> . . . to the maximum extent appropriate, handicapped children, including children in public or private institutions or other care facilities, are educated with children who are not handicapped, and that special classes, separate schooling, or other removal of handicapped children from the regular educational environment occurs only when the nature or severity of the handicap is such that education in regular classes with the use of supplementary aids and services cannot be achieved satisfactorily. . . .

The implementing regulations require each public agency to adopt a "continuum of alternative placements," which includes several alternative placements or instruction in regular classes, special classes, special schools, home instruction, and instruction in hospitals and institutions. As part of this continuum, the public agency must make provision for supplementary services (such as a resource room or itinerant instruction to be provided in conjunction with regular class placement).

In placing handicapped children, each public agency must insure that the placement is determined at least annually, is based on the child's IEP, and is as close as possible to the child's home. The alternative placement must be made available to the extent necessary to implement the IEP. Unless the IEP requires otherwise, the child is to be educated in the school which he or she would attend if not handicapped. Finally, in placing handicapped children, the regulations state that consideration is to be given "to any potential harmful effect on the child or on the quality of services" which the child needs.[36]

Does the "least restrictive alternative" concept apply in nonacademic settings?

Yes. The regulations implementing the Education for All Handicapped Children Act, as well as the HEW §504 regulations, require public agencies to insure, in providing or arranging for the provision of nonacademic and extracurricular services and activities, that each handicapped child particpate in those services to the maximum extent appropriate to the needs of the child.[37] The HEW regulations specifically mention meals and recess periods as well as other services and activities.

Do state educational agencies have an obligation to oversee the implementation of the "least restrictive alternative" requirement in public and private institutions?

Yes. The requirement applies to handicapped children in public or private institutions, and other care facilities, and the regulations implementing the Education for All Handicapped Children Act charge the state agency with implementing the requirements. A comment to the regulations provides that, regardless of the reason for institutionalization, a child capable of education in a regular school setting should not be denied access to education in that setting.[38]

Do the HEW §504 regulations have provisions requiring the placement of handicapped students with nonhandicapped students?

Yes. Recipients to whom the HEW regulations apply are required to educate, or provide for the education of, each qualified handicapped person in their jurisdictions "with persons who are not handicapped to the maximum extent appropriate to the needs of the handicapped person" in the regular educational environment unless "it is demonstrated by the recipient that the education of the person in the regular environment with the use of supplementary aids and services cannot be achieved satisfactorily." The regulations provide that placement in a setting other than the regular educational environment shall "take into account the proximity of the alternate setting to the person's home."

These principles apply to such nonacademic and extracurricular services and activities as meals, recess periods, and a wide variety of services and activities such as counseling services, health services, physical recreation, athletics, transportation, and special-interest clubs or groups sponsored by the recipient.

The regulations also provide that in situations where a recipient does operate a facility that is identifiable as being for handicapped persons (which must be themselves operated in accord with the general integrationist policy of the regulations), the facility and the services and activities provided there must be comparable to other operations of the recipient.[39]

Have physically handicapped students won court recognition of the right to placement in regular classrooms?

Yes. In *Harrison v. Drosick,* a child with spina bifida and her parents challenged her exclusion from a regular public school on the basis of §504. The case was brought before the HEW §504 regulations had been issued. The court found that her physical condition had left her with "a minor physical impairment which includes incontinence of the bowels and a noticeable limp." She was, in the opinion of the court, "clearly physically able to attend school in a regular public classroom" and "of normal mental competence and capable of performing easily in a regular classroom situation."

School officials had sought to require the child's mother to be at the regular school on a daily intermittent basis as a condition for the child's education there. The mother could not because she had other family responsibilities, had to assist her husband in his business, and had neither a driver's license nor a feasible means of transportation to the school several times a day. The court found that the requirement of the mother's frequent presence at school, coupled with the impossibility of her meeting the requirement, constituted an exclusion of the child from the regular school. The court went on to find that "even if the mother's presence were circumstantially possible, the right of a child to attend school cannot be legally conditioned upon the mother's presence at the school."

As alternatives to regular placement, the school offered to place the child in a physically handicapped class at another school or to provide homebound instruction. However, the court noted that a medical specialist had recommended that the child be permitted to attend public school. In light of this evidence, the court took a skeptical view of the school's refusal to admit the child to regular classes:

> The needless exclusion of these [spina bifida] children and other children who are able to function adequately from the regular classroom situation would be a great disservice to these children. A child's chance in this society is through the educational process. A major goal of the educational process is the socialization process that takes place in the regular classroom, with the resulting capability to interact in a social way with one's peers. It is therefore imperative that every child receive an education with his or her peers insofar as it is at all possible. This conclusion is further enforced by the critical importance of education in this society.
>
> . . . The expert testimony established that placement of children in abnormal environments outside of peer situations imposes additional psychological and emotional handicaps upon children which, added

to their existing handicaps, cause them greater difficulties in future life. A child has to learn to interact
in a social way with its peers and the denial of this
opportunity during his minor years imposes added
lifetime burdens upon a handicapped individual.

The court concluded that to deny a handicapped child
access to a regular public-school classroom which receives
federal financial assistance "without compelling educational justification" constituted discrimination and violated
§504. The court held that, "School officials must make
every effort to include such children within the regular
public classroom situation, even at great expense to the
school system."

The court also held the exclusion of a child from the
regular public classroom and placement "in a special education situation or otherwise" without prior written notice
and accompanying procedural safeguards including an opportunity to be heard violated the due process clause of
the Fourteenth Amendment. However, the court concluded the procedural safeguards set out in state regulations satisfied the mandate of due process of law.

The court then ordered the defendants to admit the
child to the regular school immediately, and further ordered that any attempt to exclude the child be based on a
legally justifiable reason and be conducted in accordance
with due process of law. Any exclusion of the child was
to be reviewed by the court prior to the action.

The *Hairston* case is a good decision for several reasons.
It focuses closely on the child's abilities and reflects an
understanding of the nature of her handicap. Second, it
rejects the approach of school officials in attempting to
place the obligation of assisting the child in her schooling
on the parents. The court refuses to allow a convenient
(from the perspective of the school officials) solution to
her problems; the decision implicitly requires the school
officials to come to terms with the child and her handicap
—a task which might not be as mysterious and discomfort-
ing as they might fear. The decision rejects the notion
that it is the families of handicapped persons who must
adjust to help those persons live. Third, the decision recognizes, in a concrete and informed way, the importance of

integration for handicapped persons. The court perceives education not merely as instruction but as a social process, and it recognizes the possible harm segregation can cause to handicapped persons.[40]

Do the regulations to implement the Education for All Handicapped Children Act address the question of confidentiality of information, including access to records, amendment of records, and destruction of information?

Yes. The act requires that action be taken to assure protection of confidentiality of personally identifiable data, information, or records collected or maintained by federal, state, or local educational authorities pursuant to the act. The implementing regulations address these issues, and also bring to bear provisions of the General Education Provision Act and the Family Educational Rights and Privacy Act of 1974. The regulations address a range of issues in connection with these rights. Among the issues are the following four:

Access rights, particularly access before a meeting regarding an IEP or hearing regarding the identification, evaluation, or placement of a child. Agencies must permit parents to inspect and review any education records relating to their children which are collected, maintained, or used by the agencies under the regulations. Requests from parents must be answered without unnecessary delay, and before an IEP meeting or hearing on the identification, placement, or evaluation of a child. In no case can the agency delay more than forty-five days after the request has been made. Included in the right to inspect and review education records are the rights to a response to reasonable requests for explanations and interpretations of the records, the right to have copies of the records containing the information if failure to provide those copies would effectively prevent the parents from exercising the right to inspect and review the records, and the right to have a representative of the parents inspect and review the records.

Fees. The regulations provide that an agency may charge a fee for copies of records which are made for

parents under the regulations if the fee does not "effectively prevent" the parents from exercising their right to
inspect and review those records. The agency may not,
however, charge a fee to search for or retrieve information
under the regulations.

Parent's request for amendment of records. A parent
who believes that information in education records collected, maintained, or used under the regulations is inaccurate, misleading, or in violation of the child's right to
privacy or other rights of the child, may request the
agency that maintains the information to amend the information. If the agency refuses, the parent has a right
to a hearing under a special procedure. If, as a result
of the hearing, the agency decides the information is
inaccurate, misleading, or otherwise in violation of the
rights of the child, the agency must amend the information
accordingly and inform the parents of the change. If, on
the other hand, the agency decides that the information is
not inaccurate, misleading, or otherwise in violation of the
rights of the child, it must inform the parents of their right
to place in the records a statement commenting on the
information or setting forth any reason for disagreeing
with the agency's decision. The parents' explanation must
be maintained as part of the records as long as the record
or contested portion of the record is maintained by the
agency, and if the records or contested portion is disclosed
by the agency to any party, the explanation must also be
disclosed.

Parental consent. The regulations implementing the Education for All Handicapped Children Act require that
parental consent must be obtained before personally identifiable information is disclosed to anyone other than officials authorized to collect or use the information or is
used for a purpose other than meeting the requirements
of the regulations. (Release of information without parental consent is also prohibited unless authorized by other
privacy regulations.) The regulations implementing the
act contain provisions relating to the eventual destruction of information and for the recognition of rights of

children themselves to privacy, distinct from the rights of their parents.[41]

Is there a public obligation to identify, locate, and evaluate children in need of special education and related services and to determine which children are or are not receiving such education and services?

Yes. This requirement has been in effect for some time. Each annual plan must include detailed policies and procedures to meet this requirement. Additionally, the HEW §504 regulations require recipients to take steps annually to identify and locate handicapped children who are not receiving a public education and to notify handicapped persons and their parents or guardians of the recipient's duties under the regulations.[42]

Does state law also have a bearing on the rights set forth in this chapter?

Yes. State statutes, administrative policies, and court cases may also address the same issues addressed by the federal provisions discussed in this chapter. These sources should always be consulted in determination of rights. While this chapter has concentrated on federal law (which will probably be the dominant factor in these matters), state law provides a concurrent basis for rights and always deserves attention.

Do the §504 regulations address the obligations of private education programs?

Yes. The regulations state that a recipient that operates a private elementary or secondary education program may not, on the basis of handicap, exclude a qualified handicapped person from the program if the person "with minor adjustments" can be provided with a free appropriate education within the recipient's program. These recipients may not charge more for providing an appropriate education to handicapped persons "except to the extent that any additional charge is justified by a substantial increase in the cost to the recipient." Recipients that do operate special education programs must operate them in accordance with the evaluation and placement and procedural safeguards provisions of the regulations. All recipients to which the "private education program" section applies are subject to the regulations governing educational setting, nonacademic services, and preschool and adult education programs.

The Analysis accompanying the regulations states that recipients that operate private education programs and activities are not required to provide an appropriate education to handicapped students with special educational needs if the recipient does not offer programs designed to meet those needs. As examples, the Analysis states that a private school with no program for mentally retarded persons is neither required to admit them nor to arrange or provide for education in another program. However, the Analysis distinguishes the situation of a blind student who could participate in the regular program with minor adjustment in the manner in which the program is normally offered. This is to be distinguished from the situation, discussed earlier, of the handicapped children in private schools not placed or referred there by public agencies, but entitled to services from public agencies.[48]

NOTES

1. See, generally, the annotations and substance of 20 U.S.C.A. §§1401–61 (1974 and 1978).
2. For a discussion of the constitutional litigation of the 1970s, see Haggerty and Sacks, *Education of the Handicapped: Toward a Definition of an Appropriate Education*, 50 Temp. L.Q. 961 (1977) and Krass, *The Right to Public Education for Handicapped Children: A Primer for the New Advocate*, 1976 U. ILL. L.F. 1016 (1976); the Congressional declaration of purpose is at 20 U.S.C.A. §1401 note (1978). Additionally, a very good source of administrative opinions by federal administrative agencies is the *Education for the Handicapped Law Reporter*. See also the cases in note 34 on the question of damages in education cases. Separate provisions pertaining to vocational education are 44 *Fed. Reg.* 17162 (March 21, 1979).
3. 20 U.S.C.A. §1401 (18) (1978).
4. 20 U.S.C.A. §1401 (16) (1978).
5. 20 U.S.C.A. §1401 (17) (1978).
6. §84.3(k)(2).
7. §84.33(a).

8. §121a.302 of the Education for All Handicapped Children Act regulation in 42 Fed. Reg. 42,488 (August 23, 1977). Citation to the regulations will be to the regulations as they appear in the *Fed. Reg.* (45 C.F.R. Part 121a). *See also* 20 U.S.C.A. §1413(a)(4)(B) (1978) (45 C.F.R. Part 121a).

9. §84.33(c)(4) refers to due process hearings in these circumstances; §84.33 sets forth general requirements for a free appropriate education under §504.

10. The term "handicapped children" is defined at 20 U.S.C.A. §1401 (1) (1978); the term "children with specific learning disabilities" is defined at U.S.C.A. §1401(15) (1978).

11. The Education for All Handicapped Children Act regulations have definitions of "handicapped children," with a definition of "specific learning disability" at §121a.5.

12. See Subpart B of the Education for All Handicapped Children Act regulations and 20 U.S.C.A. §1412, §1413 (1978).

13. §§121a.182–.184; see also 20 U.S.C.A. §1401(20), §1411, §1414(a)(1), (a)(2)(B) (1978).

14. 20 U.S.C.A. §1412 (2)(B) (1978).

15. §121a.300

16. §84.33(d)

17. *Mattie T. v. Holladay* C.A. No. DC 75-31-S (N.D. Miss. 1977), but compare *Eberle v. Bd. of Pub. Ed.*, 444 F. Supp. 41 (W.D. Pa. 1977); *Stempler v. Bd. of Educ. of Prince George's County*, 464 F. Supp. 258 (D. Md. 1979).

18. *Hairston v. Drosick*, 423 F. Supp. 180 (S.D. W.Va. 1976).

19. §121a.305; §121a.306; §121a.307; 20 U.S.C.A. §1401(16) (1978); §84.37, with Analysis at 42 *Fed. Reg.* at 22,692.

20. *Kampmeier v. Nyquist*, 553 F.2d 296 (2nd Cir. 1977), with the state court decision; *Kampmeier v. Harris*, 403 N.Y.S. 2d 638 (N.Y. Sup. Ct., Monroe County, 1978); the regulation is §84.34(b); it is unclear whether both plaintiffs continued in the state court litigation.

21. §121a.320; 20 U.S.C.A. §1412(3) (1978).

22. §§121a.340–.349; 20 U.S.C.A. §1401(19), 1412(4), (6), 1413(a)(4) (1978) are among the statutory bases for this part of the Education for All Handicapped Children Act regulations, with other statutory selections set out in the regulations; §84.33(b) (2) with Analysis at 42 *Fed. Reg.* at 22,691.

23. 20 U.S.C.A. §1415 (b)(1)(A) (1978); §121a.503.

24. §121a.504, §121a.505.

25. §84.36, with commentary on this section at 42 *Fed. Reg.* at 22,691; the Education for All Handicapped Children

regulations are at Subpart E; *see also* 20 U.S.C.A. §1415 (Supp. 1977).

26. 20 U.S.C.A. §1415 (b)(2) (1978); §121a.506, .507, with commentary at 42 Fed. Reg. at 42,511, 42,512 (August 23, 1977).

27. 20 U.S.C.A. §1415(d) (1978); §121a.508, with commentary at 42 *Fed. Reg.* at 42,512 (August 23, 1977); §121a.506(c).

28. 20 U.S.C.A. §1415(c) (1978); §121a.510.

29. 20 U.S.C.A. §1415(e) (1978); for a case considering procedural aspects of education suits after *Lloyd* and after the HEW §504 regulations and the Education for All Handicapped Children Act, *see Sherer v. Waier* 457 F. Supp. 1039 (W.D. Mo. 1977), —— F. Supp. ——, No. 78-0510-CV-W-4 (W.D. Mo., Sept. 18, 1978).

30. §121a.512.

31. §121a.512.

32. §121a.513; 20 U.S.C.A. §1415 (e)(3) (1978).

33. 20 U.S.C.A. §1415(b)(1)(B)(1978); §121a.514, with Analysis at 42 *Fed. Reg.* at 42,512 (August 23, 1977).

34. The HEW Analysis is at 42 *Fed. Reg.* at 22,690 (May 4, 1977); see also *Lougran v. Flanders,* 470 F. Supp. 110 (D. Conn. 1979), *Boxall v. Sequoia Union High School Dist.,* 464 F. Supp. 1104 (N.D. Cal. 1979).

35. 20 U.S.C.A. §1415(5)(C) (1978); §§121a.530–.533; §84.35.

36. 20 U.S.C.A. §1412(5)(B) (1978); §121a.551, .552.

37. §121a.553; §84.34(b).

38. §121a.554.

39. §84.34.

40. 423 F. Supp. 180 (S.D. W.Va. 1976).

41. 20 U.S.C.A. §1417(c) (1978); §§121a.560–.576.

42. §121a.128; §84.32.

43. §84.39, with commentary at 42 *Fed. Reg.* at 22,692.

VI

The Right to Education:
Postsecondary

Do the HEW §504 regulations apply to postsecondary education?

Yes. They apply to postsecondary education programs and activities, including postsecondary vocational education. They apply to recipients that receive or benefit from federal financial assistance and to recipients that operate, or that receive or benefit from federal financial assistance for the operation of such programs and activities.[1]

What are some of the major provisions of the HEW §504 regulations pertaining to admission and recruitment in postsecondary education?

The basic requirement is that qualified handicapped persons may not, on the basis of handicap, be denied admission, or be subjected to discrimination in admission or recruitment, by a recipient subject to the regulations. There are a number of specific prohibitions and responsibilities imposed on postsecondary recipients:

1. They may not apply limitations on the number or proportion of handicapped persons who may be admitted.
2. They may not make use of any test or criterion for admission that has "a disproportionate, adverse effect on handicapped persons or any class of handicapped persons unless (i) the test or criterion, as used by the recipient, has been validated as a predictor of success in the education program or ac-

157

tivity in question and (ii) alternate tests or criteria that have a less disproportionate, adverse effect are not shown by the Director [of the Office for Civil Rights] to be available." A recipient may base prediction equations on first year grades, but must conduct periodic validity studies "against the criterion of overall success in the education program or activity in question in order to monitor the general validity of the test scores." The Supreme Court's recent *Davis* decision may have some effect on this provision. It is discussed later.

3. They must meet the requirement, discussed earlier, in selecting and administering admissions tests, of assuring themselves that for those persons with impaired sensory, manual, or speaking skills, the test results reflect what the test purports to measure, rather than the impaired skills of the handicapped person. Moreover, admissions tests designed for persons with impaired skills must be offered "as often and in as timely a manner" as are other admissions tests. Additionally, recipients must assure themselves that admissions tests are administered in facilities that, on the whole, are accessible to handicapped persons.

4. They may not, except in certain circumstances, make preadmission inquiries as to whether an applicant for admission is a handicapped person. After admission, recipients may make inquiries "on a confidential basis as to handicaps that may require accommodation." [2]

When is a recipient permitted to make preadmission inquiries about a handicap?

The HEW §504 regulations provide that recipients may "invite applicants for admission to indicate whether and to what extent they are handicapped" when they are taking remedial action to overcome the effects of past discrimination or taking voluntary action to overcome "the effects of conditions that resulted in limited participation" in federally assisted programs or activities (conpcepts discussed in Chapter 2). However, the regulations impose strict conditions on the inquiries:

1. The recipient must state clearly on any written questionnaire used for this purpose or make clear orally if no written questionnaire is used that the information is intended for use solely in connection with remedial action or voluntary action.

2. The recipient must state clearly that the information is being requested on a voluntary basis, that it will be kept confidential, that refusal to provide the information requested will not subject an applicant to any adverse treatment, and that it will be used only in accordance with the regulations.[3]

What is an example of a case where a person's handicap has been the grounds of a college's refusal to admit the person to a postsecondary program?

In *Davis v. Southeastern Community College,* a woman with a hearing handicap brought suit against a nursing degree program that denied her admission. She challenged the denial on the constitutional grounds of due process and equal protection and on the basis of §504.

The plaintiff sought training which would have enabled her to be a registered nurse. She had already been licensed as a practical nurse for nearly ten years before the lawsuit. The district court found that she had a moderately severe hearing loss in the right ear and a severe hearing loss in the left ear, and that she had difficulty understanding speech. She used a hearing aid and the court found that she was an excellent lip reader: "although she does not possess normal hearing, she is skillful in communicating with other people if she wears her hearing aid and is allowed to see the talker and use her vision to aid her in interpreting the speech of others." But the court found that:

She is well aware of gross sounds occurring in the listening environment but can only be responsible for speech spoken to her or when the talker gets her attention and allows her to look directly at the talker. The hearing aid improves her hearing level to the outer limits of normal hearing levels.

School officials believed that her hearing handicap would prevent her from performing many of the functions of a registered nurse, particularly in emergency situations. When she was denied admission, she asked that her application be reconsidered, but she was again denied admission.

The district court concluded that there had been no violation of her constitutional rights in that the court believed that the defendants had acted reasonably in rejecting the handicapped plaintiff. In the opinion of the district court:

> The plaintiff has offered no testimony to attack the accuracy or the reasonableness of the admissions standards of the defendant institution nor has she sent in [sic] any evidence of any arbitrary or capricious action on the part of the defendant institution in denying plaintiff admission to the Associate Degree Nursing Program. Furthermore, it appears from the testimony that the single major factor in the defendant's refusal to allow admissions [sic] to the plaintiff was her projected inability to be licensed as a Registered Nurse after graduation. . . . A state has a great responsibility to provide training facilities for producing qualified persons for delivering health care to society. In view of the shortage of such personnel and the great number of applicants for the spaces available in such facilities, it is completely reasonable and logical for the state to limit enrollment to such persons as are able to meet professional qualifications upon graduation. Additionally, from the evidence presented at the trial, it appears that it would be difficult and, in fact, dangerous for plaintiff to even attempt the clinical portion of the training program.

The court also considered the plaintiff's claim that she had suffered discrimination in violation of §504, and, although the court was under the mistaken impression that §504 "has yet to be interpreted by the federal courts," considered the meaning of §504 in the plaintiff's case:

> Reasonably construed, [the words "otherwise qualified"] qualify the passage to mean that no person may be excluded from a federally assisted program

or activity solely by reason of the fact that such person is handicapped, unless the nature of the handicap renders the person unable to fully and effectively participate in the activity. By way of an illustration, under this section it would most probably be impermissible to exclude a blind or deaf person from admission to a law school, if academically qualified. However, reason dictates that it would be entirely permissible to exclude a person without sight from a position as a truck driver or to refuse a person who must read lips to [sic] a position as a telephone operator. Otherwise qualified . . . can only be read to mean otherwise able to function sufficiently in the position sought in spite of the handicap, if proper training and facilities are suitable and available. The major problem with the plaintiff's contention is that her handicap actually prevents her from safely performing in both her training program and her proposed profession. The trial testimony indicated numerous situations where plaintiff's particular disability would render her unable to function properly. Of particular concern to the court in this case is the potential of danger to future patients in such situations. Defendant presented testimony from several witnesses that plaintiff would be unable to properly perform in the program even with an improved hearing aid. The plaintiff put up no testimony at all on this point except to elicit an admission on cross-examination that with special training and individual supervision she could perform adequately in some selected fields of nursing. In view of this interpretation of the statute and the plaintiff's failure to establish her ability to complete the program and function as a Registered Nurse, the court can find no violation of [§504].

This case raises at least two questions and, indirectly, points out problems of handicapped persons in challenging discrimination. There is first the court's understanding of what registered nurses were required to do. In connection with this issue, the court attempted to distinguish the duties of a registered nurse from those of a practical

nurse—for which the plaintiff had been licensed to work
—by stating that a "Licensed Practical Nurse, unlike a
Licensed Registered Nurse, operates under constant supervision and is not allowed to perform medical tasks
which require a great degree of technical sophistication."
Yet the matters of supervision and "technical sophistication" may have little, if anything, to do with a hearing
impairment. Certainly the level of "technical sophistication" does not necessarily pertain to a handicap—indeed,
it was to increase her technical skills that the plaintiff
sought training as a registered nurse. With respect to
supervision, one of the court's concerns was that a handicapped registered nurse might not be able to take verbal
directions from physicians. Yet the court acknowledged
that practical nurses must take supervision, and there was
no suggestion the plaintiff, in her experience as a practical
nurse, had been unable to perform adequately. Therefore,
the court's analysis of what the job required and what the
plaintiff could do seems to be deficient. Throughout the
opinion, of course, the court expressed concern that the
evidence presented by the plaintiff was meager; this factor
may have influenced the court in its view of the case.

But even if we assume that the court was, on the
whole, correct in its assessment that the plaintiff, in some
situations, could not meet some urgent demand made of
registered nurses, there is the further question of whether
the plaintiff should not be allowed to have the basic training of a registered nurse. It could be that the plaintiff,
aware of her limitations, could have found or fashioned a
career for herself which would have accommodated those
limitations, but nevertheless have been fruitful. Perhaps
(although it is not certain) she should not work in critical,
emergency room situations. But there might be areas of
nursing—administrative, a doctor's office, or other alternatives—where she could have worked well. The court's
approach closes to her a range of choices because she
might be unable to deal with a limited number of problems.

These two issues—the accurate assessment of what is
required and the shaping of alternatives to enable handicapped persons to participate—are raised in many cases
involving the rights of handicapped persons.[4]

In reversing the district court, the Court of Appeals for the Fourth Circuit recognized the deficiencies in the lower court's analysis. The appellate court ordered the college to reconsider the plaintiff's application for admission to the nursing program without regard to her hearing disability. The court recognized that the college could consider the handicapped plaintiff in the context of a "fair and essentially uniform application" of subjective and objective factors utilized in the consideration of other candidates for enrollment in the nursing program.

Alternative settings existed, the court noted, in which the plaintiff could pursue a nursing career, and the entire profession should not be foreclosed to her simply because she might not be able to function in all nursing roles. The question of whether the plaintiff was "otherwise qualified," as required by §504, should not be determined by the nature of the handicap, but by the academic and technical qualifications as required by the HEW §504 regulations. Upon remand, the appellate court directed, the lower court should pay close attention to the academic requirements aspect of the regulations, together with the auxiliary aid provision, as well as considering what affirmative conduct the college might be required to take.

What did the Supreme Court hold in the Davis case?

In *Davis,* the Court of Appeals had required essentially two actions. First, the college was to reevaluate Ms. Davis without regard to her physical handicap and to concentrate on her academic and technical qualifications, just as it would for any other student. The college was not ordered to disregard her handicap entirely, but it was not allowed to give it the primary weight carried in the earlier evaluation. Instead, primary emphasis was to be placed upon her other abilities. Second, the court ordered that consideration be given to accommodations for Ms. Davis to the extent that her handicap would interfere with the ordinary curriculum for nurses training.

The Supreme Court overruled the Court of Appeals and upheld the college's exclusion of Ms. Davis from its registered nursing program. It held, first, that the college was not prohibited from considering her physical qualifications along with other criteria that it imposed on candidates for admission. Apparently this meant that the college did not have to give primary weight to academic and technical qualifications as the lower court had directed. Second, the Supreme Court held that the college was not required to make the kinds of extensive modifications to its academic curriculum that the Court felt would be required to enable Ms. Davis to participate. The college would not be required to provide individual supervision for her when she attended patients or to dispense with certain courses in her training.

The *Davis* case met immediate criticism from handicapped people and their advocates. Apart from its implications for Ms. Davis personally, the case raised many questions about the enforcement of §504 for handicapped people generally. In the opinion of many, the court was not as clear as it should have been with respect to what it was and was not deciding. For example, while it did approve of the physical requirements imposed by the college in this case, the Court also stated such requirements must be legitimate and necessary. It did not offer guidance about how one determines whether the requirements meet those standards, nor did it indicate to what kinds of programs colleges would be allowed to apply the requirements.

Second, while the Court indicated that the college did not have to modify its curriculum for her, it also stated that it could envision circumstances where the refusal to make changes or to take actions for modifications would constitute unlawful discrimination under §504. Again, we have no indication from the Court about when accommodation will be required. In short, problems arise with the *Davis* decision because it does not clearly define the limits of the ruling and its application to other cases.

While the case involves the rights of handicapped people in the context of higher education (and should properly be read as confined to that situation), it also raises questions about how the Supreme Court and lower federal courts will now interpret §504. Certainly, §504 has not been decimated by the ruling. At the same time, there are disturbing suggestions in the opinion which may imply that enforcement of the statute should be tied to the provision of financial assistance for alterations and accommodations to be provided by Congress. Additionally, it is possible to infer from the opinion that should enforcement agencies attempt to implement §504 too vigorously, the Supreme Court would regard such efforts as illegal and beyond the scope of action authorized by the statute. The result of the ruling may be that Congress will find it necessary to amend existing legislation to clarify the rights of handicapped people and the obligations of recipients under §504.

Certainly the *Davis* case demonstrates the importance of the careful preparation and trial of handicapped discrimination cases, with careful attention given to establishing in the record the abilities of handicapped people (and persons similarly situated) as well as what will be required by recipients to accommodate them. The absence of adequate information on this subject may have partially accounted for the Supreme Court's view of the case.

Do the HEW §504 regulations apply to a wide range of programs, activities, and services in postsecondary education?

Yes. In programs or activities to which the regulations apply, the antidiscrimination provisions apply to any "academic, research, occupational training, housing, health, insurance, counseling, financial aid, physical education, athletics, recreation, transportation, other extra-curricular, or other postsecondary" program or activity.[5]

Are postsecondary recipients required to assure equal opportunity for the participation of qualified handicapped persons in programs outside the school which are a part of, or equivalent to, an education program or activity?

Yes. A recipient to which the regulations apply that "considers participation by students in education programs or activities not operated wholly by the recipient as part of, or equivalent to, an education program or activity operated by the recipient" must assure itself that the other program or activity "as a whole, provides an equal opportunity for the participation of qualified handicapped persons." The Analysis accompanying the regulations illustrates the requirement by stating that "a college must ensure that discrimination on the basis of handicap does not occur in connection with teaching assignments of student teachers in elementary or secondary schools not operated by the college." The Analysis also states that a college could continue to use a school system that discriminates if the college student teaching program, when viewed in its entirety, offered handicapped student teachers "the same range and quality of choice in student teaching assignments afforded nonhandicapped students." [6]

Do the HEW §504 regulations reiterate the "most integrated setting appropriate" principle for postsecondary recipients?

Yes. This principle announced earlier in the regulation is reiterated for the part pertaining to postsecondary education.[7]

May a recipient exclude a qualified handicapped person from any course, course of study or other part of its educational program or activity?

No. Such exclusion is prohibited. The Analysis accompanying the regulations states that this provision is "designed to eliminate the practice of excluding handicapped persons from specific courses and from areas of concentration because of factors such as ambulatory difficulties of the student or assumptions by the recipient that no job would be available in the area in question for a person with that handicap." Again, however, these will be a question of the impact of the *Davis* case on this provision.[8]

Do the HEW §504 regulations require postsecondary recipients to make academic adjustments?

Yes. The regulations require "such modifications to its academic requirements as are necessary to ensure that such requirements do not discriminate or have the effect of discriminating, on the basis of handicap, against a qualified handicapped applicant or student." If an academic requirement is demonstrated by the recipient to be "essential to the program of instruction being pursued" by

a student or essential "to any directly related licensing requirement," then the regulations state that the requirement
will not be deemed discriminatory within the meaning of
that regulatory provision. Of course, continuing assessment of this provision in light of *Davis* is necessary.

Modifications may include:

1. "Changes in the length of time permitted for the
   completion of degree requirements";
2. "Substitution of specific courses required for the
   completion of degree requirements"; and
3. "Adaptation of the manner in which specific courses
   are conducted."

Additionally, recipients may not impose other rules on
handicapped students that have the effect of limiting the
participation of handicapped students in an education program or activity, such as rules which exclude tape re-
corders in classrooms or prohibit guide dogs in campus
buildings.

The provisions of the regulations requiring modifications and accommodations to the needs of handicapped
persons should be contrasted to a 1972 federal statute
prohibiting denial of admission on the ground of blindness or severely impaired vision in any course of study by
a recipient of federal financial assistance for any education program or activity, but not requiring "any special
services to such person because of his blindness or visual
impairment." Exactly what, if any, influence this statute,
which apparently also applies to preschool, elementary,
and secondary education, might have on §504 and the
regulations is unclear. Very likely §504 will now be regarded as the dominant statute governing these matters.[9]

**Must recipients conduct course examinations to accom-
modate handicapped students?**

Yes. The requirement, also established elsewhere in the
regulations, is that examinations and other procedures for
evaluation of a student's achievement must be conducted
so that test results of the examination or procedure will
not reflect impaired sensory, manual, or speaking skills,

but will represent the student's achievement in the course.[10]

Is there a requirement that recipients furnish auxiliary aids to handicapped students?

The HEW §504 regulations state that recipients "shall take such steps as are necessary" to ensure that no handicapped student suffers discrimination in programs or activities operated by the recipients because of "the absence of educational auxiliary aids for students with impaired sensory, manual, or speaking skills." The regulations go on to list what are considered auxiliary aids:

—Taped texts, interpreters, "or other effective methods of making orally delivered materials available to students with hearing impairments";
—Readers in libraries for students with visual impairments;
—Classroom equipment adapted for use by students with manual impairments;
—"Other similar services and actions."

The regulations state that recipients are not required to provide "attendants, individually prescribed devices, readers for personal use or study, or other devices or services of a personal nature."

The issue of auxiliary aids aroused controversy during the public comment period for the regulations. In the Analysis accompanying the regulations, HEW has emphasized that agencies such as state vocational rehabilitation departments and private organizations might pay for aids. Additionally, the Analysis states the recipients will have flexibility in the methods by which aids are provided—they may establish a schedule for readers for blind persons at certain times, they may seek taped texts from private organizations, and they may use students to provide aids to handicapped students. The Analysis concludes, "As long as no handicapped person is excluded from a program because of the lack of an appropriate aid, the recipient need not have all such aids on hand at all times." But the recipients themselves remain responsible for the implementation of this requirement.[11]

Have courts interpreted the requirement of the regulations that auxiliary aids be furnished?

Yes. In *Barnes v. Converse College,* a hearing impaired individual who needed an interpreter in order to participate in classroom activity brought suit under §504 to compel the college to provide an interpreter. The plaintiff was an English teacher at a school for persons with hearing and visual handicaps, and she was required to earn graduate credits in English before the next school year to meet state educational certification requirements. The court found that the plaintiff was " 'an otherwise qualified handicapped individual' who can adequately perform in the academic course in which she wishes to enroll with the help of an interpreter."

The court held the effective date of the "auxiliary aids" provision to be June 3, 1977, found that the plaintiff had a right to bring a private lawsuit to enforce §504, and issued a preliminary injunction requiring the college to provide the plaintiff with an interpreter. The court took pains to sympathize with what it considered "the plight of defendant as a private institution which may well be forced to make substantial expenditures of private monies to accommodate the federal government's generosity," and also bemoaned the "pervasive, tyrannical bureaucratic federal control [of HEW] which knows no equal or superior." It nevertheless ordered the college to "procure and compensate a qualified interpreter of its choosing for the purpose of assisting the plaintiff in her summer school classes." Subsequently the court refused to grant a permanent injunction, ruling that the plaintiff must exhaust administrative remedies.[12] An appeal was filed.

In a second case involving what the court's opinion characterized as a "deaf-handicapped" individual, a U.S. magistrate issued findings and recommendations (later adopted by the court) on the issue of the individual's right to an interpreter. The plaintiff was a deaf graduate student at a constituent institution of the University of North Carolina system. He had requested the university to provide him with interpreter services, but he had been told that the university had no funds for that purpose. He was employed at the state school for the deaf, and although his employment was not contingent upon further education, he was taking courses for a master's degree in order to "enhance his career opportunities in the field of education administration."

The plaintiff could understand speech through lipreading wtihout a sign language interpreter with 30 percent accuracy, and he needed an interpreter to make an oral presentation in classes. He had a friend who interpreted some courses for him during the summer session and he had made an unsuccessful effort to secure funds for an interpreter from other sources. His academic average was B+ for the courses he had taken.

After considerable analysis of §504, the regulations, and cases interpreting the statute and regulations, the magistrate recommended a preliminary injunction requiring the university to "procure an interpreter or other effective method of making orally delivered materials available to the plaintiff for his attendance of graduate courses. . . ." At the same time the magistrate recommended that, with the issuance of the preliminary injunction, the judicial proceedings be stayed while the plaintiff filed an administrative complaint with HEW. The court felt that the administrative enforcement of the HEW §504 regulations would aid resolution of, if not completely resolve, the complaint, without need for further judicial action. This case is noteworthy also in that, while the court distinguished the situation of the plaintiff in *Barnes* (who needed the schooling to earn required academic credit), the magistrate still recommended issuing the injunction even though the plaintiff Crawford was not in danger of losing his job. Moreover, the court recognized that the plaintiff's past academic success "does not minimize the benefits flowing to plaintiff by his being able to participate fully in classroom discussion with the aid of an interpreter." The federal district court affirmed the magistrate's ruling after both sides had filed objections.[13]

Do the HEW §504 regulations impose nondiscrimination requirements on postsecondary recipients in areas of educational programs and activities apart from academic requirements?

Yes. The regulations address a number of areas in student life apart from the classroom:

Housing. Recipients that provide housing to nonhandicapped students must provide "comparable, convenient, and accessible housing to handicapped students at the same cost as to others." At the end of the "transition period" provided for in the program-accessibility part of the HEW §504 regulations, such housing must "be available in sufficient quantity and variety so that the scope of handicapped students' choice of living accommodations is, as a whole, comparable to that of nonhandicapped students." Additionally, if a recipient assists agencies, organizations, or persons in making off-campus housing available to its students, it must "assure itself that such housing is, as a whole, made available in a manner that does not result in discrimination on the basis of handicap."

Financial assistance. In providing financial assistance to qualified handicapped individuals, recipients covered by the regulations may not:

1. On the basis of handicap provide less assistance than is provided to nonhandicapped persons, limit eligibility, or otherwise discriminate;
2. Assist any entity or person that provides assistance to any of the recipient's students in a manner that discriminates against qualified handicapped persons on the basis of handicap.

If recipients administer or assist in the administration of financial assistance established under wills, trusts, bequests, or similar legal instruments that require awards to be made on the basis of factors that discriminate or have the effect of discriminating on the basis of handicap, they must make sure that the overall effect of the provision of such financial assistance is not discriminatory on the basis of handicap. The Analysis accompanying the regulations states that with respect to athletic scholarships, it would not be considered discriminatory to deny a student with a neurological disorder a varsity football scholarship on the basis of his inability to play football because the handicap renders the person unable to qualify for the award. But a deaf person could not, on the basis of handicap, be denied a scholarship for the school's diving team, unless the denial was on the basis of comparative diving ability.

Student employment. Recipients, in their own employment of students, may not violate the part of the regulations which govern employment. (They are required to comply with those regulations in general employment practices.) A recipient must also in its assistance to agencies, organizations, or persons providing employment opportunities to any of the recipient's students, assure itself that those employment opportunities, as a whole, are made available in a manner that would not violate the §504 HEW regulations pertaining to employment if the opportunities were provided by the recipient. Whether the *Trageser* decision discussed in the employment chapter will affect this regulation is a question unsettled as this book goes to press.

Physical education and athletics. Recipients may not discriminate, on the basis of handicap, in providing physical education courses, athletics and similar programs to any of its students. If a recipient offers physical education courses, operates or sponsors intercollegiate, club, or intramural athletics, it must provide qualified handicapped students with an opportunity for participation in those activities. If recipients choose to offer separate or different physical education and athletic activities to handicapped students, they must do so only if the separation or differentiation is consistent with the "most integrated setting appropriate" principle and if no qualified handicapped student is denied the opportunity to compete for teams or to participate in courses that are not separate or different.

Counseling and placement. If a recipient provides personal, academic, or vocational counseling, guidance, or placement services to its students, it must provide those services without discrimination on the basis of handicap. Additionally, the regulations state that recipients must ensure that qualified handicapped persons "are not counseled toward more restrictive career objectives than are nonhandicapped students with similar interests and abilities." The purpose of this "nonrestrictive counseling requirement" is to combat earlier practices of directing handicapped persons toward certain careers. However, the regulations state that this requirement "does not preclude a recipient from providing factual information about licensing and certification requirements that may present obstacles to handicapped persons in their pursuit of particular careers."

Social organizations. If a recipient provides "significant assistance" to fraternities, sororities, or similar organizations, the recipient must assure itself that the membership practices of the organizations do not permit discrimination prohibited by the regulations pertaining to higher education.[14]

Has the program-accessibility provision of §504 received judicial recognition in the context of higher education?

Yes. In *Jayne v. University of Nevada, Reno,* the court, following a ruling that §504 provides a private cause of action, held that, while it was premature to charge the defendants with noncompliance, the matter should be held in abeyance until compliance or noncompliance with the HEW §504 regulation was ascertained. The Architectural and Transportation Compliance Board has invoked its jurisdiction to combat architectural barriers in a university in a second case.[15]

NOTES

1. §84.41.
2. §84.42. *Southeastern Community College v. Davis,* 99 S. Ct. 1355 (1979).
3. §84.42(c).
4. *Davis v. Southeastern Community College,* 424 F. Supp. 1341 (E.D. N.C. 1976), *aff'd., vacated and remanded* 574 F.2d 1158 (4th Cir. 1978), *reversed* 99 S. Ct. 1355 (1979).
5. §84.43(a).
6. §84.43(b); 42 *Fed. Reg.* at 22,692 (May 4, 1977).

7. §84.43(d).
8. §84.43(c); 42 *Fed. Reg.* at 22,692 (May 4, 1977); *South-eastern Community College v. Davis, supra,* note 2.
9. §84.44(a), (b); the blindness statute is 20 U.S.C.A. §1684 (1978).
10. §84.44(c).
11. §84.44(d); 42 *Fed. Reg.* 22,692–22,693 (May 4, 1977).
12. *Barnes v. Converse College,* 436 F. Supp. 635 (D.S.C. 1977), —— F. Supp. ——, Civil Action No. 77–1116 (D.S.C., March 31, 1978) and Order on Plaintiff's Motion to Reconsider Order (May 8, 1978), *appeal docketed,* No. 78–1440 (4th Cir., July 19, 1978).
13. *Crawford v. University of North Carolina,* 440 F. Supp. 1047 (M.D. N.C. 1977).
14. §§84.45–.47.
15. *Jayne v. University of Nevada, Reno,* —— F. Supp. ——, Civil No. R-76-183-BRT (D. Nev. 1977).

VII

The Right to Employment

In 1968, in enacting the Architectural Barriers Act, Congress stated its intention with regard to employment of the disabled population:

> There are approximately 22 million people in the United States, who, because of some form of physical handicap, are restricted in their ability to move from place to place. It should be the concern of all that these people are afforded every opportunity to obtain gainful employment and otherwise enter the mainstream of American life.[1]

As of 1970 one estimate was that there were approximately 10 million individuals with major activity limitations—for example, physical disabilities—in the employable age group of sixteen to sixty-four years.[2] Of this figure, 4 million received benefits from the Social Security Administration. The Social Security Disability Insurance Program paid benefits to 2.3 million handicapped individuals in 1974.[3] Also in that year, its first year of

* This chapter was prepared by Paul G. Hearne, past Executive Director of the Handicapped Persons Legal Support Unit, New York City. Mr. Hearne dedicates the chapter as follows:

"First, to my family, who have by their individual and collective sacrifices given me self-sufficiency, independence, and the desire to do good work.

"Second, to the staff of the Handicapped Persons Legal Support Unit—James Weisman, Joseph Turner, Steven Samuels, Rosalyn Vaughn, Elyse Factor, Helen Miller, and Paula Deutsch—whose support, dedication, and commitment have made this chapter as well as an entire program possible.

existence, the Supplemental Security Income program paid benefits to 1.7 million recipients.[4]

These Social Security beneficiaries received an average monthly benefit of $200 to $300 a month, $2,400 to $3,600 a year.[5] Nationally, in 1974, 24.3 million persons were below the poverty line.[6] Notwithstanding the remaining 6 million out of 10 million employable handicapped individuals who might be institutionalized, homebound, placed in sheltered workshops, or in the work force, the 4 million disabled Social Security recipients alone comprised one-sixth of the nation's poor population.

The total federal expenditure in 1974 spent on vocational-rehabilitation programs to assist handicapped individuals in attaining an employment goal was $572 million.[7] This expenditure was small in comparison to the Social Security Administration expenditure of over $8.3 billion in subsistence payments.[8] Moreover, the vocational-rehabilitation programs served a total of 1.2 million clients in 1974, while only 361,000 were rehabilitated and attained an employment goal.[9] Thus, the employed handicapped were few compared to those on public benefits.

When a handicapped person is also a member of a racial minority, or is female, the odds against employment increase. As of the 1970 census, 24 percent of all handicapped women in the employable age bracket were employed, while 42 percent of women in the national population were employed.[10] In New York City alone, there were 118,000 disabled blacks of employable age. Of those, 76,000 were unemployed or had never been in the labor force.[11] These figures indicate that the handicapped population had not begun to integrate itself into the mainstream of American life as Congress had hoped.

In the enactment and amendments to the Rehabilitation Act of 1973, which will be discussed in detail later in this chapter, Congress expressed its intention that putting severely disabled people to work was a major concern, as well as providing services to those severely disabled persons for whom traditional vocational goals were not feasible:

The key to the intent of the bill is the Committee's belief that the basic vocational rehabilitation program must not only continue to serve more individuals, but must place more emphasis on rehabilitating individuals with more severe handicaps. It is the bill's intent to be more responsive to the needs of the handicapped individual by providing a better basic program of service as well as an emphasis within special project authority for target populations whose needs are not now being met within the basic programs. Additionally, the Committee has added provisions designed to focus research and training activities on making employment and participation in society more feasible for handicapped individuals.[12]

Partly because of concern over employment barriers confronting handicapped people, Congress enacted §504 of the Rehabilitation Act of 1973.

§504, as originally enacted, stated:

No otherwise qualified handicapped individual in the United States shall, solely by reason of his handicap, be excluded from the participation in, be denied the benefits of, or be subjected to discrimination under any program or activity receiving federal financial assistance.[13]

The passage of this legislation has begun a new civil rights movement in this nation.

§504 thus represents the first Federal civil rights law protecting the rights of handicapped persons and reflects a national commitment to end discrimination on the basis of handicap. The language of §504 is almost identical to the comparable non-discrimination provisions of Title VI of the Civil Rights of 1964 and Title IX of the Education Amendments of 1972 (applying to discrimination in education on the basis of sex). It establishes a mandate to end discrimination and to bring handicapped persons into the mainstream of American life.[14]

A new body of law has been created to prevent discrimination against the handicapped. This new legal process has begun to reach into many areas of life concerning the handicapped population, such as transportation, education, employment, social welfare, and architectural access.

This chapter will deal with the legal steps that have been taken and that can be taken to ensure that the goal of equal employment for all qualified handicapped individuals is achieved.

Before the enactment of such legislation as the Rehabilitation Act, what federal legislation existed concerning the handicapped in employment? And what did it attempt to accomplish?

Congress' intent, to bring handicapped people into the mainstream of American society, with civil rights protected, is a comparatively new one.

In the past, the intended ameliorative legislation reflected stereotypical attitudes which did not serve to encourage professional advancement for the handicapped. Such statutes are still law and are poor examples of our national commitment to employ handicapped workers today.

One such statute, passed in order to promote self-sufficiency for the blind, authorized licensed blind persons to have a preference to operate vending stands on federal property.[15] The statute also authorized government agencies controlling such property to prescribe regulations that would assure these preferences without unduly inconveniencing the agencies.

Such legislation does not promote professional advancement for the blind population. While criticism should not be directed at participants in these programs, working as a news vendor does not develop adequate skills or provide experience for more advanced employment. A future employer might not be inclined to hire a blind person whose only prior experience was in a vending stand.

There is case law that suggests that employment as a vending-stand operator is considered "Sheltered Employment" and may be so removed from true self-employment that the vending stand operator could receive Social Security benefits as if he or she were not employed at all.

In the case of *Cox v. Cohen*,[16] which was an appeal

from a denial of Social Security disability benefits brought by a blind vendor, the District Court for the Northern District of California held that although the blind claimant worked a 10½-hour day, five days a week, and was mentally alert, he could not successfully operate his small vending stand without the assistance of others. His suppliers would arrange the magazines and candy for him daily, and his customers would inform him of the items they would purchase and the denominations of bills they were handing him. Even though the claimant's income was over the Social Security monthly eligibility the court held that this income was not attributed to the claimant's productivity, due to the assistance given by others. The claimant was granted disability benefits.

This case does not stand for the proposition that all blind vending operators need assistance and are therefore working in sheltered employment. However, it does imply that sheltered employment is outside the mainstream of the employment world, and that blind vending operators may be outside the mainstream as well. The vending-stand legislation is in sharp contrast to the intent of more recent legislation.

Another statute, which has since been amended, provided that blind employees of a federal agency who needed the assistance of a reader must either have the employer authorize the reader to serve as an employee *without pay*, or the blind employee must pay the reader for his assistance from his own wages.[17] The effect of this statute is obvious; the burden for reading assistance fell entirely on the blind employee. Perhaps the intention of this statute was to encourage the employer to hire the blind employee; nevertheless, the effect was to put an unconscionable expense on the blind applicant. The amendments in the Civil Service Reform Act of 1978 now authorize the heads of federal agencies to employ paid readers and interpreters for employees who are blind or deaf. The reader or interpreter may also be paid by the blind or deaf employee or from a not-for-profit agency.[18]

What are sheltered work-activity centers?

A work-activity center is a center planned and designed exclusively to provide therapeutic activities for handicapped persons whose physical or mental impairments are so severe as to make their productive capacity inconsequential. Work and production are not the main purpose of a work-activity center.

The Fair Labor Standards Act [19] provides that in order to promote employment of severely handicapped and multiply handicapped persons whose earning and productive capacity is impaired by severe physical or mental deficiency, the Secretary of Labor may issue a special exemption certificate to an employer who files for an exemption to the minimum-wage requirement. If the exemption is granted, the employer may then pay less than the minimum wage to those handicapped individuals whose productivity is hampered, but no less than 50 percent of the minimum wage, or wages commensurate with those paid nonhandicapped workers in the industry for the same type, quality, and quantity of work in that area, unless the Secretary allows a lower wage.

Under regulations, no program that has an annual average labor rate of over certain limits can be eligible for the minimum-wage exemption. Moreover, no individual client who earns substantially more than that average annual labor rate can receive below the minimum wage under an exemption certificate, except in certain cases.[20]

These regulations are an important step in implementing the intention behind the work-activity centers. They narrowly define the segment of the handicapped population that belongs in the work-activity centers, as well as the criteria for eligibility for the minimum wage exemption. Prior to these regulations, abuses of handicapped workers was possible. However blind individuals are continuing to challenge some aspects of these policies.[21]

The Employment Opportunities for Handicapped Individuals Act,[22] creates a community service employment pilot program for the handicapped. It is interesting to note that *any* employer who has handicapped persons employed under this act will not be eligible to receive an exemption of the minimum wage under the Fair Labor Standards Act. It is clear that the legislative emphasis is shifting from merely hiring a handicapped person to assigning a job and wage commensurate with his ability.

What are examples of early efforts to combat employment discrimination by the federal government?

Civil Service legislation guaranteeing equality in employment for the handicapped appeared in 1948. One such statute authorized the President to prescribe rules to prohibit discrimination on the basis of physical handicap in an executive agency or competitive service.[23] The Civil Service Commission was charged with determining if the handicapped person could efficiently perform the duties of the position; however, the statute expressly forbid any employment of a handicapped person that endangers the health and safety of that person or of others.

Pursuant to an amended version of this statute, the Civil Service Commission promulgated regulations in 1969 that gave handicapped people equal opportunity in appointments and positions.[24] Moreover, the regulations proscribe discrimination on the basis of physical handicap and specifically prohibit any agency from taking adverse action against a handicapped employee whose duties may be efficiently performed by a handicapped person. These provisions were an early effort to combat employment discrimination at the federal level.[24]

One case brought under these provisions was *Smith v. Fletcher*.[25] A federal district court in Texas ordered promotion of the plaintiff after a finding of discrimination on the basis of sex and physical disability.

Ms. Smith, a paraplegic confined to a wheelchair, was employed by the National Aeronautic and Space Administration in 1962 at a grade of GS-7. In 1963, Ms. Smith was promoted to GS-9, reduced to GS-5 due to a reduction in force, and repromoted to GS-7 in 1973 and GS-9 in 1974.

Two male employees, hired at about the same time as Ms. Smith, with almost identical qualifications, began at GS-9 levels, and one was promoted to GS-11. Neither was ever reduced in classification.

Ms. Smith was given routine clerical assignments, while other employees with similar qualifications were given advanced research projects to work on. She filed a written complaint of discrimination based on both her sex and her physical disability before the Civil Service Commission on December of 1971. The commission failed to order any specific relief.

In reviewing the adminstrative record, the district court held that Ms. Smith, due both to her sex and handicap, had been denied assignment to positions she could have physically performed and in which she could have achieved promotion and advancement. The court further determined that this was a violation of both the Civil Service statute and its regulations and ordered retroactive promotion of Ms. Smith with back pay. The case was affirmed in the Court of Appeals, although the handicapped discrimination issue was not clearly before the court.

Similar issues were addressed in *Shaposka v. United States.*[26] Bert Shaposka was a physically handicapped employee who had been discharged by the National Archives and Records Service. His employer argued that Mr. Shaposka was only a temporary employee under a trial procedure for physically handicapped employees and therefore was not subject to Civil Service procedural guidelines.

The U.S. Court of Claims held that this temporary program was not designed to hinder handicapped employees in the exercise of their procedural rights and that Mr. Shaposka was entitled to those rights prior to his discharge. The court reinstated him with full back pay.

The Shaposka case also involved the "700 hours" appointment program for severely handicapped people for initial or trial temporary employment. The Court noted the consistency of the liberal approach with the purpose of 5 U.S.C. §7153, the old federal employment discrimination law. On March 15, 1979, President Carter signed Executive Order 12125 allowing severely physically handicapped federal employees (as well as mentally retarded employees) who have completed at least two years of satisfactory service, in a position excepted from the competitive service, to obtain civil service competitive status. Of related interest are recently promulgated regulations concerning noncompetitive appointment of disabled veterans.[27]

Is there now a government plan to hire qualified handicapped people?

Although the *Smith* case was successful, no affirmative-action plans or minimum requirements existed at that time for the hiring of handicapped personnel, and the language of the Civil Service Act was too vague to justify large-scale compliance litigation.

However, in 1973, §501 of the Rehabilitation Act [28] provided that within 180 days of its enactment, each department, instrumentality, or agency in the executive branch was to promulgate a written affirmative action plan for hiring, placing, and advancing handicapped individuals, and submit this to the Civil Service Commission. These plans are to be updated annually, and are to include a description of the methods used to meet the special needs of handicapped individuals. The Commission was then to report to Congress each year on the progress of these plans.

Subsection (c) provides for the Commission to recommend to appropriate state agencies policies and procedures which will facilitate the hiring, placement, and advancement in employment of persons who have benefited from state vocational rehabilitation or veterans programs.

§501 also provided for an Interagency Committee on Handicapped Employees comprised of such appointees as the President might select plus the Chairman or Administrator of the Civil Service Commission, Veterans Administration, General Services Administration, the Federal Communications Commission and the Department of Health, Education and Welfare. The Chairman of the Civil Service Commission and the Secretary of HEW acted as co-chairmen of the committee.

The job of this committee was to cooperate with the President's Committee on Employment of the Handicapped and develop policies and procedures, as well as systems for effective review, to facilitate the hiring, placement, and advancement of handicapped employees in the executive branch of government. Moreover, in selecting personnel for the President's committee, special preference would be given to qualified handicapped individuals. The Civil Service Commission was also able to make legislative and administrative recommendations to further employment efforts for the handicapped to the appropriate committees of Congress.

With the reorganization of the Equal Employment Opportunity Commission to take over many of the functions previously performed by the Civil Service Commission, handicapped persons will await better enforcement of §501. §505, created in the Rehabilitation Amendments of 1978 provides that the remedies, procedures, and rights set forth under certain sections of the Civil Rights Act of 1964 shall be available with respect to any complaint brought under §501 to any employee or applicant for employment aggrieved by the final disposition of a complaint or by the failure to take final action on the complaint. Courts, in fashioning equitable or affirmative action remedies under this provision, may take into account the reasonableness of the cost of any necessary work place accommodation, and the availability of alternatives or other appropriate relief in order to achieve an equitable and appropriate remedy. Attorney fees may be awarded under the 1978 Rehabilitation Amendments.[29]

What procedures are available to a handicapped person challenging employment discrimination prohibited by §501?

In the 1978 amendments to the Rehabilitation Act, Congress provided that the remedies, procedures, and rights set forth in specified provisions of the Civil Rights Act of 1964 shall be available with respect to any complaint brought under §501.[30] Any employee or applicant for employment aggrieved by the final disposition of a complaint, or by the failure of a final action on a complaint, may invoke these remedies. The statutes allow an aggrieved individual, within specified time periods, to seek redress of grievances or to bring actions against the head of the department that discriminates. Enforcement is vested in the Equal Employment Opportunities Commission. Additionally, under the Civil Rights Act provisions, individuals may, under certain conditions, bring private law suits to enforce their rights under §501.

A court may enjoin unlawful employment practices, order affirmative action as may be appropriate (including, but not limited to, reinstatement or hiring, with or without backpay or other appropriate relief). Courts may award attorney fees in these cases.

However, before action is started with the E.E.O.C., an aggrieved individual files a complaint with the agency against which the discrimination is alleged. Under the Civil Service regulations promulgated in 1978, agencies are required to provide regulations governing the existence and processing of complaints of discrimination based on physical and mental handicap. Time limits within which to file complaints under these regulations can be quite short. Generally, a person has 30 calendar days to notify an equal employment opportunity counselor of the complaint, with 15 days after the final conference to file a complaint. These time limits can, in some cases, be extended. Different periods apply in taking further actions against the agency. It should also be noted that the Civil Service regulations are promulgated not only on the basis of §501, but also under the earlier statute, 5 U.S.C. §7153, which derives from the earlier federal antidiscrimination employment legislation.

The concern handicapped persons have had over whether a private right of action will exist under §501 may be somewhat abated by these amendments. Recently, the United States Court of Appeals for the Tenth Circuit held in *Coleman v. Darden* that a private right of action does not exist. The court's opinion does not appear to be well reasoned, but distinguished *Coleman* from other cases in which individuals have sought judicial review of discriminatory agency action pursuant to the Administrative Procedure Act.[30]

What are the general provisions and subjects addressed by the 1978 §501 regulations?

The general policy of the regulations is stated as follows:

> Agencies shall give full consideration to the hiring, placement, and advancement of qualified mentally and physically handicapped persons. The Federal Government shall become a model employer of handicapped individuals. An agency shall not dis-

criminate against a qualified physically or mentally handicapped person.

Agencies must make reasonable accommodation to the known physical or mental limitations of qualified handicapped applicants or employees unless the agencies can demonstrate that the accommodation would impose an undue hardship on the operation of their programs. In the 1978 Amendments,[31] Congress specified that a court may take into account the reasonableness of the cost of any necessary work-place accommodation, and the availability of alternatives or other appropriate relief needed to achieve an equitable and appropriate remedy. Examples of reasonable accommodations given by the regulations are making facilities readily accessible and usable by handicapped persons, job restructure, acquisition or modification of equipment or devices, the provision of readers and interpreters, as well as other actions. Factors to be taken into account in determining whether a particular accommodation would impose an undue hardship are the overall size of the agency's program with respect to the number of employees, number and type of facilities, and size of budget; the type of agency operation, including the composition and structure of the agency's work force; and the nature and cost of the accommodation.

With respect to employment criteria, agencies may not make use of any employment test or other selection criterion that screens out or tends to screen out qualified handicapped persons or any class of handicapped persons unless:

1. The test score or other selection criteria, as used by the agency, is shown to be job-related to the position in question and
2. Alternative job-related tests or criteria that do not screen out or tend to screen out as many handicapped persons are not shown to be available.

Under the 1978 regulations the burden for showing the availability of an alternative test was on the Civil Service Commission Director of Personnel Research and Development Center.

Agencies must select and administer tests concerning employment to ensure that, when administered to applicants or employees who are handicapped in ways that impair sensory, manual, or speaking skills, the test results accurately reflect the applicant's or employee's ability to perform the job. The test should not reflect the applicant's or employee's impaired sensory, manual, or speaking skills, except where those skills are the factors which the test purports to measure.

With respect to preemployment inquiries, agencies may not conduct a preemployment medical examination and may not make preemployment inquiries as to whether the applicant is a handicapped person or as to the nature of the severity of a handicap. Agencies are permitted to make preemployment inquiries into an applicant's ability to meet the medical qualification requirements, with or without reasonable accommodation, of the position in question. The agency may inquire as to whether the applicant has the minimum abilities necessary for safe and efficient performance of the duties of the position in question. Under the 1978 Civil Service regulations, the Civil Service Commission could also make an inquiry as to the nature and extent of a handicap for the purpose of special testing.

Agencies are permitted to condition an offer of employment on the results of a medical examination conducted prior to the employee's entrance on duty, if:

1. All entering employees are subjected to such an examination regardless of a handicap or when the preemployment medical questionnaire used for positions which do not routinely require medical examination indicates a condition for which further examination is required because of the job-related nature of the condition.
2. And the results of the examination are used only in accordance with the requirements of the regulations.

Preemployment medical information may be gathered for purposes of special appointing authorities for handicapped persons. Information obtained in accordance with the preemployment inquiries regulation as to medical condition or history must be collected and maintained according to the existing procedures as a medical record. However, supervisors and managers may be informed of necessary accommodations, and first-aid and safety personnel may be informed, where appropriate, if the condition may require emergency treatment.

Finally, agencies may not discriminate against qualified handicapped applicants or employees due to inaccessible facilities. Accessibility is defined as compliance with the Architectural Barriers Act of 1968.[32]

Will §504 also be available in employment discrimination by the federal government itself?

Possibly. The 1978 Amendments to the Rehabilitation Act applied §504 to the federal government itself, in addition to recipients of federal financial assistance. Depending upon how §504 is interpreted by courts to apply to employment discrimination matters, it could become an additional resource for handicapped persons challenging employment discrimination against the federal government.[33]

What coverage is provided in the regulations under §503 of the Rehabilitation Act?

While §501 of the Rehabilitation Act covers employment in the executive branch, §503 provides that any federal contract over $2,500 for the procurement of personal property or nonpersonal services (including construction contracts) requires the contracting party to take affirmative action to employ qualified handicapped employees in carrying out the contract. (This section also applies to subcontracts over $2,500 entered into by a prime contractor.)

Employers who enter into a contract for $50,000 or more with the federal government and have fifty or more employees must also prepare and maintain at each establishment a written affirmative action plan, which will be reviewed and updated annually, and which will set forth the policies and procedures affecting the employment of qualified handicapped individuals.[34]

It should be noted that the §503 regulations are under revision at the present time.

How does the affirmative action plan work?

The affirmative action plan under §503 is a written plan which includes an agreement that the contractor plans not to discriminate against qualified handicapped individuals and authorizes the implementation of affirmative action hiring for the employer's program.

The plan must be reviewed and updated annually. Each employer-contractor is responsible for updating his policies and practices in order to enhance efforts in both the recruitment and upgrading of handicapped employees.

The contractor must invite all applicants and employees to identify themselves in order to benefit from the affirmative action program. However, this invitation must emphasize that it seeks only a voluntary response and that refusal to provide the information will not subject an individual to adverse treatment. Additionally, the information can be used only in accordance with the regulations. Employees are not precluded from informing the employer at a later time of a handicap, and employers are not relieved of the obligation to take affirmative action where they know an employee is handicapped.[35]

§503 also provides that as part of their affirmative action to employ qualified handicapped individuals, employers must develop internal procedures throughout their programs to implement their plans. These procedures would include periodic meetings with managers to inform them of the intent of the affirmative action plan and to make them responsible for its implementation. The managers should also be aware that their affirmative action efforts will be evaluated as part of their job performance.

The affirmative action policy should be included in all orientation programs for new employees. Handicapped workers must be a part of the programs' publications both internally and externally for recruitment, and should be encouraged to participate in career days and community relations for the contractor. A special effort should be made to have qualified handicapped individuals on the contractor's personnel relations staff.[36]

If a union exists, its cooperation should be requested and it should be fully informed of the contractor's obligations.[37]

The contractor should review internal practices to implement affirmative action. The contractor must also disseminate this policy to the public by informing them of his commitment to seek out and employ handicapped people. This outreach program can include, but is not limited to, vocational rehabilitation agencies, college placement offices, sheltered workshops, and labor organizations. These should be ongoing contacts so the agencies can recommend prospective employees. Also, their technical assistance would be helpful in the future placement of qualified handicapped personnel and in making reasonable accommodation to these applicants.[38]

All publicity for the contractor, whether for recruitment, sales, or promotions, should include qualified handicapped employees. This would create a positive atmosphere to attract handicapped people not now working who have the skills but are difficult to locate. These individuals may also come to the contractor's attention through his liaison with disabled community groups or service providers.

It is interesting to note that contracts with sheltered workshops do not constitute affirmative action in lieu of employment and advancement of qualified handicapped individuals in the contractor's own workforce. They may only fall under an affirmative action plan if the sheltered workshop trains severely handicapped people to work for the contractor at full compensation when they become qualified in the training program.[39] This provision attempts to limit sheltered workshops and attempts to check the possible abuses under the minimum wage exception previously mentioned in the Fair Labor Standards Act.

These regulations also provide for equal pay for equal work for handicapped employees. A handicapped employee may not have his or her income reduced because of any collateral source of disability pension or benefit.[40]

When considering a handicapped individual for an employment position, what steps must contractors take under §503?

The regulations provide that contractors must review their personnel practices and procedures to assure careful and systematic consideration of the job qualifications of the handicapped applicant. This section is designed to prevent the traditional stereotyping of handicapped applicants without considering their ability to perform the job in question.

In determining the physical and mental qualifications of handicapped applicants, contractors must review their requirements to ensure that, to the extent qualification requirements tend to screen out qualified handicapped individuals, they are job related and are consistent with business necessity and safe performance of the job.[41]

These requirements must be specifically related to the job for which the individual is being considered while being consistent with business necessity and safe performance of the job. The prospective employee must be able to perform the job-related tasks, and perform them in a safe fashion. However, an applicant cannot be rejected without a case-by-case evaluation of his specific capability to perform. Moreover, the employer-contractor must, within cost and business necessity, make a reasonable accommodation to the physical and mental limitations of the employee or applicant under §503, a concept discussed more fully later.

May a contractor give a preemployment medical exam to an applicant under §503?

A contractor, under §503, may conduct a comprehensive medical examination prior to employment if the results are used in accordance with the regulations.

The results of such medical exams must be confidential except:

1. supervisors and managers may be informed regarding restrictions on the work or duties of qualified handicapped individuals and regarding accomodations;
2. first-aid and safety personnel may be informed where, to the extent appropriate, a condition may require emergency treatment;
3. government officials investigating compliance with the act may be informed.[42]

The point is that any physical or mental requirements *must* be job related, and cannot screen out handicapped employees except on a case-by-case basis. The burden of showing an applicant's inability to perform job-related tasks is on the contractor whenever job qualifications are disputed in a specific case.[43] Requirements under §504 concerning preemployment examination are different and are discussed later.

What recourse may an individual who feels he has suffered discrimination pursue under §503?

When an aggrieved handicapped person feels that a contractor is not fulfilling his obligations under §503, he or she may institute a written complaint to the Office of Federal Contract Compliance (OFCCP) of the Department of Labor (DOL) within 180 days of the occurrence of the alleged violation. At that time the DOL refers the matter back to the contractor for internal review. If no favorable action is taken within 60 days—a cooling off period to attempt resolution through the contractor's established internal procedure—then the DOL or the OFCCP may designate an agency that initiates its own formal investigation. If a violation of §503 is found, efforts are made to secure compliance through informal means; negotiation, conciliation, and persuasion are used whenever possible. If noncompliance persists, the Director of the OFCCP can go to court or can withhold payments under the contract to the contractor. He can ultimately terminate the contract with the contractor for failure to comply. The contractor does have a right to a predetermination hearing. Amendments to the Rehabilitation Act provide attorneys' fees in §503 lawsuits brought by individuals, but it is unsettled as to whether an individual must first exhaust administrative remedies before going to court.[44] Additionally, see the questions below on a private right of action.

A recently published periodical, *Affirmative Action for Handicapped People,* included this table of Affirmative Action Complaints to the Department of Labor under §503, which indicated that administrative complaints have increased threefold in the last three months of 1977.[45]

COMPLAINT REPORTS: AFFIRMATIVE ACTION FOR HANDICAPPED PERSONS UNDER SECTION 503

	10/1/75 to 9/30/76	10/1/76 to 9/30/77	Three Months 10/1/77 to 12/31/77
Complaints			
Received	785	1453	4481
Closed	416	800	2487
Open	823	653	2560
Type of Complaints			
Hiring	248	674	1808
Promotion	32	90	245
Discharge	206	545	1583
Other (fringe benefits, requests for irregular hours, time off, etc.)	134	144	670
Reason for Closure			
No coverage	149	252	796
Complaint withdrawn	24	92	233
No violation	84	145	477
Conciliated	92	166	566
No reply over 60 days	42	121	333
Transferred	24	24	98
Status of Open Cases			
Initial stages of investigation	524	456	1956
Referred to solicitor's office	103	21	218
In negotiation for conciliation			
Referred to national office	231	176	410

Readers should also be aware that the DOL plan to revise the §503 regulations to be more consistent with the HEW §504 rules.

How does the coverage of §504 with respect to employment compare to that of §503?

After much delay, the Secretary of Health, Education and Welfare signed the §504 regulations for that department on April 28, 1977. Subpart B of the regulations concerns employment and bars discrimination by all recipients of HEW assistance in recruitment, hiring, compensation, job assignment, classification, and fringe benefits.[46] The regulations call for written assurances from all potential recipients as a condition of eligibility for funds.

In furtherance of the governmental policy that all federal agencies and programs must comply with §504, an Executive Order signed by President Ford made all agencies responsible for promulgation of appropriate regulations for that compliance.[47] Regulations implementing §504 are being published pursuant to Executive Order 11914 which requires all federal agencies to promulgate §504 regulations that would apply to all recipients of funds from those agencies. At this writing, many agencies have proposed or promulgated such regulations.[48]

In summary, §503 provides for affirmative action in employment as well as policies and procedures for all those who contract with the federal government in excess of $2,500. §504 applies to all recipients of federal assistance. In 1978, Congress amended §504 to apply to the federal executive branch itself. The legislative history of §504 indicates a congressional basis for affirmative action under the statute.

Both the §503 and §504 regulations set policies and procedures for the employment of qualified handicapped individuals. These policies and procedures include general concepts fundamental to an understanding of employment law in relation to the handicapped.

How does the concept of reasonable accommodation apply under §503 and §504 regulations?

The regulations promulgated under §504 provide definitions of a "Qualified Handicapped Person."

A handicapped individual means any person who (1) has a physical or mental impairment which substantially limits one or more of such person's major life activities, (2) has a record of such impairment, or (3) is regarded as having such an impairment.

A qualified handicapped individual is a handicapped individual who is capable of performing a particular job, with reasonable accommodation by the employer to the physical or mental limitations of his or her handicap.[49]

The qualified handicapped individual is capable of performing job-related tasks. For example, a qualified handicapped individual who is in a wheelchair can be an editor in a publishing house; the skills needed are the ability to read, write, and think clearly. If that individual was denied the job simply because he or she is in a wheelchair, that would be a discriminatory practice, due to the recipient's failure to hire an otherwise qualified applicant who could perform the job.

In the same case, if there were two steps to enter the building, and a $50 plywood ramp would allow the qualified handicapped individual to enter and do his daily work, the employer could not deny employment due to his failure to provide reasonable accommodation (in this case, a ramp). The lack of access to the publishing house is not related to the handicapped applicant's job functions.

An employer may not deny any employment opportunity to a qualified handicapped individual if the basis for the denial is the need to make reasonable accommodation to the physical and mental limitations of the applicant or employee. Accommodations such as making facilities accessible and restructuring jobs are reasonable if they do not impose an undue hardship on the recipient's program.[50]

Therefore, a qualified handicapped individual is one who can perform job-related tasks despite his or her handicap but who may need these accommodations. A hearing-impaired job applicant may need an interpreter in order to perform daily tasks, or a telephone amplifier in order to communicate. If an assigned desk was too high above an employee's wheelchair, it might be a "reasonable accommodation" to furnish a new desk. However, if the firm were on the third floor, it might be reasonable to transfer the employee to an accessible local office but not reasonable to spend $50,000 for an elevator.

The commentary Analysis to the §504 regulations include specific examples of reasonable accommodation. The examples, while not exhaustive, provide guidance to the employer as to what actions constitute reasonable accommodation, without undue hardship:

Thus, a small day care center might not be required to expend more than a nominal sum, such as that necessary to equip a telephone for use by a secretary with impaired hearing, but a large school district might be required to make available a teacher's aide to a blind applicant for a teaching job. Further, it might be considered reasonable to require a state welfare agency to accommodate a deaf employee by providing an interpreter, while it would constitute an undue hardship to impose that requirement on a provider of foster home care services.[51]

The reasonable-accommodation requirement is a flexible one which looks to size, type of operation, and nature and cost of the accommodation.

Under §503, the factors in determining undue hardship in reasonable accommodations include business necessity and financial cost and expense.[52]

The potential of state law in requiring reasonable accommodations is discussed later.

What other conditions are imposed by employers covered in the §504 regulations?

All recipients are forbidden to limit, classify, or segregate their employees in any way that adversely affects their opportunities or status because of handicap. Recipients may not participate in contractual or other relationships that have the effect of subjecting qualified handicapped employees to discrimination. This provision includes relationships with employment and referral agencies, labor unions, organizations providing or administering fringe benefits, and with organizations providing training and apprenticeship programs.

The above provisions apply an overall standard of non-discrimination on the basis of handicap to the following:

1. Recruitment, advertising, and processing of applications for employment.
2. Hiring, upgrading, promotion, award of tenure, demotion, transfer, layoff, termination, right of return from layoff, and rehiring.
3. Rates of pay or any other form of compensation and changes in compensation.

4. Job assignments, job classifications, organizational structures, position descriptions, lines of progression, and seniority lists.
5. Leaves of absence, sick leave, or any other leave.
6. Fringe benefits available by virtue of employment, whether or not administered by the recipient.
7. Selection and financial support for training, including apprenticeship, professional meetings, conferences, and other related activities, and selection for leaves of absence to pursue training.
8. Employer-sponsored activities, including social or recreational programs.
9. Any other term, condition, or privilege of employment.

These obligations would not be affected by any contradictory clause included in a collective-bargaining agreement to which the HEW recipient is a party.[53]

What standards apply to HEW recipients in the selection of employees?

The requirements of the HEW §504 regulations have similarities and differences from those under §503 discussed earlier. A §504 recipient may not make use of any employment test or other selection criterion that screens out or tends to screen out handicapped persons or any class of handicapped persons unless:

1. The test score or other selection criterion, as used by the recipient, is shown to be job-related for the position in question and
2. Alternative tests or criteria that do not screen out or tend to screen out as many handicapped persons are not shown by the Director [of HEW's Office for Civil Rights] to be available.[54]

§504 recipients must select and administer tests concerning employment so as best to ensure that, when administered to an applicant or employee who has a handicap which impairs sensory, manual, or speaking skills, the test results accurately reflect job skills, aptitude, or whatever other factor they purport to measure. The test should not reflect the applicant's or employee's impaired skills, except

where those skills are the factors which the test purports
to measure.[55]

§504 recipients may not make preemployment inquiries
of an applicant as to whether the applicant is a handicapped person or as to the nature or severity of the
handicap with several exceptions. The exceptions are:

1. If the recipient is taking remedial action to correct
   the effects of past discrimination, or
2. If the recipient is attempting to take action to overcome the effects of conditions that resulted in limited
   participation by handicapped persons in its federally
   assisted program or activity, or
3. If the recipient is taking affirmative action pursuant
   to Section 503.

In these exceptional cases, recipients may invite applicants
for employment to indicate whether and to what extent
they are handicapped. However, the recipient must state
clearly on any written questionnaire used for the purpose,
or make clear orally if no written questionnaire is used,
that the information requested is intended for use solely
in connection with remedial action or affirmative action
efforts and that the information is being requested on a
voluntary basis. It must also state that the information
will be confidential and that refusal to provide it will not
subject the applicant or employee to any adverse treatment, and that the information will be used only in
accordance with the Rehabilitation Act and §504 regulations.

§504 recipients are permitted to conduct medical examinations prior to an employee's entrance on duty only
if all prospective employees are subjected to such examinations regardless of handicap and results of the examination are used only in accordance with regulations. §504
employers are somewhat more restricted at present in this
respect. Under the HEW §504 regulations, the information obtained with respect to medical history must be
collected and maintained on separate forms which are accorded confidentiality as medical records. Supervisors and
managers may be informed regarding restrictions on the
work or duty of handicapped persons and regarding necessary accommodations; first-aid and safety personnel may

be informed, where appropriate, if the condition might require emergency treatment; and investigating government officials concerned with compliance of the act must be provided relevant information upon request.[56]

Do other federal statutes provide for affirmative action in hiring qualified handicapped individuals?

Yes, the Education for All Handicapped Children Act of 1975 provides for federal assistance to the states to initiate and provide a free, adequate and appropriate education to all handicapped children. As a condition to such a grant-in-aid, the recipient must provide an assurance that it will seek out, employ, and advance qualified handicapped people.

The Developmentally Disabled Assistance and Bill of Rights Act of 1975 provides for federal grants-in-aid to the states in areas such as education, architectural barriers, and any projects concerning the full participation of the developmentally disabled in society. This statute still incorporates the obligations under the Rehabilitation Act of 1973 in a provision entitled "Employment of Handicapped Individuals":

> As a condition of providing assistance under this chapter, the Secretary shall require that each recipient of such assistance take affirmative action to employ and advance in employment qualified handicapped individuals on the same terms and conditions required with respect to the employment of such individuals by the provisions of the Rehabilitation Act of 1973 which govern employment (1) by state rehabilitation agencies and rehabilitation facilities, and (2) under federal contracts and subcontracts.

Although both of these statutes mandate affirmative action in employment for qualified handicapped personnel, neither statute provides a procedural mechanism for compliance that would provide direct relief to an aggrieved claimant. An individual aggrieved under the provisions of either one of these statutes could still pursue remedies under the Rehabilitation Act. These statutes are illustrative; other laws have similar provisions.[57]

Do disabled veterans qualify for affirmative action in employment?

Although disabled veterans would qualify for affirmative action under the Rehabilitation Act due to their disability, they have their own separate affirmative action programs.

One plan parallels §501 of the Rehabilitation Act. It is a matter of national policy to promote a maximum of employment and job advancement within the federal government for disabled veterans. Similar to §501, the veterans program requires a separate affirmative action plan for each part of the executive branch. The Civil Service Commission was originally responsible for review and evaluation of these plans,[58] a function now carried out by EEOC.

Additionally paralleling §503, any contractor with a federal contract to supply personal property or nonpersonal services (including construction) worth $10,000 or more must take affirmative action to employ qualified disabled veterans and Vietnam era veterans.[59]

An aggrieved disabled veteran may file a noncompliance complaint with the Secretary of Labor.[60] While this book does not go extensively into the rights of veterans (covered in another ACLU Handbook), readers should be aware of these provisions. Additionally, the Supreme Court has upheld a state "veterans preference law" against a claim of sex discrimination.[61]

Prior to the 1978 amendments to the Rehabilitation Act, did any courts indicate that an aggrieved handicapped individual could pursue a remedy in federal court under §503 or §504?

In order for an individual to bring an action in federal court, some statutory authority must exist that authorizes jurisdiction, and the aggrieved individual must have a "private cause of action," a right to bring his or her complaint before the court. Prior to the 1978 amendments to the Rehabilitation Act, which will be discussed in the next question, neither §503 nor §504 explicitly authorized such action, although the legislative history indicated that some kind of judicial action was contemplated at some time. Without explicit authority in either the statute or the regulations, the courts must decide whether a private right of action exists. Although a statute called the Administrative Procedure Act states that all administrative decisions are subject to judicial review, most cases sought federal court review on the basis of the Rehabilitation Act itself.

Courts generally have held that no private right of action exists under §503. The U.S. Court of Appeals for the Fifth Circuit is now considering a case involving this issue.

Other courts have been reluctant to bestow a private right of action under this section.[62] In a case in U.S. District Court in Pennsylvania, *Drennon v. Philadelphia General Hospital*,[63] there is language in the opinion to the effect that §503 could bestow a private cause of action to handicapped employees.

Ms. Drennon was a highly qualified laboratory technician who was denied employment at Philadelphia General Hospital because she had epilepsy. She alleged that the hospital had a policy that denied employment to anyone who had experienced an epileptic seizure within two years from the date of his or her job application.

Although the court in *Drennon* remanded her case to the Department of Labor for Ms. Drennon to exhaust her administrative remedies, it did not specifically rule out the possibility that §503 does provide a private cause of action to a handicapped litigant. In fact, the court did state that a showing of specific intention to bestow a private right of action is not necessary to create one. In referring to the legislative history of the Rehabilitation Act, the court said there was no controlling specific exclusion of a private right.

§504 however, has been more successfully advanced as a private cause of action. In fact, §504 has become the keystone for all federal litigation concerning discrimination on the basis of handicap.

The case of *Lloyd v. the Regional Transportation Authority* [64] was a class action brought on behalf of all mobility disabled persons in northeastern Illinois, alleging that the plaintiff class was unable to use public transportation operated by the municipal defendants.

On appeal, the U.S. Court of Appeals for the Seventh

Circuit found that no administrative remedy existed for the plaintiffs and their only remedy was to pursue an action in federal court under §504. The court reasoned that the language in §504 was patterned after, and almost identical to, the Civil Rights Act of 1964. Like the Civil Rights Act, the Rehabilitation Act was viewed by the court in *Lloyd* as granting a private cause of action to the handicapped. §504 became the Civil Rights Act for the handicapped.

This section and its regulations will provide judicial access to determine the scope of the law with regard to discrimination on the basis of handicap. Now that attorneys' fees are provided for by the 1978 Rehabilitation Act Amendments, for causes brought under the civil rights provision of the act, handicapped persons may have more resources with which to challenge discrimination. With a private cause of action, a handicapped individual can be heard in federal court.

Another important case is *Whitaker v. the Board of Higher Education,*[65] which concerned a Brooklyn College professor who was being denied tenure and was being denied a permanent appointment as a Martin Luther King professor of African Studies. The denial was based on the professor's history of alcoholism.

The professor brought an action for a preliminary injunction as an individual who was "handicapped" under §504. The University contended that he did not have a private right of action in federal court, nor had he exhausted his administrative remedies prior to bringing suit. No complaint had been filed with the Office for Civil Rights under the §504 regulations.

However, at that time, the Office for Civil Rights was operating with a backlog which would have rendered the procedure useless for all purposes.

In deciding *Whitaker,* the District Court in the Eastern District of New York indicated that §504 provided a private right of action and in doing so expanded the right somewhat. The court held that where the administrative process would be rendered ineffective, or is simply not provided for in a particular case, an aggrieved individual would not be required to pursue these remedies prior to bringing a private action in federal court.

Since these cases, have their been any amendments to the Rehabilitation Act affecting the private right of action?

Yes, the new Rehabilitation Comprehensive Services, and Developmental Disabilities Amendments of 1978 have added a new area of legal remedies in this area,[66] as well as applying §504 to cover the federal executive branch itself.

This creates an entirely new system of remedies which would include a civil action by the EEOC or U.S. Attorney General, as well as a private right of action under §501 on behalf of the aggrieved party.

§505(B) applies the remedies, procedures, and rights in Title VI of the Civil Rights Act of 1964 to an aggrieved individual under §504. Although as previously mentioned, these remedies were established at the procedural level in the §504 regulations, now the statute as amended guarantees their application to an aggrieved individual.

These provisions do not settle all the questions which have arisen about remedies for discrimination, but they do establish some rights.

What is the Trageser Case and what is its significance?

In *Trageser v. Libbie Rehabilitation Center,*[67] the United States Court of Appeals for the Fourth Circuit considered an employment discrimination claim brought by a woman under §504 against a private nursing home which received substantial income in the form of Medicare, Medicaid, Veterans Administration, and welfare payments. She alleged that because of a visual impairment, she was about to be dismissed before she had resigned.

The Court of Appeals considered her case in light of the 1978 Rehabilitation Amendments. It noted the provision which incorporates the "remedies, procedures, and rights" set forth in Title VI of the Civil Rights Act of 1964 as available to any person aggrieved by any act or failure to act by a recipient or provider covered under §504. Noting the close relationship between §504 and Title VI, the court looked at another provision of Title VI, §604, which prohibits any action by any department or agency with respect to any employment practice of an employer, employment agency, or labor organization except "where a primary objective of the Federal financial assistance is to provide employment." The court concluded that because §604 of Title VI does not provide a judicial remedy for employment discrimination by institutions receiving federal funds unless (1) providing employment is a primary objective of the federal aid, or (2) discrimination in employment necessarily causes discrimination against the primary beneficiaries of the federal aid, the same limitation would be applied to §504. As the court stated:

> A private action under §504 to redress employment discrimination therefore may not be maintained unless a primary objective of the federal financial assistance is to provide employment.

Concluding that the nursing home was not such a program, the court refused to grant relief under §504. It also denied relief under the plaintiff's general civil rights claim.

The holding of the court in *Trageser* could severely limit the application of §504 in employment discrimination matters. The Supreme Court refused to review the case. Advocates for handicapped persons consider the court's reading as too narrow in light of the broad intentions of Congress in enacting both §504 and the 1978 Rehabilitation Amendments. Moreover, there is scant evidence that Congress intended to impose any limitation on the broad reach of the HEW §504 employment regulations. Indeed, there are indications that Congress expressly affirmed the HEW §504 regulations and their application to employment programs of all HEW recipients.

Can a handicapped litigant receive attorneys' fees under the Rehabilitation Act and what significance does that have?

Yes, the new section of the act provides that in any action or proceeding to enforce or charge a violation of Title V of the Rehabilitation Act, a court in its discretion may allow the winning party, other than the U.S., to receive a reasonable attorneys' fee as part of the costs.[68]

This is a most important tool for handicapped litigants to gain access to the courts. Litigation in this new field of law is costly and time consuming, and if it cannot be motivated by the possibility of payment of counsel fees at the successful termination of a case, it is certain that many issues will not be fully litigated. In fact, a substantial percentage of the disabled population cannot afford private counsel. The appellate process would be severely limited without a provision for attorneys' fees.

Moreover, the case of *Johnson v. the Department of Administrative Service*,[69] awarded attorneys' fees prior to enactment of their provisions.

Gary Johnson, a blind employee of the Ohio Civil Service Commission, received low scores on the Civil Service competitive exam and as a result was due to be dismissed from his position. He attacked the test as being discriminatory in that additional time should be given him since he had to use a reader for the test.

While this action was pending, a state law was passed giving to provisional employees who had passed the exam and who had served for at least six months permanent employee status. Mr. Johnson was in this category and had no further need for the suit.

However, Mr. Johnson's attorney was awarded $3,000 in fees under the Civil Rights Attorneys' Fees Awards Act of 1976.[70] The use of this statute in future handicap discrimination cases provides another alternative that will allow the courts to award fees to handicapped litigants. However, the ideal remedy is §505, which authorizes awarding attorneys' fees in all of these cases.

Can aggrieved handicapped employees receive an award of back pay under §503 or §504?

There is no specific provision for back pay awards in any section of the Rehabilitation Act of 1973. This acts as a disincentive for possible litigants who wish to pursue an appeal in court, but who would have little reason for lengthy litigation if there is no possibility of monetary relief.

However, since the application of sections of Title VII the Civil Rights Act of 1964 in the new §505, it can be argued that back pay is now an included remedy within the scope of the Rehabilitation Act, at least for §501.

In *McNutt v. Hills,* the U.S. District Court for the

District of Columbia considered the questions of back pay for federal employees under the provision.[71]

Plaintiff McNutt was a blind employee of Department of Housing and Urban Development (HUD) who was informally placed in 1968 in the Office of Congressional Services for Model Cities. This informal position did not allow his formal evaluation for promotion purposes by superiors. In November of 1969, he was transferred on twenty-four hours' notice to the administrative division. This resulted in his dissatisfaction with his position, and after each request for reassignment he received a GS grade increase. These increases were not on the basis of merit after an evaluation, but only in response to his expressions of dissatisfaction.

Mr. McNutt filed an informal grievance in 1973 as a result of the denial of his promotion through HUD procedures. After this proved fruitless, he filed a formal grievance for retroactive promotion in order to challenge the HUD affirmative action policy. The Secretary of HUD denied back pay stating no authority for such relief existed.

As a result, he filed suit in federal court. In its opinion, the court stated that back pay was not available to redress discrimination against the physically handicapped. Although the basis for the court's denial was that the government had not explicitly waived its sovereign immunity, the court also mentioned a statute called the Federal Back Pay Act, which awards back pay to Federal employees due to unjustified personnel actions. This statute could not apply in the McNutt case because he did not allege that he was demoted, only that on merit he should be placed on a higher level.

At present, through the negotiating process described in §503 regulations, an award of back pay agreed upon between a federal contractor and the Office of Contract Compliance could be possible under what the regulations call a "corrective action." Through these provisions, it would be possible for a claimant to be awarded back pay at the administrative level under §503, although no statutory mandate for an award of back pay in federal court is included in either §503 or §504. Either section could be amended to include specific statutory basis for back pay.

In the previously mentioned case of *Smith v. Fletcher,* back pay was awarded to Ms. Smith. In that situation, the court found Ms. Smith to be a victim of dual discrimination on the basis of both sex and handicap. Because she was a victim of sex discrimination, her remedies under the Civil Rights Act of 1964 allowed her to receive back pay.

Do the 1978 amendments create any new programs in employment?

Yes, two programs will provide direct employment opportunities for handicapped individuals and are designed to remove the traditional barriers to employment.

Title VI of the 1978 amendments, part A, creates a new Community Service Employment Program for Handicapped Individuals.[72] This program authorizes the Secretary of Labor to enter into agreements with public or nonprofit agencies or organizations to provide for employment of qualified handicapped individuals in communities where they reside, or in nearby communities.

These programs are to promote the employment of handicapped individuals while contributing to the general welfare of the community. The projects will provide for the necessary vocational training as well as the payment of reasonable expenses and subsistence allowance during training.

Placement services will also be provided if at the termination of federal financial assistance the eligible people need assistance in locating unsubsidized employment.

The rate of pay for eligible handicapped employees will be the prevailing rate of pay for persons employed in similar occupations by the employer, or the minimum wage. As previously mentioned, no certificate of exemption for the minimum wage under the Fair Labor Standards Act will be allowed with respect to any person employed in a community service project.

Individuals employed under the community service programs will not be considered federal employees for the purposes of this employment. No employer exempt from the operation of workmen's compensation program shall be eligible for assistance under this program unless the employer makes other provisions through insurance.

Of all these provisions, the one which clearly promotes employment for more severely handicapped workers is the provision which disallows any part of wages, allowances, or reimbursement for transportation and attendant care costs, from the income of an employed individual under the program. In exceptional cases, this exclusion may not be permitted, but it applies to state and federal programs.[73]

Also, in order to reach into the private sector subpart B of Title VI creates a new Projects with Industry and Business Opportunities for Handicapped Individuals program.

This program is designed to provide training and employment in a realistic work setting in order to prepare the individual for work in the competitive market. It must provide handicapped individuals with needed supportive services while expanding job opportunities by providing for:

1) the development and modification of jobs to accommodate the special needs of such individuals;

2) the distribution of special aids, appliances, or adapted equipment to such individuals;

3) the establishment of appropriate job placement services; and,

4) the modification of any facilities or equipment of the employer.

The program also includes guarantees that handicapped people will receive the applicable minimum wage under the program. Moreover, equal terms and benefits of employment with other employers are guaranteed, as well as an assurance that handicapped persons should not be unreasonably segregated from the other employees. A right of review by the Commissioner of the Rehabilitation Services Administration with regard to any employment termination is also authorized to determine the reasonableness of such termination. The Commissioner of RSA, in conjunction with the Secretaries of Labor and Commerce, is authorized to contract or grant to handicapped persons for the purpose of establishing or operating small businesses or enterprises.[74]

A new Title VII added to the Rehabilitation Act, and entitled: "Comprehensive Services for Independent Living" includes a provision to provide vocational and or rehabilitation grants and services to any handicapped individual whose ability to function independently in his family or community, or whose ability to engage or continue in employment, is so limited by the severity of that handicap that these services will be necessarily more costly and of longer duration. These services must be necessary to significantly improve his or her ability to engage in employment or to function independently in the family or community.[75]

Has the Fourteenth Amendment to the United States Constitution served as a basis for successful attacks against employment discrimination by handicapped persons?

Yes. *Gurmankin v. Costanzo* [76] was a case brought by a blind graduate of Temple University, certified to teach English in Pennsylvania, who sought a teaching position in the Philadelphia Public Schools system. Initially rejected by school officials on the basis of a policy that blind teachers could teach only blind students and that in no event could a person having what the school system considered a chronic or acute physical defect take the Philadelphia teachers examination (a prerequisite to a job), the plaintiff brought suit on the basis of §504 and of the due process and equal protection clauses of the Fourteenth Amendment to the United States Constitution.

Both the district court and the Court of Appeals were of the view that §504 was not in effect at the time the alleged violations took place (a conclusion open to question). However, both courts went on to hold that the denial to the plaintiff of the opportunity to take the qualifying examination violated her due process rights guaranteed by the Fourteenth Amendment. The violation of her constitutional rights occurred because defendants deprived the plaintiff of the opportunity to present evidence of her qualifications. The relief ordered by the courts was that the defendants must offer her employment with seniority rights and all other rights accruing to a secondary school English teacher commencing employment in September, 1970. In a subsequent ruling, the District Court refused to certify the case as a class action. It did order that the plaintiff be granted "building seniority" at a specific school as if she had been employed there since September, 1970. Additionally, she was to be credited with sick and personal days accruing from September, 1970, and the school district was to make contributions to the pension and retirement fund as if she had been employed there since September, 1970. She had requested the court to order that she be given tenure, but the court declined to do so. Back pay continues to be an issue before the Court of Appeals.

Can the Revenue Sharing Act be used to combat employment discrimination?

Yes. The revenue sharing legislation incorporates §504 into its provisions, and regulations adopted under the act also prohibit employment discrimination. This is an additional basis to use against recipients that receive federal revenue sharing money, such as municipalities.[77]

Are there states with employment antidiscrimination legislation protecting the handicapped?

Yes, many states have such legislation. As illustrations of the type of legislation, consider New York, Illinois, and North Carolina.

The Executive Law of New York prohibits discrimination on the basis of disability by an employer, employment agency, or labor organization in terms, conditions, or privileges of employment.[78] It also forbids discriminatory practices with regard to the terms, rates, renewal extension, or conditions of credit to a disabled individual.[78]

The statute provides that any limitation, specification, or discrimination that is due to disability may be based only upon a bona fide occupational qualification. It means that an employer must limit his specifications to the individual's ability to perform job-related functions. The Executive Law also prohibits preemployment inquiries concerning disability, unless used for the purposes of recruitment to remedy past practices.

An individual aggrieved by an unlawful discriminatory practice may file a written complaint with the State Division of Human Rights, which, within 180 days of the filing, shall determine if it has jurisdiction to decide the case, and if so, whether there is probable cause to believe there has been an unlawful practice.

If the division judges that an unlawful practice has taken place, it shall endeavor to eliminate the practice by conciliation or persuasion. If unsuccessful, the division may apply for a remedial decree in the state supreme court.

The burden on the Human Rights Division would be decreased, as would administrative delay, if there were such a private cause of action, opening a new avenue of judicial review having legal authority superior to mere persuasion and conciliation.

The New York Civil Service Law prohibits civil-service employment discrimination based on handicap.[79] The statute also provides, however, that blind or otherwise handicapped individuals must be certified by the State Education Department to be physically eligible to perform the duties of the position. This certification step causes much administrative delay and twists the concept of bona fide occupational qualification so that it militates against the employee rather than acting as a protective standard. Moreover, the employability of mentally retarded persons must also be certified by the State Education Department.[80]

Another section of the New York Civil Service Law provides for a number of positions to be set aside by the State Civil Service Commission as noncompetitive and reserved for handicapped employees. The section, called "Employment of Handicapped Persons by the State," reads:

> The state civil service commission may determine up to two hundred positions with duties such as can be performed by physically or mentally handicapped persons who are found otherwise qualified to perform satisfactorily the duties of any such position. Upon such determination the said positions shall be classified in the noncompetitive class, and may be filled only by persons who shall have been certified by the employee health service of the department of civil

service as being either physically or mentally handicapped, but capable of performing the duties of such positions. The number of persons appointed pursuant to this section shall not exceed two hundred.[81]

This statute is of limited use in that it authorized only two hundred noncompetitive civil-service positions for the entire state. At best, it could not be looked upon as an affirmative action effort.

Nevertheless, New York does provide a comprehensive system of vocational-rehabilitation services under the State Education Department. Such services are provided to train a handicapped person for a gainful occupation.

The Office of Vocational Rehabilitation is authorized by statute to render such services as evaluation, training, counseling, placement, and to pay attendants, readers, transportation costs, fees, maintenance payments, and a list of other expenses necessary to render a handicapped person employable and to maintain him until he realizes that goal.[82]

The New York Civil Rights Law specifically prohibits employment discrimination due to blindness. It also prohibits employer discrimination against blind employees due to the necessity of having their seeing-eye dogs on business premises.[83]

Another significant state law is that of North Carolina. (See Appendix D.) As in the New York Law, North Carolina guarantees a visually handicapped person the right to be accompanied by a guide dog in places of public accommodation, provided he or she is liable for damage done by the dog on the premises. A 1977 amendment states that no person, firm, or corporation shall refuse to sell, rent, lease, or shall otherwise disallow a visually handicapped person to use any premises for the reason that said person has or will obtain a guide dog for mobility purposes.[84] Moreover, similar to the federal law, North Carolina sets a public policy to encourage and enable handicapped persons to participate fully in the social and economic life of the state and to engage in remunerative employment. This policy can be both criminally and civilly enforced.

Although the right to equal employment is not guaranteed in detail, the statute does require a showing that the individual's particular disability impairs performance of the work involved in order to discriminate on the basis of handicap.

In October of 1975, the Illinois Fair Employment Practice Act [85] was amended to prohibit discrimination in employment based on physical or mental handicap unrelated to ability. The act provides for reasonable accommodations to be made by the employer so the handicapped employee can perform the essential functions of the job. Like federal law, reasonable accommodation must be made unless an employer can show undue hardship on the conduct of the business. The act also forbids discrimination except where a handicap interferes with bona fide occupational qualifications. In doing so, the act states that refusing to select a handicapped individual for a position due to preferences of coworkers, clients, or customers, or due to uninsurability or increased cost of insurance, actual or anticipated, is not a bona fide occupational qualification.

As with the federal regulations, employers have a positive duty to recruit handicapped employees. The Illinois statute forbids employers from using recruitment or referral services which are known to exclude the handicapped.

Preemployment inquiries with regard to physical handicaps are not prohibited, but the information may be used only to question bona fide occupational qualifications. Physical examinations are also allowed but cannot exclude qualified handicapped individuals except as to their relationship with a bona fide occupational qualification.

However, when it can be demonstrated that hiring a handicapped employee is a threat to the health and safety of that individual or his coworkers, a bona fide occupational qualification may be established.[85]

Has there been significant case law in this area at the state level?

Yes, many states have had litigation either in the courts or at the administrative level interpreting the application of their nondiscrimination laws.

An example of the establishment of a bona fide occupational qualification based upon health and safety is

Rhodes v. Longview Fibre Company, heard before the Washington State Human Rights Commission in 1974.[86]

In that case Mr. Rhodes and Mr. Fisher were two persons with epilepsy who had prior work experience. They applied for laborer positions with the Longview Fibre Paper Company. Both were denied positions, due to their epilepsy. The respondent, Longview Fibre, indicated that working on the floor of the mill required constant exposure to dangerous machinery as well as caustic chemicals, making alertness a bona fide occupational qualification.

Longview Fibre claimed that had Mr. Rhodes or Mr. Fisher applied for clerical or office work they would have been considered. However, neither one had prior clerical experience.

The Washington statutes make it an unfair labor practice to refuse to hire any person because of the presence of any sensory, mental, or physical handicap. Another regulation promulgated by the Washington State Department of Labor and Industries stated: "No employee known to have . . . epilepsy or similar ailments which may suddenly incapacitate him shall be permitted to operate a crane, winch, or other power operated hoisting apparatus or power operated vehicle." [87]

Starting employees were required to use motorized vehicles as well as heavy machinery on the floor of the mill. Epilepsy controlled by medication would not necessarily prevent the operation of such apparatus under existing Washington State Law, but the Human Rights Commission felt that even people who took medicine for epilepsy were a threat to the safety of other workers in the mill. Moreover, some people had been known to forget occasionally to take their medication, increasing the chance of seizure.

The Washington State Human Rights Commission denied relief to both Mr. Rhodes and Mr. Fisher. In doing so they stated:

> In reaching our conclusion we have also given consideration to the fact that one employee with a condition controlled by epilepsy has been employed at Respondent's mill since 1966. That fact suggests that such an employee may be safely employed in some

of the job classifications at the mill. But we also note that the employee did experience one seizure soon after his employment. He experienced another seizure in January, 1973. His record of employment thus does not offer an assurance that other employees with a condition of epilepsy would not have seizures at work, nor does his experience guarantee that they would be equally fortunate in not suffering injuries or death or causing injuries to others during a seizure.

Even if four out of five, or nine out of ten employees with epilepsy controlled by medication could work in Respondent's mill without experiencing seizures, we do not believe it would be proper to expose the fifth or tenth employee and his fellow employees to the hazards associated with a loss of consciousness in that mill.

Because the hazards to an employee with such a condition are pervasive in the mill, particularly with respect to all those positions to which a newly hired employee might be assigned, we do not find it necessary to pass upon the Commission's contention that Respondent is under an obligation to negotiate with the collective bargaining representative at the mill to obtain an exception to the seniority rules governing job assignments from the "extra board." Because no violation has been established we also find it unnecessary to pass upon the contention that the refusal to employ Mr. Rhodes or Mr. Fisher was a part of a pattern or practice violating the Washington State Law Against Discrimination.[88]

The rationale in the *Longview Fibre* decision is a dangerous one. The degrees of epilepsy vary with the individual and correspond to the amount of control medication administered. Cases such as *Longview Fibre* could bar even the most well-controlled persons with epilepsy from employment under a safety rationale.[89]

Regardless of the type of disability and how it relates to the individual's ability to perform job-related tasks, employers with stereotypical attitudes concerning the handicapped tend to find that handicapped applicants are per se unqualified. Two Wisconsin cases concerning totally different disabilities reflect this stereotyped rationale.

In *Bucyrus-Erie v. the Department of Industry, Labor, and Human Relations*,[90] Thomas Parks was a qualified applicant for a position as a welder. However, upon a medical examination by the employer's physician he was found to have some congenital back defects and was rejected. Mr. Parks did not complain of any back problem at that time.

The employer's medical examiner was not an orthopedic specialist; subsequent examinations by orthopedic specialists indicated only a possible back condition. Furthermore, the specialists felt Mr. Parks was qualified for the position.

The Wisconsin Court agreed, finding that the burden is on the employer to prove that the potential employee cannot safely and efficiently perform the job, and the failure to do so leaves the opposing presumption intact.

Another Wisconsin case, *Chrysler Outboard Corp. v. Department of Industry, Labor and Human Relations*,[91] was based on the same rationale. Following the finding of the medical examiner that the applicant, who had leukemia, would be frequently absent and would cause group insurance rates to be raised, the employer denied employment, without considering job-related abilities. The court found this to be unlawful discrimination.

Two New York cases, again concerning different disabilities, were decided on this issue. In the case of *Parolisi v. Board of Examiners*,[92] Ms. Parolisi was a substitute teacher in the New York City school system. Legislation required all substitute teachers to be examined as to their health and fitness by the Board of Examiners prior to licensing. She was denied a substitute teacher's license due to being 76 percent overweight at 221 pounds. No test was given as to her ability to perform on the job, and her prior teaching record was excellent.

The court found this to violate her constitutional due process rights in that the denial was not based on an objective determination that she was unable to perform on the job.

In this second New York case, the issue of ability to do the job actually arose only after the individual became disabled. In *Bevan v. NYS Teachers Retirement Board*,[93] the plaintiff had been a public-school teacher who had been tenured and teaching for eight years. In September of 1970, Mr. Bevan experienced visual difficulty and took an extended sick leave for two years. During that time he became totally blind. However, he was rehabilitated and examined by the medical supervisor of his former school district and found qualified.

Before returning to his position, he was informed by the superintendant of schools that he was going to be placed on a disability retirement due to his blindness. Nevertheless, he reported for work as planned in September of 1972 and was told his position no longer existed. A second medical examination concurred that he should not return to his duties. Mr. Bevan was afforded no opportunity to rebut this decision at a hearing, and sued in the New York State Supreme Court.

In rendering its decision that Mr. Bevan was denied due process, and in ordering that he be reinstated with full back pay, the court noted:

> The question to be decided at the hearing will not be whether plaintiff is blind, but whether he is physically incapacitated from performing his duties as a teacher. The articles in the appendices to the plaintiff's memorandum of law reveal that there are numerous teachers throughout the United States who are both successful and competent notwithstanding their lack of sight. This court will not rule, as the defendants implicitly urge, that blindness per se disqualifies one to teach. Indeed, such a ruling would be directly contrary to the express policy of the Legislature as expressed in Section 3004 of the Education Law.

> Section 3004, insofar as it pertains to blindness, provides that no regulation established by the Commissioner or by any school district shall disqualify any person, otherwise qualified, from qualifying for a position as a teacher solely by reason of his or her blindness or physical handicap, provided such physical handicap does not interfere with such person's ability to perform teaching duties. While the appli-

cability and construction of this section is not at this time before this court, it might be useful to make some comments thereon. Whether directly applicable or not, the section expresses a strong legislative policy that a teacher shall not be denied a position because of blindness. It is also apparent from a reading of the section and its predecessor that the words "provided such physical handicap does not interfere with such person's ability to perform teaching duties" pertain only to a physical handicap other than blindness. In other words, it is premised in the statute itself that blindness per se will not interfere with a person's ability to perform teaching duties.

It is clear that many state cases have turned on combating employers' stereotypical attitudes that handicapped employees or applicants are per se unqualified.

Do state workers' compensation laws affect handicapped employment?

State workers' compensation laws have long had an effect on employment of the handicapped.

In the past, employers were reluctant to hire handicapped individuals due to the prospect of increased workers' compensation costs. An already handicapped employee was deemed by the employer more likely to be injured on the job. Once injured, the second injury would render him far more disabled, and would be more expensive to the employer than a singly injured nondisabled employee.

This successive-injury problem raised the issue of who would bear the cost. Under a full-responsibility rule, a handicapped employee who had one leg initially and lost the other leg on the job would receive compensation from the employer for his total disability. Under this rule, employers simply did not want to be liable and would not hire the handicapped individual. Moreover, in states which had full-responsibility statutes, employers would have a financial incentive to discharge presently employed handicapped workers.

However, the establishment of "second injury funds" has alleviated some of their problems. Here the state may step in to cover said injuries, protecting employers from some claims and providing more complete compensation for workers.[94]

Are tax incentives available to encourage employers to hire handicapped people?

Yes. One example is the federal tax provision that provides a tax credit for hiring new handicapped employees who have gone through vocational rehabilitation. Employers should check state and federal tax provisions for other incentives, as well as the limits of the one mentioned.[95]

NOTES

1. 3 U.S. Code, Cong. & Admin. News 3214 (1967).
2. Current estimates from the Health Interview Survey, U.S. Census, 1970.
3. Statistical Abstract of the United States, U.S. Department of Commerce, Bureau of the Census, 96 Ed. Table 459, p. 288.
4. *Ibid*. Table 487, p. 305.
5. *Ibid*. Table 458, p. 288, Table 487, p. 305.
6. *Ibid*. Table 652, p. 349.
7. *Ibid*. Table 473, p. 295.
8. *Ibid*. Table 459, p. 288; Table 487, p. 305.
9. *Ibid*. Table 473, p. 295.
10. President's Committee on Employment of the Handicapped, Bureau of the Census, *One in Eleven Handicapped Adults in America*, 1970.
11. New York City Department of City Planning, Annual Report, Educ. Sec. 1973.
12. 2 U.S. Code, Cong. & Admin. News 2076, 2092 (1973).
13. 29 U.S.C.A. §794 (1975), with amended statute at 29 U.S.C.A. §794 (Supp. 1979).
14. 42 *Fed. Reg.* 22,676 (May 4, 1977).
15. 20 U.S.C.A. §107 (1974, as amended, Supp. 1979).
16. 321 F. Supp. 534 (N.D. Cal. 1971).
17. 5 U.S.C.A. §3102 (1974, as amended Supp. 1979).
18. *Ibid*.
19. 29 U.S.C.A. §214(c) (Supp. 1979).
20. 29 C.F.R. (§525).
21. For a discussion of the minimum wage requirements of mentally retarded workers and examples of abuses, *see*

Souder v. Brennan, 367 F. Supp. 808 (D.D.C. 1971); 44 *Fed. Reg.* 38,910 (July 3, 1979).

22. 29 U.S.C.A. §795(b)(2) (Supp. 1979).
23. The original statute, enacted in 1948, was at 5 U.S.C. §633(2)(9) (1948). The present version is at 5 U.S.C.A. §7153 (1967).
24. 5 C.F.R. §713.401 which, because of the EEOC reorganization, is now found at 5 C.F.R. §720.901.
25. 559 F.2d 1014 (5th Cir. 1977).
26. 563 F.2d 1013 (Ct. Cl. 1977).
27. 44 *Fed. Reg.* 44,812 (July 31, 1979); *see also* proposed regulations implementing the Executive Order, 44 *Fed. Reg.* 37,232 (June 26, 1979) related also are interim regulation at 44 *Fed. Reg.* 20,699 (April 6, 1979), with reference to recent legislative changes.
28. 29 U.S.C.A. §791 (1975).
29. 29 U.S.C.A. §794(a)(1) (Supp. 1979).
30. *Ibid. Coleman v. Darden,* 595 F.2d 533 (10th Cir. 1979), *petition for certiorari filed* (U.S. August 10, 1979), No. 79–224; the old Civil Service procedural regulations were at 5 C.F.R. §713.708–.710 and §713.214(a), but will now be codified at 29 C.F.R. §1613.201 *et seq.*, with minor changes, see 43 *Fed. Reg.* 60,900 (Dec. 29, 1978) and 44 *Fed. Reg.* 37,888 (June 29, 1979); see also *McNutt v. Hills,* 426 F. 990 (D.D.C. 1977), for a case brought under the Administrative Procedure Act.
31. 29 U.S.C.A. §794(a).
32. §.701–§.707, *supra,* note 31; for a general discussion of the federal government's policy toward employment of handicapped individuals, see Linn, *Uncle Sam Doesn't Want You: Entering the Federal Stronghold of Employment Discrimination against Handicapped Individuals,* 27 DePaul Law Review 1047 (1978).
33. 29 U.S.C.A. §794 (Sup. 1979).
34. 29 U.S.C.A. §793 (Supp. 1979); 41 C.F.R. §60–741.5.
35. 41 C.F.R. §60–741.5(c).
36. §741.6(g), (h).
37. §741.6(g)(6).
38. §741.6 generally.
39. §741.6(j).
40. §741.6(e).
41. §741.6(c)(1).
42. §741.6(c)(3).
43. §741.6(c)(2).
44. 29 U.S.C.A. §794(a) (Supp. 1979); the private right of action under §503 is pending in the consolidated cases of

Rogers v. Frito-Lay, Inc., 433 F. Supp. 200 (N.D. Tex. 1977), and *Moon v. Roadway Express, Inc.*, 15 E.P.D. §7903 (N.D. Ga. 1977), *appeal docketed* No. 77–2443 (5th Cir., July 13, 1977) for a case recognizing a private right to sue under §503, see *Hart v. County of Alameda*, No. C-79-0091WH0, (N.D. Cal. Sept. 6, 1979).

45. Newsletter for Industry, Affirmative Action for Handicapped People, Vol. 2, no. 9, March, 1978, p. 3.

46. 45 C.F.R. part 84.

47. Executive Order 11914, 41 *Fed. Reg.* 17,871 (April 28, 1976).

48. For example, see the Department of Transportation regulations at 49 C.F.R. §27.31 *et seq.*

49. 45 C.F.R. §84.3(k).

50. 45 C.F.R. §84.12.

51. 42 *Fed. Reg.* 22,688 (May 4, 1977).

52. 41 C.F.R. §60–741.6(d).

53. 45 C.F.R. §84.11.

54. 45 C.F.R. §84.13(a).

55. 45 C.F.R. §84.13(b).

56. 45 C.F.R. §84.14.

57. 20 U.S.C.A. §1406 (1978).

58. 38 U.S.C.A. §2014 (1979).

59. 38 U.S.C.A. §2012 (1979), as amended by Pub. L. 95–520, 92 Stat. 1820 (October 26, 1978).

60. 41 C.F.R. §60–250 *et seq.*

61. *Personnel Administrator of Massachusetts v. Feeney*, 99 S. Ct. 2282 (1979).

62. *Supra*, note 44.

63. 428 F. Supp. 809 (E.D. Pa. 1977).

64. 548 F.2d 1277 (7th Cir. 1977).

65. 461 F. Supp. 99 (E.D. N.Y. 1978).

66. 29 U.S.C.A. §794(a) (Supp. 1979).

67. 590 F.2d 87 (4th Cir. 1978), *cert. den.* 442 U.S. —— (1979); additionally see the Hart case, *supra* note 44 for its refusal to follow the Fourth Circuit, Paula Wiseman has examined legislative history in an unpublished memorandum for the National Center for Law and the Handicapped.

68. 29 U.S.C.A. §794(a) (Supp. 1979).

69. Civ. No. 1–77–348 (S.D. Oh., Jan. 5, 1978).

70. 42 U.S.C.A. §1988 (Supp. 1979).

71. *Supra*, note 30.

72. 29 U.S.C.A. §795 (Supp. 1979).

73. 29 U.S.C.A. §795(b) (Supp. 1979).

74. 29 U.S.C.A. §795(g)-(h) (Supp. 1979).

75. 29 U.S.C.A. §796 (Supp. 1979).
76. 411 F. Supp. 982 (E.D. Pa. 1976), aff'd. 556 F.2d 184 (3d Cir. 1977); of whether opinions and orders are in No. 74–2980 (E.D. Pa.), with appeals still underway.
77. 31 U.S.C.A. §1242(g) (Supp. 1979); 31 C.F.R. §51.53; readers should be alert to imminent changes in these regulations.
78. N.Y. Exec. Law 296 (McKinney 1977).
79. N.Y. Civil Service Law 55 (McKinney 1977).
80. Ibid. at 55A.
81. Ibid. at 55B.
82. N.Y. Educ. Law 1002 (McKinney 1977).
83. N.Y. Civil Rights Law (McKinney 1977).
84. N.C. Gen. Stat. §168–7; this law received judicial interpretation in Burgess v. Jos. Schlitz Brewing Co., 18 FEP 1518 (January 16, 1979).
85. Ill. Rev. Stat., Ch. 48, §§851, 853, 854.
86. Washington State Human Rights Comm., V. 27–74 (1974).
87. W.A.C. 296.46 44615(2).
88. Supra note 86.
89. See also Silverstein v. Sisters of Charity, 559 P.2d 716 (Colo. Ct. of Appeals 1976).
90. 13 E.P.D. §11,580 (Wis. Cir. Ct. 1977), aff'd. 20 E.P.D. §30,105 (June 29, 1979, Sup. Ct. of Wis.)
91. 13 E.P.D. §11,526 (Wis. Cir. Ct. 1976).
92. Misc. 2d 546, 285 N.Y.S. 2d 936 (1967).
93. 74 Misc. 2d 446, 345 N.Y.S. 2d 921 (1973).
94. See generally Larsen, WORKMEN'S COMPENSATION LAW (1976).
95. 26 U.S.C.A. §51 (Supp. 1979).

VIII

The Right to Live in the World

The title of this chapter is borrowed from a famous article by Jacobus ten Broek. His description of the social situation of handicapped persons and the impediments to their achievement of equality is an apt summary of the opposition they may encounter in securing their rights:

> The actual physical limitations resulting from the disability more often than not play little role in determining whether the physically disabled are allowed to move about and be in public places. Rather, that judgment for the most part results from a variety of considerations related to public attitudes, attitudes which not infrequently are quite erroneous and misconceived. These include public imaginings about what the inherent physical limitations must be; public solicitude about the safety to be achieved by keeping the disabled out of harm's way; public feelings of protective care and custodial security; public doubts about why the disabled should want to be abroad anyway; and public aversion to the sight of them and the conspicuous reminder of their plight.

Professor ten Broek's assessment of the consequences of that situation is an appropriate way to conclude this book: "For our purposes, there is no reason to judge these attitudes as to whether they do credit or discredit to the human head and heart. Our concern is with their existence and their consequences."

The purpose of this final chapter is to describe briefly

some of the remedies that exist under three of the major federal statutes (§504, the Architectural Barriers Act, and the Revenue Sharing Act; the remedies under §501 and §503 have been considered in Chapter VII) and to discuss some issues that may be expected to arise as handicapped persons seek to overcome the consequences of the attitudes described by Professor ten Broek.[1]

Are there administrative procedures by which complaints under §504 may be made?

Yes. In the HEW §504 regulations, HEW has utilized the existing procedural regulations for Title VI complaints and adopted them for implementation of §504. HEW has stated that it expects to have a consolidated procedural regulation applicable to all of the civil rights statutes and executive orders administered by the department in the future.

The Title VI procedural regulations emphasize cooperation and assistance by the department in obtaining compliance and in bringing about voluntary compliance. A person who believes himself or any specific class of individuals to be subjected to discrimination by an HEW recipient may by himself or by a representative file a complaint with HEW, most likely with the Office for Civil Rights. The Title VI regulations state that a complaint must be filed not later than 180 days from the date of the alleged discrimination unless the time for filing is extended by the responsible HEW official or his designee. The complaint should trigger an investigation resulting in either an attempt to resolve the matter informally or a decision that the investigation does not warrant action (in which case the complainant and recipient are so notified.) The regulation prohibits recipients from intimidating, threatening, coercing, or discriminating against any individual as an attempt to interfere with rights under the act or because an individual has made a complaint, or has testified, assisted, or participated in an investigation, proceeding, or hearing. The identity of complainants is to be kept confidential except to the extent necessary to carry out enforcement of the regulations.

Among the procedures available to enforce the law are referral of the case to the Justice Department for prosecution, an action under state or local laws, or termination or refusal to grant or to continue federal financial assistance. Rights and procedures are set up for hearings by the Department, as well as requirements for the making of decisions and review of those decisions. The capacity of the Office for Civil Rights to handle all the complaints has raised questions about the adequacy of those procedures, and questions remain about the exhaustion of these remedies as a prerequisite to filing lawsuits. In recent cases, HEW has taken the position that exhaustion is not required. Some courts indicate exhaustion of administrative remedies is necessary, but this view is being actively questioned. The 1978 Rehabilitation Act amendments make explicit the application of the remedies, procedures, and rights of Title VI of the Civil Rights Act of 1964 to §504 cases, as well as allowing courts to award attorneys' fees to prevailing parties.[2]

Where a complaint involves a recipient receiving assistance from another department or agency, two alternatives are available. If the department has a procedural mechanism established, that remedy may be used. If not, direct litigation is a second choice (and may be an alternative even where administration procedures are established).

Does the Architectural and Transportation Barriers Compliance Board have procedures for compliance with the Architectural Barriers Act?

Yes. The Compliance Board has procedures to enforce the act. Complaints may be submitted to the board. Complaints are to be served on relevant agencies and interested parties. The regulations promise confidentiality to complaining parties, unless they request otherwise. A person filing a complaint does not automatically become a "party" to the proceeding, but may petition for party status. If there appears to be a violation or a threatened violation, the executive director must issue a citation to the offending party if informal means of resolution have failed. The decision whether or not to issue a citation must be made within sixty days of receipt of the complaint. The citation will set forth, among other information, the relief which the executive director will request the board to grant. A hearing may be set by the board

or requested by the agency, at which an administrative
law judge will preside.

Procedures are set forth for the conduct of the hearing,
eventually leading to possible judicial review. The board
also has a provision for "Provisional Expedited Relief"
(PER) in cases where "immediate and irreparable
harm" from noncompliance is threatened.[3]

What procedures are available to challenge discrimination in revenue sharing programs?

This provision is relatively new and, apparently, has
not been used very much. Administrative complaints may
be filed with the Director of the Office of Revenue Sharing, and an investigation can be made. The director must
make a finding within ninety days of the filing of the complaint. Upon written request of the complaining party,
the director must advise complainants of the status of the
investigation or review of the administrative complaint.
Within ten days after the director's finding, the director
must notify the complainant or the complainant's counsel,
if any, of the nature of the finding. A recipient is deemed
to have exhausted administrative remedies upon the expiration of ninety days from the date the administrative
complaint was filed with the director or when a determination has been made or failure to make a determination occurs, either by the director or with one of the
other agencies with which the director has an agreement
to investigate noncompliance.[4]

Will the matter of public housing for handicapped persons be an important issue in the future?

Probably. Federal housing policies toward handicapped
persons has been under strong criticism for sometime. At
least three questions are raised. First, is the overall federal
commitment and the corresponding local response to public housing for handicapped persons sufficient? Second,
are appropriately designed housing units for handicapped
persons available in sufficient numbers and integrated
adequately in the overall housing program to meet the
needs and preferences of handicapped persons? Third,
are there adequate support services in these housing programs for handicapped persons? With the passage of

legislation in the last several years to deal with housing for handicapped persons and the stated commitment by federal housing officials to infuse new directions and energy into the programs, handicapped persons may be expected to make this an increasingly important issue. Of related importance is recent federal legislation authorizing grants for independent living for severely handicapped people.[5]

Will rehabilitation programs also be a focus for handicapped persons to assert rights?

Probably. The Rehabilitation Act of 1973 includes important provisions for client participation, among them the individual written rehabilitation program. The program is to be developed jointly by vocational rehabilitation personnel and a handicapped client (or, in appropriate cases, by a handicapped person's parents or guardian). Among the requirements for the plan are: a statement of long-range rehabilitation goals for the individual and intermediate rehabilitation objectives related to the attainment of those goals; a statement of the specific vocational rehabilitation services to be provided; the projected date for starting and the anticipated duration of each such service; objective criteria and an evaluation procedure and schedule for determining achievement of goals and objectives; and, when appropriate, a detailed explanation of another client assistance project. The written program must set forth terms and conditions, rights and remedies in the vocational rehabilitation arrangement. Likewise a determination of ineligibility must set forth rights and remedies. A provision for annual review is also required by the act. Important rights to appeal before the state VR director and high HEW officials were included in the 1978 amendments.[6]

Will state and local laws guaranteeing rights to handicapped persons play an important part in the effort to secure legal equality for handicapped persons?

Probably. While a great deal of the early legal activity in the handicapped rights area was at the federal level, many state and local provisions hold potential as bases for reform. Among these laws are both specific laws enacted to meet problems of handicapped persons, and general, broader civil rights laws, covering several protected groups, which have been amended to include handicapped persons.[7]

What is the function of the Protection and Advocacy Systems for developmentally disabled persons?

In 1975, Congress enacted the Developmentally Disabled Assistance and Bill of Rights Act. Among the major purposes of the law are assistance to states in the development of a comprehensive plan to provide services to developmentally disabled persons and to assure the rights and dignity of persons served. The term "developmentally disabled" under this legislation included mental retardation, cerebral palsy, epilepsy, autism, or any other closely related condition which results in an impairment similar to that of mental retardation or which requires treatment or services required by mentally retarded persons. A disability attributable to dyslexia was also included if it results from one of the listed conditions.

In the 1978 amendments to the Rehabilitation Act, the term "developmental disability" was amended to mean a severe, chronic disability of a person which:

1. is attributable to a mental or physical impairment or combination of mental and physical impairments;
2. is manifested before the person attains age 22;
3. is likely to continue indefinitely;
4. results in substantial functional limitations in three or more of the following areas of major life activity: (a) Self-care, (b) Receptive and expressive language, (c) Learning, (d) Mobility, (e) Self-direction, (f) Capacity for independent living, and (g) Economic sufficiency; and
5. reflects the person's need for a combination and sequence of special, interdisciplinary, or generic care, treatment, or other services which are of lifelong or extended duration and are individually planned and coordinated.

There was controversy about this definition of developmentally disabled persons and the 1978 amendments direct the Secretary to complete a special report concerning the impact of the definition.

The Protection and Advocacy Systems (called P & A Systems) are independent agencies which the act mandates for the protection of the legal rights of these groups of handicapped persons. The systems have a wide range of advocacy powers including the right to bring suits. In implementation of rights, they may represent, educate, and investigate, as well as conduct other activities.[8]

NOTES

1. ten Broek, *The Right to Live in the World: The Disabled in the Law of Torts*, 54 Calif. L. Rev. 841, 842 (1966).
2. The Title VI procedural regulations are appended to the May 4, 1977 HEW §504 regulations at 42 *Fed. Reg.* 22,695–22,702, and are found at 45 C.F.R. (Part 80); compare *Lloyd v. Regional Transportation Authority*, 548 F.2d 1277 (7th Cir. 1977), *Doe v. New York University*, 442 F. Supp. 522 (S.D.N.Y. 1978), and *Crawford v. University of North Carolina*, 440 F. Supp. 1047 (M.D.N.C. 1977); Rehabilitation, Comp. Servc., and D.D. Amend. of 1978, Pub. L. 95–602, §120, 29 U.S.C.A. §794(a) (Supp. 1979); the HEW position was taken in its "Memorandum of the United States as Amicus Curiae . . ." in *Whitaker v. City University of New York*, 75C iv 2258 (JM) (E.D.N.Y. 1978) a recent decision on exhaustion is *NAACP v. Wilmington*, 599 F.2d 1247 (3rd Cir. 1979).
3. The ATBCB practice and procedures regulations are at 36 C.F.R. Part 1150 and were published at 41 Fed. Reg. 55,442–55,451 (December 20, 1976).
4. Interim regulations for revenue sharing were published at 42 *Fed. Reg.* 18,362 (April 6, 1977), 31 C.F.R. (Part 51), *et seq.* Final regulations are imminent.
5. Two discussions of the housing and community development legislation and issues are E. Clarke Ross, *The Department of Housing and Urban Development: Influence and Impact on Supporting Alternative Community Based Living Arrangements for Persons with Disabilities* (1976) and Marie McGuire Thompson, *Housing and Handicapped People* (1976); see also the Housing and Community Development Act of 1977, Pub. L. 95–128, 91 Stat. 1111 (October 12, 1977), 29 U.S.C.A. §796 (Supp. 1979).

6. The Act is at 29 U.S.C.A. §§701–794 (1975 and Supp. 1979).

7. See Chapter 1, note 5 and examples of state statutes given there. Additionally, cities and counties may have pertinent local legislation.

8. 42 U.S.C.A. §6000 *et seq.*, with HEW regulations at 42 *Fed. Reg.* 5273 (January 27, 1977).

Conclusion

The decade since the passage of the Architectural Barrier Act in 1968 has shown much national progress in removing employment obstacles of the handicapped.

Now there is some public awareness of the situation of handicapped people. There is new federal and state legislation. As with every civil-rights movement, the next job is to enhance public awareness by enforcing the legislation both locally and nationally in order to promote the reality of employment for qualified handicapped people. Additional stereotypes about handicapped people must be broken down as employers learn to treat each applicant as an individual with capacities and talents.

Compliance must be the next step. The Rehabilitation Act has been strengthened with the comprehensive amendments of 1978 so that attorneys' fees and back pay will promote litigation. The regulations must be strengthened to provide for these incentives as well. Administrative solutions must be more effective and responsive to the needs of the disabled complainant.

Government agencies must be regulated more strictly by Congress to provide for compliance with their affirmative action requirements under §501.

Each state that has not already done so should adopt antidiscrimination legislation for the handicapped. All states should adopt strict compliance procedures.

If as a nation we are to provide equal opportunity in employment to a long-ignored minority, legislation is just the beginning. Compliance with that legislation is the next long, tedious, and necessary step. Placing the disabled in the mainstream of American life is the ultimate goal.

APPENDIX A

Model White Cane Law

§ 1—It is the policy of this State to encourage and enable the blind, the visually handicapped, and the otherwise physically disabled to participate fully in the social and economic life of the State and to engage in remunerative employment.

§ 2—(a) The blind, the visually handicapped, and the otherwise physically disabled have the same right as the able-bodied to the full and free use of the streets, highways, sidewalks, public buildings, public facilities, and other public places. (b) The blind, the visually handicapped, and the otherwise physically disabled are entitled to full and equal accommodations, advantages, facilities, and privileges of all common carriers, airplanes, motor vehicles, railroad trains, motor buses, streetcars, boats or any other public conveyances or modes of transportation, hotels, lodging places, places of public accommodation, amusement or resort, and other places to which the general public is invited, subject only to the conditions and limitations established by law and applicable alike to all persons. (c) Every totally or partially blind person shall have the right to be accompanied by a guide dog, especially trained for the purpose, in any of the places listed in section 2(b) without being required to pay an extra charge for the guide dog; provided that he shall be liable for any damage done to the premises or facilities by such dog.

§ 3—The driver of a vehicle approaching a totally or partially blind pedestrian who is carrying a cane predominately white or metallic in color (with or without a red tip) or using a guide dog shall take all necessary precautions to avoid injury to such blind pedestrian, and any driver who fails to take such precautions shall be liable in damages for any injury caused such pedestrian; provided that a totally or partially blind pedestrian not carrying such a cane or using a guide dog in any of the places, accommodations or conveyances listed in section 2, shall have all of the rights and privileges conferred by law upon other persons, and the failure of a totally or partially blind pedestrian to carry such a cane or to use a guide dog in any such places, accommodations or conveyances shall not be held to constitute nor be evidence of contributory negligence.

§ 4—Any person or persons, firm or corporation, or the agent of any person or persons, firm or corporation who denies or interferes with admittance to or enjoyment of the public facilities enumerated in section 2 or otherwise interferes with the rights of a totally or partially blind or otherwise disabled person under section 2 shall be guilty of a misdemeanor.

§ 5—Each year, the Governor shall take suitable public notice of October 15 as White Cane Safety Day. He shall issue a proclamation in which:

(a) he comments upon the significance of the white cane;

(b) he calls upon the citizens of the State to observe the provisions of the White Cane Law and to take precautions necessary to the safety of the disabled;

(c) he reminds the citizens of the State of the policies with respect to the disabled herein declared and urges the citizens to cooperate in giving effect to them;

(d) he emphasizes the need of the citizens to be aware of the presence of disabled persons in the community and to keep safe and functional for the disabled the streets, highways, sidewalks, walkways, public buildings, public facilities, other public places, places of public accommodation, amusement and resort, and other places to which the public is invited, and to offer assistance to disabled persons upon appropriate occasions.

§ 6—It is the policy of this State that the blind, the visually handicapped, and the otherwise physically disabled shall be employed in the State Service, the service of the political subdivisions of the State, in the public schools, and in all other employment supported in whole or in part by public funds on the same terms and conditions as the able-bodied, unless it is shown that the particular disability prevents the performance of the work involved.

APPENDIX B

Michigan Handicappers' Civil Rights Act

Act No. 220
Public Acts of 1976
Approved by Governor
July 28, 1976

STATE OF MICHIGAN
78TH LEGISLATURE
REGULAR SESSION OF 1976

Introduced by Senators Otterbacher, Corbin, Nelson, Cartwright, Holmes and Kildee

ENROLLED SENATE BILL No. 749

AN ACT to define the civil rights of individuals who have handicaps; and to prohibit discriminatory practices, policies, and customs in the exercise of those rights.

The People of the State of Michigan enact:

ARTICLE 1

Sec. 101. This act shall be known and may be cited as the "Michigan handicappers' civil rights act."

Sec. 102. The opportunity to obtain employment, housing and other real estate and full and equal utilization of public accommodations, public services, and educational facilities without discrimination because of a handicap is guaranteed by this act and is a civil right.

Sec. 103. As used in this act:

(a) "Commission" means the civil rights commission established by section 29 of article 5 of the state constitution of 1963.

(b) "Handicap" means a determinable physical or mental characteristic of an individual or the history of the characteristic which may result from disease, injury, congenital condition of birth, or functional disorder which characteristic:

(i) for purposes of article 2, is unrelated to the individual's ability to perform the duties of a particular job or position, or is unrelated to the individual's qualifications for employment or promotion.

(ii) for purposes of article 3, is unrelated to the individual's ability to utilize and benefit from a place of public accommodation or public service.

(iii) for purposes of article 4, is unrelated to the individual's ability to utilize and benefit from educational opportunities, programs, and facilities at an educational institution.

(iv) for purposes of article 5, is unrelated to the individual's ability to acquire, rent, or maintain property.

(c) "Handicapper" means an indvidual who has a handicap.

(d) "Mental characteristic" is limited to mental retardation which is significantly subaverage general intellectual functioning, and for purposes of article 5 only to a determinable mental condition of an individual or a history of such condition which may result from disease, accident, condition of birth, or functional disorder which constitutes a mental limitation which is unrelated to an individual's ability to acquire, rent, or maintain property.

(e) "Person" includes an individual, agent, association, corporation, joint apprenticeship committee, joint-stock company, labor union, legal representative, mutual company, partnership, receiver, trust, trustee in bankruptcy, unincorporated organization, the state, or any other legal or commercial entity or governmental entity or agency.

ARTICLE 2

Sec. 201. As used in this article:

(a) "Employee" does not include an individual employed in domestic service of any person.

(b) "Employer" means a person who has 4 or more employees or a person who as contractor or subcontractor is furnishing material or performing work for the state or a governmental entity or agency of the state and includes an agent of such a person.

(c) "Employment agency" means a person regularly undertaking with or without compensation to procure employees for an employer or to procure for employees opportunities to work for an employer and includes an agent of such a person.

(d) "Labor organization" includes:

(i) An organization of any kind, an agency or employee representation committee, group, association, or plan in which employees participate and which exists for the purpose, in whole or in part, of dealing with employers concerning grievances, labor disputes, wages, rates of pay, hours, or other terms or conditions of employment.

(ii) A conference, general committee, joint or system board, or joint council which is subordinate to a national or international labor organization.

(iii) An agent of a labor organization.

Sec. 202.(1) An employer shall not:

(a) Fail or refuse to hire, recruit, or promote an individual because of a handicap that is unrelated to the individual's ability to perform the duties of a particular job or position.

(b) Discharge or otherwise discriminate against an individual with respect to compensation or the terms, conditions, or privileges of employment, because of a handicap that is unrelated to the individual's ability to perform the duties of a particular job or position.

(c) Limit, segregate, or classify an employee or applicant for employment in a way which deprives or tends to deprive an individual of employment opportunities or otherwise adversely affects the status of an employee because of a handicap that is unrelated to the individual's ability to perform the duties of a particular job or position.

(d) Fail or refuse to hire, recruit, or promote an individual on the basis of physical or mental examinations that are not directly related to the requirements of the specific job.

(e) Discharge or take other discriminatory action against an individual on the basis of physical or mental examinations that are not directly related to the requirements of the specific job.

(f) Fail or refuse to hire, recruit, or promote an individual when adaptive devices or aids may be utilized thereby enabling that individual to perform the specific requirements of the job.

(g) Discharge or take other discriminatory action against an individual when adaptive devices or aids may be utilized thereby enabling that individual to perform the specific requirements of the job.

(2) This section shall not apply to the employment of an individual by his parent, spouse, or child.

Sec. 203. An employment agency shall not fail or refuse to refer for employment, or otherwise discriminate against an individual because of a handicap or classify or refer for employment an individual on the basis of a handicap that is unrelated to the individual's ability to perform the duties of a particular job or position.

Sec. 204. A labor organization shall not:

(a) Exclude or expel from membership, or otherwise discriminate against a member or applicant for membership because of a handicap that is unrelated to the individual's ability to perform the duties of a particular job or position which entitles him to membership.

(b) Limit, segregate, or classify membership, or applicants for membership, or classify or fail or refuse to refer for employment an individual in a way which would deprive or tend to deprive an individual of employment opportunities, or which would limit employment opportunities or otherwise adversely affect the status of an employee or of an applicant for employment, because of a handicap that is unrelated to the individual's ability to perform the duties of a particular job or position.

(c) Cause or attempt to cause an employer to violate this article.

Sec. 205. An employer, labor organization, or joint labor management committee controlling apprenticeship, on the job, or other training or retraining programs shall not discriminate against an individual because of a handicap in admission to, or employment or continuation in, a program established to provide apprenticeship or other training.

Sec. 206. (1) An employer, labor organization, or employment agency shall not print or publish or cause to be printed or published a notice or advertisement relating to employment by the employer or membership in or a classification or referral for employment by the labor organization, or relating to a classification or referral for employment by the employment agency, indicating a preference, limitation, specification, or discrimination, based on a handicap that is unrelated to the individual's ability to perform the duties of a particular job or position.

(2) Except as permitted by applicable federal law, an employer or employment agency shall not:

(a) Make or use a written or oral inquiry or form of application that elicits or attempts to elicit information concerning the handicap of a prospective employee for reasons contrary to the provisions or purposes of this act.

(b) Make or keep a record of information or disclose information concerning the handicap of a prospective employee for reasons contrary to the provisions or purposes of this act.

(c) Make or use a written or oral inquiry or form of application that expresses a preference, limitation, or specification based on the handicap of a prospective employee for reasons contrary to the provisions or purposes of this act.

Sec. 207. Nothing in this article shall be interpreted to exempt a person from the obligation to accommodate an employee or applicant with a handicap for employment unless the person demonstrates that the accommodation would impose an undue hardship in the conduct of the business.

Sec. 208. A person subject to this article may adopt and carry out a plan to eliminate present effects of past discriminatory practices or assure equal opportunity with respect to individuals who have handicaps if the plan has been filed with the commission under rules of the commission and the commission has not disapproved the plan.

ARTICLE 3

Sec. 301. As used in this article:

(a) "Place of public accommodation" means a business, educational institution, refreshment, entertainment, recreation, or transportation facility of any kind, whether licensed or not, whose goods, services, facilities, privileges, advantages, or accommodations are extended, offered, sold, or otherwise made available to the public.

(b) "Public service" means a public facility, department, agency, board, or commission, owned, operated, or managed by or on behalf of the state or a subdivision thereof; a county, city, village, township, or independent or regional district in the state, or a tax exempt private agency established to provide service to the public.

Sec. 302. Except where permitted by law, a person shall not:

(a) Deny an individual the full and equal enjoyment of the goods, services, facilities, privileges, advantages, and accommodations of a place of public accommodation or public service because of a handicap that is unrelated to the individual's ability to utilize and benefit from the goods, services, facilties, privileges, advantages, or accommodations or because of the use by an individual of adaptive devices or aids.

(b) Print, circulate, post, mail, or otherwise cause to be published a statement, advertisement, or sign which indicates that the full and equal enjoyment of the goods, services, facilities, privileges, advantages, and accommodations of a place of public accommodation or public service will be refused, withheld from, or denied an individual because of a handicap that is unrelated to the individual's ability to utilize and benefit from the goods, services, facilities, privileges, advantages, or accommodations or because of the use by an individual of adaptive devices or aids, or that an individual's patronage of or presence at a place of public accommodation is objectionable, unwelcome, unacceptable, or undesirable because of a handicap that is unrelated to the individual's ability to utilize and benefit from the goods, services, facilities, privileges, advantages, or accommodations or because of the use by an individual of adaptive devices or aids.

Sec. 303. This article shall not apply to a private club, or other establishment not in fact open to the public, except to the extent that the goods, services, facilities, privileges, advantages, or accommodations of the private club or establishment are made available to the customers or patrons of another establishment that is a place of public accommodation, or if it is licensed, chartered, or certified by the state or any of its political subdivisions.

ARTICLE 4

Sec. 401. As used in this article, "educational institution" means a public or private institution and includes an academy, college, elementary or secondary school, extension course, kindergarten, nursery, school system, school district, or university, and a business, nursing, professional, secretarial, technical, or vocational school; and includes an agent of an educational institution.

Sec. 402. An educational institution shall not:

(a) Discriminate in any manner in the full utilization of or benefit from the institution, or the services provided and rendered thereby to an individual because of a handicap that is unrelated to the individual's ability to utilize and benefit from the institution or its services, or because of the use by an individual of adaptive devices or aids.

(b) Exclude, expel, limit, or otherwise discriminate against an individual seeking admission as a student or an individual enrolled as a student in the terms, conditions, and privileges of the institution, because of a handicap that is unrelated to the individual's ability to utilize and benefit from the institution, or because of the use by an individual of adaptive devices or aids.

(c) Make or use a written or oral inquiry or form of application for admission that elicits or attempts to elicit information, or make or keep a record, concerning the handicap of an applicant for admission for reasons contrary to the provisions or purposes of this act.

(d) Print or publish or cause to be printed or published a catalog or other notice or advertisement indicating a preference, limitation, specification, or discrimination based on the handicap of an applicant that is unrelated to the applicant's ability to utilize and benefit from the institution or its services, or the use of adaptive devices or aids by an applicant for admission.

(e) Announce or follow a policy of denial or limitation through a quota or otherwise of educational opportunities of a group or its members because of a handicap that is unrelated to the group or members' ability to utilize and benefit from the institution or its services, or because of the use by the members of a group or an individual in the group of adaptive devices or aids.

(f) Develop a curriculum or utilize textbooks and training or learning materials which promote or foster physical or mental stereotypes.

Sec. 403. An educational institution may adopt and carry out a plan to eliminate present effects of past discriminatory practices or assure equal opportunity with respect to individuals who have handicaps if the plan is filed with the commission under rules of the commission and the commission has not disapproved the plan.

ARTICLE 5

Sec. 501. As used in this article:

(a) "Housing accommodation" includes improved or unimproved real property, or a part thereof, which is used or occupied, or is intended, arranged, or designed to be used or occupied, as the home or residence of 1 or more persons.

(b) "Immediate family" means a spouse, parent, child, or sibling.

(c) "Real estate broker or salesman" means a person, whether licensed or not, who, for or with the expectation of receiving a consideration, lists, sells, purchases, exchanges, rents, or leases real property, or who negotiates or attempts to negotiate any of these activities, or who holds himself out as engaged in these activities, or who negotiates or attempts to negotiate a loan secured or to be secured by a mortgage or other encumbrance upon real property, or who is engaged in the business of listing real property in a publication; or a person employed by or acting on behalf of any of these persons.

(d) "Real estate transaction" means the sale, exchange, rental, or lease of real property, or an interest therein.

(e) "Real property" includes a building, structure, mobile home, real estate, land, mobile home park, trailer park, tenement, leasehold, or an interest in a real estate cooperative or condominium.

Sec. 502. An owner or any other person engaging in a real estate transaction, or a real estate broker or salesman shall not, on the basis of a handicap that is unrelated to the individual's ability to acquire, rent, or maintain property or use by an individual of adaptive devices or aids:

(a) Refuse to engage in a real estate transaction with a person.

(b) Discriminate against a person in the terms, conditions, or privileges of a real estate transaction or in the furnishing of facilities or services in connection therewith.

(c) Refuse to receive or fail to transmit a bona fide offer to engage in a real estate transaction from a person.

(d) Refuse to negotiate for a real estate transaction with a person.

(e) Represent to a person that real property is not available for inspection, sale, rental, or lease when in fact it is available, or fail to bring a property listing to a person's attention, or refuse to permit a person to inspect real property.

(f) Print, circulate, post, or mail or cause to be so published a statement, advertisement, or sign, or use a form of application for a real estate transaction, or make a record of inquiry in connection with a prospective real estate transaction, which indicates, directly or indirectly, an intent to make a limitation, specification, or discrimination with respect thereto.

(g) Offer, solicit, accept, use, or retain a listing of real property with the understanding that a person may be discriminated against in a real estate transaction or in the furnishing of facilities or services in connection therewith.

Sec. 503. Section 502 shall not apply to the rental of a housing accommodation in a building which contains housing accommodations for not more than 2 families living independently of each other, if the owner or a member of the owner's immediate family resides in 1 of the housing accommodations, or to the rental of a room or rooms in a single housing dwelling by a person if the lessor or a member of the lessor's immediate family resides therein.

Sec. 504. A person to whom application is made for financial assistance or financing in connection with a real estate transaction or for the construction, rehabilitation, repair, maintenance, or improvement of real property, or a representative of such a person shall not discriminate against the applicant because of a handicap that is unrelated to the individual's ability to acquire, rent, or maintain property or use a form of application for financial assistance or financing or make or keep a record or inquiry for reasons contrary to the provisions or purposes of this act in connection with applications for financial assistance or financing which indicates, directly or indirectly, a limitation, specification, or discrimination based on a handicap that is unrelated to the individual's ability to acquire, rent, or maintain property.

Sec. 505. Nothing in this article shall be deemed to prohibit an owner, lender, or his agent from requiring that an applicant who seeks to buy, rent, lease, or obtain financial assistance for housing accommodations supply information concerning the applicant's financial, business, or employment status or other information designed solely to determine the applicant's credit worthiness, but not concerning handicaps for reasons contrary to the provisions or purposes of this act.

Sec. 506. A person shall not represent, for the purpose of inducing a real estate transaction from which he may benefit financially or otherwise, that a change has occurred or will or may occur in the composition with respect to handicappers of the owners or occupants in the block, neighborhood, or area in which the real property is located, or represent that this change will or may result in the lowering of property values, an increase in criminal or antisocial behavior, or a decline in the quality of schools in the block, neighborhood, or area in which the real property is located.

Sec. 507. A person subject to this article may adopt and carry out a plan to eliminate present effects of past discriminatory practices or assure equal opportunity with respect to individuals who have handicaps, if the plan is filed with the commission under rules of the commission and the commission has not disapproved the plan.

ARTICLE 6

Sec. 601. This act shall be administered by the civil rights commission.

Sec. 602. A person or 2 or more persons shall not:

(a) Retaliate or discriminate against a person because the person has opposed a violation of this act, or because the person has made a charge, filed a complaint, testified, assisted, or participated in an investigation, proceeding, or hearing under this act.

(b) Aid, abet, incite, compel, or coerce a person to engage in a violation of this act.

(c) Attempt directly or indirectly to commit an act prohibited by this act.

(d) Willfully interfere with the performance of a duty or the exercise of a power by the commission or any of its authorized representatives.

(e) Willfully obstruct or prevent a person from complying with this act or an order issued.

Sec. 603. A person shall not violate the terms of an adjustment order made under this act.

Sec. 604. Nothing in this act shall be interpreted as invalidating any other act that establishes or provides programs or services for individuals with handicaps.

Sec. 605. A complaint alleging an act prohibited by this act shall be subject to the same procedures as a complaint alleging an unfair employment practice under Act No. 251 of the Public Acts of 1955, as amended, being sections 423.301 to 423.311 of the Michigan Compiled Laws, or under the existing state law dealing with unfair employment practices if Act No. 251 of the Public Acts of 1951, as amended, is repealed.

Billie S. Farnum
_____
Secretary of the Senate.

T. Thos. Thatcher
_____
Clerk of the House of Representatives.

Approved___July 28, 1976_____

/s/ William G. Milliken
_____
Governor.

APPENDIX C

Architectural Barriers Ordinance of Prince George's County, Maryland—Declaration of Purpose

COUNTY COUNCIL OF PRINCE GEORGE'S COUNTY, MARYLAND

Legislative Session ___1976___

Proposed and Presented by Council Members D. White, Bogley,

Francois, Koonce, and Casula

Introduced by Council Members D. White, Bogley, Francois,

Koonce, Casula, F. White, and Amonett

Bill No. ___CB-49-1976___

Chapter No. ___85___

Introduced by Council on___October 19, 1976___

A BILL ENTITLED

AN ACT to amend the Building Code for Prince George's County, Maryland, being Chapter 4 of the Prince George's County Code of Ordinances and Resolutions, 1967 Edition, as amended, so as to set forth certain requirements with regard to building, construction, alteration or addition in order to aid the physically handicapped, requiring architectural barrier free design in new construction, alteration or addition; and otherwise requiring increased accessibility for handicapped persons.

WHEREAS, there exists a class of people who are physically handicapped, with total or partial impairments, whether such impairments be temporary or permanent, of the manual, orthopedic, visual, auditory or other functions that prevent such people from enjoying total access to physical structures within their environment; and,

WHEREAS, there exists a substantial percentage of the population within Prince George's County who are afflicted with one or more physical handicaps; and,

WHEREAS, according to the National Center for Health Statistics "At least 67,900,000 Americans suffer from limiting physical conditions and would benefit from a more accessible environment. An additional 20 million or more Americans over the age of 65 and limited in mobility as a result of the aging process are not included in this figure"; and,

WHEREAS, the people so afflicted are limited in their mobility by lack of accessibility into and within physical structures, which adversely affects their health and welfare; and,

WHEREAS, all persons are exposed to a significant risk that they at some time during their lifetime will directly be in need of one or more features of a barrier free environment; and,

WHEREAS, such legislation is necessary and proper to provide adequate conditions to accommodate the needs of the handicapped, which have been so long neglected.

APPENDIX D

North Carolina Statute

ARTICLE 1

Rights

§ 168–1. Purpose and definition.—The State shall encourage and enable handicapped persons to participate fully in the social and economic life of the State and to engage in remunerative employment. The definition of "handicapped persons" shall include those individuals with physical, mental and visual disabilities. For the purposes of this Article the definition of "visually handicapped" in G.S. 111–11 shall apply. (1973, c. 493, s. 1.)

§ 168–2. Right of access to and use of public places.— Handicapped persons have the same right as the ablebodied to the full and free use of the streets, highways, sidewalks, walkways, public buildings, public facilities, and all other buildings and facilities, both publicly and privately owned, which serve the public. (1973, c. 493, s. 1.)

§ 168–3. Right to use of public conveyances, accommodations, etc.—The handicapped and physically disabled are entitled to accommodations, advantages, facilities, and privileges of all common carriers, airplanes, motor vehicles, railroad trains, motor buses, streetcars, boats, or any other public conveyances or modes of transportation; hotels, lodging places, places of public accommodation, amusement or resort to which the general public is invited, subject only to the conditions and limitations established by law and applicable alike to all persons. (1973, c. 493, s. 1.)

§ 168–4. May be accompanied by guide dog.—Every visually handicapped person shall have the right to be accompanied by a guide dog, especially trained for the purpose, in any of the places listed in G.S. 168-3 provided that he shall be liable for any damage done to the premises or facilities by such dog. (1973, c. 493, s. 1.)

§ 168-5. Traffic and other rights of persons using certain canes.—The driver of a vehicle approaching a visually handicapped pedestrian who is carrying a cane predominantly white or silver in color (with or without a red tip) or using a guide dog shall take all necessary precautions to avoid injury to such pedestrian. (1973, c. 493, s. 1.)

§168-6. Right to employment.—Handicapped persons shall be employed in the State service, the service of the political subdivisions of the State, in the public schools, and in all other employment, both public and private, on the same terms and conditions as the ablebodied, unless it is shown that the particular disability impairs the performance of the work involved. (1973, c. 493, s. 1.)

§ 168-7. Guide dogs.—Every visually handicapped person who has a guide dog, or who obtains a guide dog, shall be entitled to keep the guide dog on the premises leased, rented or used by such handicapped person. He shall not be required to pay extra compensation for such guide dog but shall be liable for any damage done to the premises by such a guide dog. No person, firm or corporation shall refuse to sell, rent, lease or otherwise disallow a visually handicapped person to use any premises for the reason that said visually handicapped person has or will obtain a guide dog for mobility purposes. (1973, c. 493, s. 1; 1977, c. 659.)

§168-8. Right to habilitation and rehabilitation services.—Handicapped persons shall be entitled to such habilitation and rehabilitation services as available and needed for the development or restoration of their capabilities to the fullest extent possible. Such services shall include, but not be limited to, education, training, treatment and other services to provide for adequate food, clothing, housing and transportation during the course of education, training and treatment. Handicapped persons shall be entitled to these rights subject only to the conditions and limitations established by law and applicable alike to all persons. (1973, c. 493, s. 1.)

§ 168-9. Right to housing.—Each handicapped citizen shall have the same right as any other citizen to live and reside in residential communities, homes, and group homes, and no person or group of persons, including governmental bodies or political subdivisions of the State, shall be permitted, or have the authority, to prevent any handicapped citizen, on the basis of his or her handicap, from living and residing in residential communities, homes, and group homes on the same basis and conditions as any other citizen. Nothing herein shall be construed to conflict with provisions of Chapter 122 of the General Statutes. (1975, c. 635.)

§ 168–10. Eliminate discrimination in treatment of handicapped and disabled.—Each handicapped person shall have the same consideration as any other person for individual accident and health insurance coverage, and no insurer, solely on the basis of such person's handicap, shall deny such coverage or benefits. The availability of such insurance shall not be denied solely due to the handicap, provided, however, that no such insurer shall be prohibited from excluding by waiver or otherwise, any pre-existing conditions from such coverage, and further provided that any such insurer may charge the appropriate premiums or fees for the risk insured on the same basis and conditions as insurance issued to other persons. Nothing contained herein or in any other statute shall restrict or preclude any insurer governed by Chapter 57 or Chapter 58 of the General Statutes from setting and charging a premium or fee based upon the class or classes of risks and on sound actuarial and underwriting principles as determined by such insurer, or from applying its regular underwriting standards applicable to all classes of risks. The provisions of this section shall apply to both corporations governed by Chapter 57 and Chapter 58 of the General Statutes. (1977, c. 894, ss. 1, 2.)

Are you a member?

The ACLU needs the strength of your membership to continue defending civil liberties. If you have not renewed, we urge you to do so today. If you are not a member, please join.

Fill out the membership form below and send, with the mailing label on the right, to: **American Civil Liberties Union, 22 East 40 Street, New York, N.Y. 10016. Att: Membership Dept.**

If you have already renewed, give this issue to a friend and ask them to join.

	Individual	Joint
Basic Membership	☐ $20	☐ $30
Contributing Membership	☐ $35	☐ $50
Supporting Membership	☐ $75	☐ $75
Sustaining Membership	☐ $125	☐ $125
Life Membership	☐ $1,000	☐ $1,000
☐ $5 Limited Income Member	☐ Other $_____	

Enclosed is my check for $_____.
(Make your check payable to the American Civil Liberties Union.)

PLEASE PRINT
☐ Renewal of membership
☐ New membership

NAME_____

ADDRESS_____

CITY_____STATE_____ZIP_____

ACLU-H

ACLU HANDBOOKS

MAY 1 3 1992

◆ DISCUS BOOKS

DISTINGUISHED NON-FICTION

MAR 1 8 1997

MOZART Marcia Davenport	45534	3.50
NATURE OF POLITICS M. Curtis	12401	1.95
THE NEW GROUP THERAPIES Hendrick M. Ruitenbeek	27995	1.95
NOTES OF A PROCESSED BROTHER Donald Reeves	14175	1.95
OF TIME AND SPACE AND OTHER THINGS Isaac Asimov	24166	1.50
DELMORE SCHWARTZ James Atlas	41038	2.95
THE RISE AND FALL OF LIN PIAO Japp Van Ginneken	32656	2.50
POLITICS AND THE NOVEL Irving Howe	11932	1.65
THE POWER TACTICS OF JESUS CHRIST AND OTHER ESSAYS Jay Haley	11924	1.65
PRISONERS OF PSYCHIATRY Bruce Ennis	19299	1.65
THE LIFE OF EZRA POUND Noel Stock	20909	2.65
THE QUIET CRISIS Stewart Udall	24406	1.75
RADICAL SOAP OPERA David Zane Mairowitz	28308	2.45
THE ROMAN WAY Edith Hamilton	33993	1.95
SHOULD TREES HAVE STANDING? Christopher Stone	25569	1.50
STUDIES ON HYSTERIA Freud and Breuer	16923	1.95
THE TALES OF RABBI NACHMAN Martin Buber	11106	1.45
TERROR OUT OF ZION J. Bowyer Bell	39396	2.95
THINKING ABOUT THE UNTHINKABLE Herman Kahn	12013	1.65
THINKING IS CHILD'S PLAY Evelyn Sharp	29611	1.75
THOMAS WOODROW WILSON Freud and Bullitt	08680	1.25
THREE NEGRO CLASSICS Introduction by John Hope Franklin	16931	1.65
THREE ESSAYS ON THE THEORY OF SEXUALITY Sigmund Freud	29116	1.95
TOO STRONG FOR FANTASY Marcia Davenport	45195	3.50
TOWARDS A VISUAL CULTURE Caleb Gattegno	11940	1.65
THE WAR BUSINESS George Thayer	09308	1.25
WHAT WE OWE CHILDREN Caleb Gattegno	12005	1.65
WHEN THIS YOU SEE, REMEMBER ME: GERTRUDE STEIN IN PERSON W. G. Rogers	15610	1.65
WILHELM REICH: A PERSONAL BIOGRAPHY I. O. Reich	12138	1.65
WOMEN'S ROLE IN CONTEMPORARY SOCIETY	12641	2.45
WRITERS ON THE LEFT Daniel Aaron	12187	1.65